Mail this card TODAY for John T. Reed's **Football Coaching Lessons Learned booklet**

Yes, please send my l̶ and any other products

Name _____

Address _____

City _____ State __ Zip_____

sent to buyers of this book who send in this card.

Coaching Youth Football .... $19.95_____

Coaching Youth Football Defense .... $19.95___ ___

Prices effective March 1996 and are subject to change.
Call **Toll Free:** 800-635-5425.
E-mail to johntreed@aol.com

Subtotal _____

CA residents add sales tax _____

Shipping: $4 for first item, $2 for EACH additional item _____

Total _____

☐ Check enclosed   ☐ Visa   ☐ MasterCard

Card # _____   Exp. _____

Signature _____   Tel. _____

Mail to: John T. Reed, 342 Bryan Drive, Danville, CA 94526

John T. "Jack" Reed
342 Bryan Drive
Danville, CA 94526

Coaching Youth Football Defense
Second Edition

By

John T. Reed
342 Bryan Drive
Danville, CA 94526
510-820-6292
Fax: 510-820-1259
E-mail: JohnTReed@AOL.COM

Thanks to...

My sons, Daniel and Steven, for agreeing to my recommendation that they try football for a year before deciding whether they wanted to play soccer or football...my other, younger son Michael for not complaining too much about having to attend football practice when Mom's busy...my wife for being a football widow to an extent during coaches meetings, scouting trips, practice, and games...to the San Ramon Bears for taking my oldest son in after he was cut by another team and for giving me the opportunity to coach my son's team...Pat Elliott for selecting me as defensive coach for the 1991 season...Steve Noon for selecting me as assistant head coach and defense/special teams coach in the 1992 season...Jim Monroe for helping me design my defensive system...Kathryn Steele, Bears trainer for her counsel on injury prevention and treatment...my fellow coaches for putting up with my foibles and faults...our cameramen without whose videotaping of games we coaches wouldn't know what the heck happened out there...the Bears players who also put up with my faults and foibles as we struggled together through their early years as players and my early years as coach...Miramonte High School coaches Richard Blaisdell, Floyd Burnsed, Paul Yriberri, Vince Dell'Aquilla for their instruction and encouragement.

Cover photography: David Fischer, San Francisco; Hand model, Michael Reed
Copyright 1993, 1996 by John T. Reed All rights reserved. Manufactured in U.S.A.
Published by John T. Reed, 342 Bryan Drive, Danville, CA 94526
Library of Congress Catalog Card Number: 95-092927; ISBN: 0-939224-36-4

Table of Contents

1

Overview

What offense do your toughest opponents use?

Before the season starts, you need to figure out what offense your typical opponent will use. Actually, you probably have to face one or two powerhouse teams and you should design your defense to stop **them**. You can probably stop the weaker teams with **any** defense. But you have to use the optimum system to stop the toughest teams.

In youth football, the toughest teams generally have a fast player who can run sweeps or a powerful inside running game. You occasionally see a team that can throw passes. But it is very rare that you will be defeated by another youth team's passing game. You cannot ignore the pass in youth football defense. But you **almost** can.

In some cases, the toughest team in your league may use a **contrarian** offense. That's what I use and advocate in my book, *Coaching Youth Football*. The contrarian offense is simply an unusual offense unlike any other offense in the league. An unusual offense gives the team that uses it an advantage. Defenses aren't used to it so they do not know how to line up against it and/or what techniques to use to stop it.

If there is an unusual offense on your schedule, you should either design your main defense to stop that unusual offense or at least have a second defense to stop that offense.

What are the strengths and weaknesses of your players?

Once you know who your players are and get an idea of their strengths and weaknesses, you should modify your defense accordingly. In recent years, both the San Francisco 49ers and the Dallas Cowboys have modified their defenses to take advantage of the strengths of Deion Sanders. They let him cover almost half the field and concentrate their other defensive backs on the other side.

I have seen teams that have no good linebackers trying to play a 4-4 or a 5-3 defense. Those defense are fine if you have three or four good linebackers. But if you do **not** have three or four good linebackers, you'd better look at the 7-diamond, 10-1, or 8-2-1.

The contrarian defense

Your choices are more limited in defense than on offense. But wherever possible, you should apply the contrarian principle to defense as well. That is, you want your defense to be **different** than any other in the league. That will probably confuse your opponent's blockers. Also, your opponent's offense has probably evolved over the years to involve whatever plays worked best against the typical defenses in the league. It is therefore probably **not** suited to succeed against a contrarian defense.

I used an 8-2-1 defense one season and a 10-1 the other two seasons. I prefer the 10-1 even though the 8-2-1 team had slightly better numbers.

The defense must be sound

"Sound" is a frequently used word in football coaching circles. There are many defenses you can use. Teams have been successful with virtually every well-known defense. But you cannot be successful with an unsound defense. To be sound, a defense must cover every possible offensive play and the technique required by the defensive players must be feasible. For example, you could say that the free safety is responsible to stop the dive play. But since the free safety is also responsible for stopping the deep pass, he cannot reasonably be expected to stop the dive.

Here are all the things that every defense must stop in order to be sound:

Running plays
- Left A gap
- Left B gap
- Left C gap
- Left D gap (containment)
- Right A gap
- Right B gap
- Right C gap
- Right D gap (containment)
- Reverse
- Draw play
- Option dive
- Option keep
- Option pitch

Passing plays with man defense
- Assign a defender to each eligible receiver including the quarterback
- Left contain rush
- Right contain rush
- Inside rush

Passing plays with zone defense
- Deep zone(s)
- Shallow zones
- Flats (to either side of offensive backfield)
- Left contain rush
- Right contain rush
- Inside rush
- Left screen pass
- Middle screen pass
- Right screen pass

Sound alignment, stance, and technique

In addition to making sure all the above points of attack are covered, you have to make sure your players are aligned soundly, are in a sound stance, and use the correct technique in their initial movement and pursuit.

For example, it would be unsound to assign a player containment (prevent running back from getting outside the tight end) responsibility while having him **align** on the **inside** shoulder of the tight end. To contain, he must have freedom of movement to the outside. That's almost impossible unless he lines up with his outside arm **away from** the tight end. It would also be unsound to have your defensive linemen line up **on** offensive linemen if those offensive linemen take **large splits** (more than a foot or so from the lineman next to them). In that case, you should tell your defensive linemen to line up in the gap between the offensive linemen.

It would be an unsound **stance** for the defensive end to be in a **two**-point stance when he is lined up on the outside shoulder of the tight end and there is a wing outside the tight end. He has to get down in a **three**-point stance to have any chance of defeating a double-team block by the wing and tight end.

It would be unsound **pursuit**—I know because I made this mistake—to have everyone run to the sideline on a sweep. At least one defender has to trail the play through the offensive backfield to stop a possible **reverse** and at least one other player must stay behind a laterally moving ball carrier to prevent him from **cutting back** against the grain.

Old, goal–line stuff

Youth football is different from high school, college, and pro football. Youth passers cannot throw very far. But there are still eleven defenders on the field. It's easier for them to cover all the ground within the passer's range radius than it is at higher levels where the quarterbacks can throw much farther.

Youth receivers also have a lower fielding percentage than older receivers. That is, they drop a higher percentage of the passes that reach them. Finally, youth passers are less accurate than older passers. All of this combines to make youth football teams lousy at passing. Many books aimed at **high school** coaches state that it is very hard for teams at **that** level to have a real passing game. So it's pretty unrealistic for youth teams to try to do what high school teams have trouble doing. In short, the youth passing game is not much of a threat and you should focus on the run.

In the early days of football, there was little effective passing. At all levels of football, goal-line defenses recognize that the quarterback cannot throw very far—not because of arm strength—but because of the end line at the back of the end zone.

Accordingly, you should study two kinds of defenses: those used today for **goal-line** defense and those used decades ago in football's **pre-forward-pass era**. In general, that means the gap 8, the seven diamond, and the 10-1. Those defenses, in turn, imply **man-to-man** pass coverage. In theory, man pass defense is vulnerable to physical mismatches. In theory, **zone** pass defense is better when your pass defenders are not as fast as the opponent's receivers. But zone is quite complicated. Your pass defenders will become tentative in zone defense and that tentativeness will more than cancel out the theoretical benefits. Use man-to-man pass coverage—in particular, the **bump-and-run** version of man. With a goal-line defense, you will have heavy pressure on the quarterback. Bump and run delays the receiver and delay is the last thing a pressured quarterback wants.

Don't do what you see on TV or use a high school defense

I get the impression that most youth coaches get their defensive ideas from college and pro games on TV. Or they use the defense they remember from high school or the one their local high school uses. Don't do that. Those defense are designed to stop vastly different offenses. They are relatively weak against the run in order to beef up against the pass. The run-oriented offenses in youth football will chew up a defense that is scattered all over the field to stop nonexistent passes.

2

Our record

I do not claim to be the world's greatest youth football defensive coach. But I will accept some of the coaching credit for the 1991 and 1992 San Ramon Bears Jr. Pee Wee defenses. The same is true of the 1994 Miramonte junior varsity defense which was 9-1 and won the league championship.

We were probably the second or third best defense in the Western League of the California Youth Football program in 1991 and 1992. We played only one Eastern League team, Elk Grove, and beat them 25-8 in 1992. Interleague play by other Western League teams both years suggested we would have been in the top two or three over there as well.

My hat's off to the two teams that seemed to have **better** defenses than us in the Western League: The Oakland Dynamites in 1991 and the Fairfield Falcons both years. Our offense did well against the Falcons in '91—although we didn't score on offense. But the Falcons held the Dynamites to just seven points the two times they lost to them in '91. In contrast, we lost to Oakland by scores of 18-0 and 25-0.

If the defensive coaches of the Dynamites or Falcons write books on youth football defense, buy them. I will. But **until** they do—and they probably won't—this book should be helpful to the **other** coaches in our league—and perhaps the coaches of teams that finished in the middle or bottom of other leagues. And it should be helpful to **all** rookie coaches as well as to **offensive** coaches who haven't had time to see themselves as opposing defensive coaches do. And it should help non-coaching parents better understand how they can best support their football-playing child and his or her coaches.

1991			Points scored against Bear defense	Points scored by Bears defense	Net yards by opponent
Date opponent	Bears	Opponent			
9/7 Napa	18	0	0	6	32
9/15 Fairfield	2	6	0	2	-18
9/21 Oakland	0	18	18	0	100+
9/28 Berkeley	12	0	0	0	-36
10/5 Bye					
10/12 Benicia	24	0	0	16	-1
10/19 Manteca	31	0	0	0	-28
10/26 Richmond	8	13	13	8	100+
11/2 Napa	7	0	0	0	86
11/9 Vacaville	6	0	0	0	20
11/16 Oakland	0	25	25	0	159
Totals	108	62	56	32	
Avg. per game	10.8	6.2	5.6	3.2	

1992			Points scored against Bear defense	Points scored by Bears defense	Net yards by opponent
Date opponent	Bears	Opponent			
9/5 Elk Grove	25	8	8	0	not
9/13 Pittsburgh	22	0	0	2	calculated
9/19 Berkeley	2	19	19	2	
9/26 Manteca	19	0	0	0	
10/3 Woodland	39	0	0	0	
10/10 Vallejo	13	6	6	0	
10/17 Napa	27	7	7	6	
10/24 Richmond	18	6	6	0	
10/31 Manteca	26	0	0	6	
11/7 Vacaville	26	0	0	6	
11/14 Falcons	7	19	19	0	
Totals	224	65	65	22	
Avg. per game	20.4	5.9	5.9	2	

In 1993, I was **head** coach and my defense was generally terrible. We were 3-6. As far as I can tell, we had a personnel problem. We only had one player who had ever played defense before and only three who had ever played football before. There were only two or three kids on the 1993 defense who would have been first-string on the 1992 defense—or on our 1989 and 1990 defenses for that matter. The 1989 through 1992 teams each had about **seven** defensive veterans.

In 1993, I should have constantly shifted my best players from position to position so that the opposing offenses could not find a hole they could consistently run successfully. I did not figure that out until after the season ended. I also had the most successful **offense** in the history of the Bears in 1993. We generally ran a **hurry-up, no-huddle offense** that got off as many as 80 plays a game. In our game against Pittsburgh, my only defensive veteran had to leave the game exhausted. He was also our tailback and gained 354 yards and scored 25 points that day. Pittsburgh scored 57.

We should have run a **slow-down** offense instead to keep our defense off the field as much as possible. We did that in the last regular season game and held our opponent, River City, to just seven plays in the second half. We beat them 25-6 in a game in which my only defensive veteran felt ill and did not play defense and only played tailback in the second half.

3

8-2-1 and 10-1 defenses

Another youth football coach I know asked me how my son's team did his first year (1989). When I told him they went one and seven he immediately asked, "How many offensive plays did his team have?" When I said, "25 or 30" he smiled knowingly and said, "We had six." I asked how his team had done. "Eleven and 0." Hmmm.

Our 1990 team had **16** defenses in the pre-season handout given to the players by that year's defensive coordinator. Although we only used four or five of the sixteen. I've also read in books on coaching youth sports like baseball that you should, "Keep it simple." So when it was time for me to come up with our defensive play book, I decided to make it **real** simple: **one** defense.

Other coaches criticized me for only having one defense. They said opposing teams would see what I was doing and adjust. I thought they might be right about that. And I suspected that I'd have to add at least one other defensive alignment. But I figured there was no point in having two until the players mastered the first one.

In 1991 and 1992, we won the Valley Conference Championship and thereby got to the semifinals of the California Youth Football League before being knocked out by the eventual CYF champions, the Oakland Dynamites and Fairfield Falcons.

I never added that second defense. Never needed to. One defense was enough. In 1992, I started with the 8-2-1 which evolved into a 10-1. I also modified it slightly from week to week according to the scouting report on the upcoming opponent. And we added a special rather large modification when we played a team with a shotgun formation.

Goal-line stand

The defense I chose was an 8-2-1. That also caused criticism. People said it was a goal-line stand defense—which it is. People said, "You can't use a goal-line stand defense everywhere on the field and in every situation." I can and I did. As you can see from the record in the previous chapter, it worked pretty well most of the time. And when we lost, our X's and O's were not the cause.

Weak against the pass?

The 8-2-1 and 10-1 would appear to be weak against the pass. Not so fast. We got seven interceptions in 1991. There are no league statistics on such things. But I never saw any comparable team in that category in the games we played or the many games we scouted. We may have led the league in interceptions with our 8-2-1. And I'm almost certain we did in 1992 with the 10-1.

One reason was we had five boys who had pass-coverage responsibilities in 1991 and three in 1992. That's enough to cover just about any pass pattern. An 8-2-1 doesn't mean only the 2 and the 1 cover passes.

Not very good at passing

Another reason for our success against the pass is that most youth football teams aren't very good at passes. Most passes fall incomplete—if they're not picked off. We kind of liked to see them thrown because of the opportunity to intercept.

I believe only Oakland and Napa completed passes against us in 1991. And three of the four completions were halfback passes in which the quarterback pitched to a halfback who then threw the pass. Our pass defenders released their receivers thinking the play was a run because of the exchange.

Our scouting report said Berkeley was a big passing team in '91. We worked very hard at pass coverage during that week—even trying temporarily to switch to a **zone** defense before switching back to man-to-man. Berkeley never even **threw** a pass against us. Their quarterback dropped back to do so on a couple occasions but was sacked before he could throw. The 8-2-1 gave us a six-man pass rush; the 10-1, an eight-man pass rush. An ounce of pass rush is worth a pound of defensive secondary.

Can't throw far

In addition to not being very good at passing, most young quarterbacks can't throw very far. That phrase "can't throw very far" applies to a particular situation at the high school, college, and pro level, too. What situation is that? Red-zone offense, or as the defense knows it: goal-line stands. Youth football is essentially the goal-line portion of higher level football.

Put it in writing

You may decide to use a defense other than the 8-2-1 or 10-1. Heck, **I** may decide to use a different one.

But whatever defense you use, make sure you put it in writing and hand it out to your coaches and players. You should put it in diagram and written form. Try to keep it to two sides of one sheet. Multi-page playbooks are thorough and impressive. But they probably intimidate and overwhelm young kids. Cover the following:

- How to line up in response to various offensive formations
- How to respond to an opposing player going in motion
- What to do when the ball moves

Diagrams

Here are the diagrams I gave to our players during the preseason.

Bears Jr. Pee Wee Defensive alignment

● = eligible receiver

T formation with split end

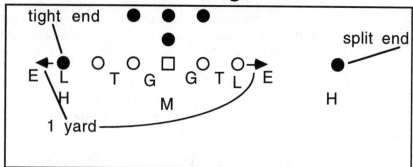

I formation with wingback and wide slot

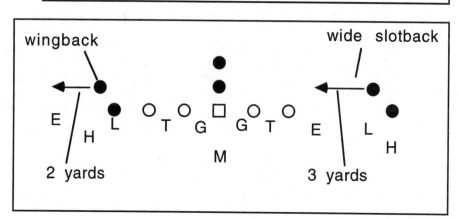

I formation with tight slot

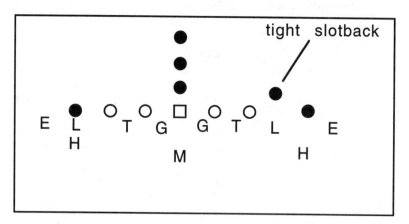

Shotgun with split end and split wingback

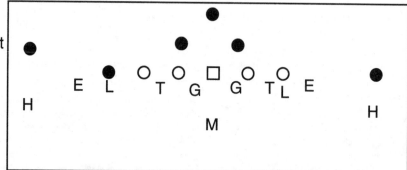

Always keep your head up when you block or tackle.

Preseason diagram

That was the diagram I handed out during the '91 preseason. Actually, it's a modified version reflecting the lessons I learned during the season. During the preseason you don't know what offensive formations you'll face so you need to be ready for anything.

The only time we used these diagrams as our play preparation was in our preseason Jamboree against Benicia and Manteca. This preparation worked quite well. We allowed Manteca only one gain of five yards—and review of the video revealed that our left defensive guard had lined up in the guard-tackle gap instead of the center-guard gap where he should have been. The five-yard dive went through the unmanned center-guard gap. Benicia only managed about two yards total against us during the scrimmage.

Once the real season began, we gave our players scouting report diagrams of the opposing team's offensive formations and plays and those showed where our defensive players were to line up in response to each formation.

In one case, our playoff game against Napa, they came out with a totally different offense than we had seen in our first game with them. And we had not scouted them again because we assumed they would not change their whole offense during the season.

Also, I had indiscreetly told a Napa coach that we had scouted them in the snack bar line after we beat them 18-0 on opening day. That may have inspired them to change their offense when they found out they were playing us in the playoffs.

No problem though. In the Napa playoff game, our defense simply ignored the stuff we had been working on all week and reverted to their recollection of the preseason diagrams and written job descriptions. We shut them out again 7-0.

The diagram above was done on an Apple Macintosh computer using MacDraw software. You could do it by hand about as well.

On the same page

In addition to the diagrams, we gave the players and coaches a companion written job description sheet. When I gave this job description sheet to an assistant coach who was helping me in the preseason, he said, "I guess this is so we'll all be on the same page, literally?" Well put.

I read in a coaching book somewhere that one of the best ways to make sure a player does not do well is to **confuse** him about what he's supposed to do. In *Option Football*, authors Stan Scarborough and William E. Warren say,

> *Coaches have known for years that indecision, whether offensive or defensive, leads to lack of aggressiveness.*

John Durham expressed a similar thought in his book, *Football's Modular Defense*,

> *When there is too much for the players to think about and too many things to do, there tends to be a "paralysis of analysis" destroying the athlete's aggressiveness and putting him in a state of confusion.*

My job description sheet is supposed to at least make sure each boy **knows** what he's **supposed** to do. Getting him to do it remains a challenging task. But at least he knows what he's supposed to do.

The job description also performs the important function of making sure the coaches **are** all on the same page and teaching the same approach. During practice, each coach should be assigned to coach a specific boy or group of boys. During the start of the season, the coaches should have copies of the written job descriptions and diagrams (I put them on opposite sides of the same sheet). As the season progresses, the coaches will learn the job descriptions by heart.

Bears Jr. Pee Wee 8-2-1 defensive alignment

Position	Where to line up before snap	What to do when the ball moves
Guards	On line of scrimmage between center and player next to him. That's the center player of the offensive team's seven-man line, not necessarily the guy who hikes the ball.	Burst through gap and tackle the **ball carrier** or any back **pretending** to be the ball carrier and trying to penetrate your gap. Rush a passer with **hands high.**
Tackles	On line of scrimmage in the next gap out from the gap our defensive guard is in.	Explode **one step** into opposing backfield, find ball then tackle **ball carrier** or any back **pretending** to be the ball carrier and trying to penetrate your gap. Rush a passer with **hands high.**
Ends	On line of scrimmage **one yard** outside the **end; two yards** outside a **wingback.** If the end or wingback is split out, so far that you can surely get to the depth of the ball untouched, line up one yard outside the **tackle.** If the end or wingback is split but **not** far enough that you can get to the depth of the ball untouched, line up **outside** the split end or wingback.	Penetrate immediately to the depth of the ball and keep the ball carrier from getting **wider than your starting position.** Tackle him only if you can do it without risking his getting outside. If the ball carrier runs around the **other end**, pursue under control **through the other team's backfield** at the depth of the deepest offensive back in case the play is a **reverse.** Rush a passer with **hands high.**
Linebackers	On line of scrimmage nose to nose with tight end, tackle eligible, or guard eligible. If there is no tight end, tackle eligible, or guard eligible, line up two yards in front of the second-widest receiver on your side. If your man goes in motion, go with him.	Keep the tight eligible receiver on the line of scrimmage. Use both hands to keep him at arms length away from your body. Be prepared to slide off to the right or left if the ball carrier tries to run through your area. If your man gets away, stay with him until you're sure no pass will be thrown to him, then tackle the ball carrier.
Cornerbacks	Two yards in front of widest receiver other than tight end, tackle eligible or guard eligible. If your man is behind his center, guard or tackle, line up one yard behind our linebacker. If your man goes in motion, go with him.	Stay with your man until you're sure no pass will be thrown to him then tackle the ball carrier. If your man attempts to block our end, immediately **blitz** outside him and **contain** the sweep or reverse.
Middle linebacker	Halfway between the widest offensive players at whatever depth you think best for the situation.	Stay behind the deepest receiver if it's a pass. If it's a pass, go to the ball and tackle, intercept, or bat down. When you're sure it's not a pass, go to the ball carrier and tackle him.

Effective 8/17/92

Always keep your head up when you block or tackle.

I heard of one youth football team where different coaches disagreed on what to teach the kids and contradicted each other when talking to the kids. The team did very poorly. Coaches who disagree with the defensive job descriptions ought to bring it up in a **coach's meeting** or with the defensive coordinator **privately**. But once they've been heard, they should conform to the defensive coordinator's decision on the matter.

Assistant coaches who deviate from the "party line" on job descriptions should be spoken to. And if they persist, they jeopardize your program's success both at winning on the field and at teaching teamwork and good citizenship to the players. A coach who refuses to conform to the defensive coordinator's job descriptions after repeated warnings should be fired. These job descriptions were done on the Macintosh with Pagemaker software. A typewriter would do almost as well.

Guards

Our defensive guards were supposed to line up in the gap between the center and offensive guard and shoot that gap when the ball moves. If the line is **unbalanced**, line up on the **center player, not the ball**. Most players were required to keep their hands on the ground until they got past the offensive blocker. We permitted the rare (one player every other year) very strong player to charge without keeping his hands on the ground. If such a strong player felt himself getting beat, he was to drop down on all fours and clog up that gap. They were not allowed to go after the ball carrier until **after** they had gone through that gap. This is a good position for less disciplined players. The job description is so simple refusal to do it right is obvious. But undisciplined players can claim mitigating circumstances when they deviate from their assigned task in other positions.

Stunt rarely

Always lining up in the same place and going through the same gap gives the offensive linemen an advantage. He knows where the guard is going to be when he wants to block him. Before the season, I suspected we'd have to teach stunts to overcome that advantage. As the season progressed, however, I dropped that idea.

With an 8-2-1 or 10-1, we can't afford any breach in the line. There aren't enough backup tacklers. Stunts are complicated and possibly confusing. Plus a stunting lineman might not make it to his destination because of tripping over a teammate or opponent. Our opponents could count on us coming through those gaps on every play. But the advantage of knowing that almost never enabled them to gain yards through those gaps.

We stunted twice against Oakland. One resulted in a 60-yard touchdown; the other in a 36-yard touchdown. Stunting is generally an anti-pass maneuver. In our league there were so few passes that stunting was a low-percentage play. In 1992, I only stunted when I knew from the formation that the ball was going to be at a particular vulnerable spot at a particular time. By vulnerable spot I mean other than immediately behind the center or guards. For example, if scouting revealed that a particular formation meant they were going to do a roll-out right pass, I'd have a back blitz to the quarterback's set-up-and-pass spot.

Minimum-play players

Another reason to avoid stunting by down linemen is that those positions are the best ones at which to play your large, minimum-play defensive players.

Youth football rules require all players to get a minimum number of plays. We had to give everyone at least six plays according to California Youth Football rules in '91 and '92.

Minimum play players are generally struggling with just basics like keeping their head up and charging forward on the snap. The **last** thing they need is to have to learn stunts.

Free-lance stunts

In spite of my policy on stunts, my players would sometimes stunt on their own initiative. Perhaps they learned to do so with a previous team. Or their father may have taught them to stunt as a way of being helpful and playing the role of wise father. Or maybe it was the player's own bright idea.

Your parents meeting should include a **warning** against teaching such a thing without coach approval. Explain that defense relies on each player carrying out his assigned task—that the coaches and team are **counting** on each player to be exactly where he's supposed to be and be doing exactly what he's supposed to be doing. Players who deviate from their assigned job description should be told in crystal clear terms that they have committed a serious violation of team policy and that they will be benched if it happens again.

That may sound a bit harsh, but I found it necessary. Furthermore, I rarely benched players for subsequent transgressions. Not because I ignored such transgressions. You must carry out your threat when the subsequent violation occurs. Rather the **deterrent** effect I intended took hold. The players didn't **do** any more free-lance stunts because they knew I wasn't kidding about benching them. Little discussions and policies like that are the building blocks of a disciplined team and **only** disciplined teams are successful on defense.

Tackles

The tackle's job description is about the same as the guard's except that tackles have to pause after they burst through the line to check for a diagonally-originated **off-tackle play** which would go right behind their penetration if they did not stop.

Ends

We had a slow team in 1991. Except for Napa, every other team could outrun our team. Whenever you play faster teams, the end sweep is generally the most dangerous play. That means your ends are the most important defenders. They **must** contain the sweep.

That is, they must block the runner's path. It is **not** important for them to make the tackle. Indeed, attempts to tackle ball carriers by ends are one of the main reasons sweeps succeed. My ends were to force the end to change direction or break stride. Tackles by ends were frosting on the cake and they'd darned well better not lose a ball carrier because they were trying to make a tackle. The ends played the role a ranch dog does in a cattle round up. He just keeps them in the middle. Ranch dogs don't rope and brand cattle, cowboys do. And ends don't tackle, linemen and linebackers do.

Hitting the tight end

Every book you read on football says the defensive end lines up on the outside shoulder of the tight end and hits him as he goes in. I was taught to do it that way when I played high school football.

But for Jr. Pee Wees, forget it. The end must run immediately to the depth of the deepest running back and the only way he's going to make it on time is if he is **untouched**. At least that's been my observation in five years of watching Jr. Pee Wee football games. Ends must be hyper disciplined. Replace a kid who takes short cuts.

I want the ends to line up where they can get to their depth-of-the-ball containment spot **untouched**. I suggest one yard outside a tight end and two yards outside a wingback. But I really want the ends to decide for themselves based on the speed of the offensive player, their own speed, and the formation keys, if any. (Some teams give away that a sweep is coming by the formation they come out in or the pre-snap motion of their backs.)

High school technique

When I began coaching high school football in '94, coaches there said my ends' boxing technique was unsound—made you vulnerable to the off-tackle play. In off tackle plays, the contain men are blocked out by the offensive end, a cross-blocking tackle, a pulling trap-blocking guard, or a lead kick-out-blocking running back. Penetration across the line of scrimmage by defensive ends makes it easier to block them on this play.

At Miramonte High School the defensive end was to read the helmet of the mar lined up on—either the tight end or weakside tackle. If the helmet went to his i meant the play was an off-tackle play and the defensive end was to **squeeze i** close that hole. The same was true if the man tried to block the defensive end out. L... ... helmet tried to get **outside** the defensive end, indicating a **sweep** to that side, he was to put his hands on the offensive player's shoulder pads, extend his arms and and lock his elbows to keep the man away from his body and slide sideways with the ball carrier along the line of scrimmage. Miramonte's defensive ends were **not** to penetrate across the line of scrimmage unless the play was a pass or a sweep the other way. They stopped the sweep at the line of scrimmage, not in the backfield so they could also stop the off tackle play.

In my youth defense, the defensive end does **not** have to stop the off-tackle play because there are ten guys on the line. But at Miramonte, we only had four to six guys on the line of scrimmage. So the defensive ends had to perform double duty. I suggest you use my boxing technique and the 10-1. But if you are getting hurt at the off-tackle hole, switch to the stay-on-the-line-of-scrimmage approach.

Split ends and wingbacks

When there is a split end or wingback, I told my kids to make a judgment call. If the split guy was far enough away from the offensive tackle that the defensive end could surely get to his containment spot untouched, the defensive end was to line up one yard outside the offensive **tackle**. But if the split guy was only two or three yards away from the offensive tackle, I wanted the end to line up **outside** the split guy.

Make a pile

Defensive ends understand the need to contain pretty readily. But they tend to think they are containing when a sweep comes their way and they run backwards toward the sideline. Heck, if that's all containment was you could let the sideline do it. Containment means containing **on the line perpendicular to the line of scrimmage where the defensive end lines up**. If the defensive end lines up on the hash mark, for example, he must not let the ball carrier get wider than that hash mark.

In many cases, the end finds himself attacked by several blocking backs and possibly a pulling guard—the legendary "student body left" play. Ends typically think that their role in such cases is to preserve their own ability to make the tackle. So they retreat to avoid being knocked down or blocked. In fact, retreating is the **same** as being blocked. What they must do is get to their containment spot, then **get low and fight** right there.

They probably won't make the tackle. But they will make a **pile**. And that's almost as good. The main thing is to make the ball carrier break stride—to slow him down so the defensive end's teammates can catch up.

Linebackers

The linebackers have the most varied job. In the 8-2-1, they have pass responsibility for the tight end or eligible tackle or guard. They are also to stop the run through their area or environs. In the 10-1, they have pass responsibility for the second widest wide receiver. If there was no second wide receiver, I just had them go to the ball carrier. And if there was only a tight end, I had the linebacker and cornerback blow through the tight end on their way to the ball carrier. They have to keep their eyes open for a back swinging out of the backfield for a pass out to the side. Such a back becomes the second widest receiver during the play and is therefore the man of the linebacker on that side.

In the 8-2-1, they first try to stop the receiver from catching a pass by **prevention**— they hit him and keep him on the line. The standard way of doing this is to hit the receiver with both hands in the numbers and stand him up.

The 8-2-1 linebacker is also to keep the receiver at **arm's length** so he cannot block the linebacker—and so the linebacker can slide off to either the right or left if the play is a run. If the receiver escapes, the 8-2-1 linebacker is to go with him **man-to-man**. That means, the linebacker watches the receiver only. He does **not** watch the quarterback or any one else. In a '91 San Francisco 49ers game, I saw a pass defender run right past a ball carrier without tackling him. The reason was he was in man-to-man coverage and he was properly focused completely on the receiver and did not see the ball carrier.

I told my players man-to-man means you stay with your man and watch only him. If he goes to the men's room, I want you at the next urinal. If the stadium burns down while you're in man-to-man, I don't want you to find out until the evening news.

Hitting the tight receiver should keep him on the line of scrimmage at least momentarily. And that should stop the **look-in or slant pass** which is one of the few patterns that youth players can successfully complete.

If the second-widest receiver is lined up in his backfield behind his own center, guard, or tackle, the linebacker just lines up between the defensive end and defensive tackle. In the 8-2-1, if his man goes out for a pass, the linebacker goes with him. If his man blocks, the linebacker tackles the ball carrier. If the linebacker's man goes in motion before the snap, he mirrors that motion.

Cornerbacks

Now we're finally in the backfield. The cornerbacks are the 2 in the 8-2-1. They line up on the widest receiver. If their man is lined up in his own backfield behind the offensive center, guard, or tackle, the halfback lines up a yard behind our linebackers in the 8-2-1 and between the linebacker and end on the line of scrimmage in the 10-1.

They cover their guy man-to-man. They also read their keys to support the run defense if the play is a run. They go in motion with their man if he goes in motion.

Man-to-man versus zone

I get the impression from other books on football that **zone** is the main pass defense in youth ball. I don't understand that. Remember, you want the players to be crystal clear as to their assignment. Man-to-man is simple. "You stay with that guy."

With zone, you cover a rectangular shaped, unmarked area. Furthermore, there is no rule against the other team flooding your zone. You're supposed to stay behind the deepest guy in your zone if there's more than one guy in it and wider than the widest guy if two receivers are at the same depth. And you're supposed to drift over near someone else's zone if there's no one in yours. Finally, the zones disappear as soon as the ball is in the air. That sounds a lot more complicated than, "Stay with that guy."

As I said earlier, we had a phenomenal interception rate. And darned few passes were completed against us in two years of using this defense. I prefer experience over logic when designing defenses. Maybe the zone is more logical in an academic discussion. But we could not have had much more success than we did.

Safety

Our 8-2-1 safety did so little I wonder if we need one at all. We should have an 8-3 defense with the safety playing middle linebacker. In 1992, we had no safety. Our safety became a middle linebacker playing only a few yards off the line of scrimmage.

Our 1991 safety occasionally made a touchdown-saving tackle. But only once every other game or so. Mostly, he was an insurance policy. Our 1992 middle linebacker led the team in assists. Our middle back was told to line up halfway between the offense's widest receivers. For example, if the offense split an end out to their right, our safety would shift that way a little.

The '91 safety was also told to line up eight yards from the line of scrimmage—too deep I now believe. The '91 safety was not allowed to ever move forward until the ball crossed the line of scrimmage—either in the air or in someone's hand. The '92 middle linebacker was allowed to use his judgment to decide when to go forward or back.

Finally, they were to stay behind all potential pass receivers. They had no man to cover. Actually, they operated a one-man zone defense. Only their zone was marked: The entire field downstream of the current down marker.

One of our safeties picked off a pass. Another was hit square in the chest by one which he inexplicably made no effort to catch. But in general, our safety was bored stiff back there in 1991. I put one of my best athletes there in the first game of the '91 season. Then I decided that was a waste of talent. In 1992, the middle linebacker was very important to us.

Numbering system

There is a standard numbering system in defensive football. When I started reading *Coach of the Year Clinic Manuals*, I kept coming across references to "5-technique tackles" and "1-technique guards" and such. I had no idea what they were talking about. The same thing happened when I attended the Frank Glazier Football Clinic in San Ramon, CA on February 7-9, 1992. However, a company called Quality Coaching was selling football books. One of the ones I bought was *Principles of Coaching Football* by Mike Bobo. On page 29, it has the positioning, at least, of these various numbers. It looks like this:

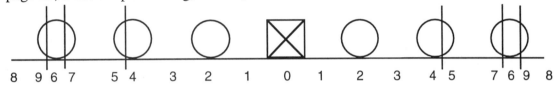

8 9 6 7   5 4   3   2   1   0   1   2   3   4 5   7 6 9 8

Here's my understanding of the meaning of the numbers:

0 Nose-to-nose with the center
1 In the center-guard gap
2 Nose-to-nose with the guard
3 In the guard-tackle gap
4 Nose-to-nose with the tackle
5 On the tackle's outside shoulder
6 Nose-to-nose with the end
7 On the end's inside shoulder
8 Outside the end
9 On the end's outside shoulder.

My 8-2-1 had a two 1-technique guards, two 3-technique tackles, two 8-technique ends, and two linebackers lined up in the 6-technique positions.

The techniques seem to involve the way the defender deals with his responsibilities. Guys in gaps like 1 and 3 just blow through like I told my guys to do. Guys who are lined up on an offensive lineman have more complicated techniques which they employ. Many are supposed to fend off the blocker with one arm while keeping the other free for tackling.

You can number your defenses based on this numbering system. For example, my 8-2-1 was a 138 because I had a 1-technique guard, 3-technique tackle, and an 8-technique end.

You should also know the standard gap lettering. It looks like this:

O C O B O A □ A O B O C O

I do not believe the 8-2-1 or 10-1 is the best defense. I don't believe it is the best defense for youth football. I don't even believe it is the best defense for Jr. Pee Wee level football. I actually don't even believe it is the best defense for a Jr. Pee Wee team coached by me. If I had been the head coach of the Oakland team, with all their speed, I, too, probably would have put my linebackers in the middle to stop the quick hitting dive and relied on speed to catch up with plays to the outside.

If you have a significant number of defensive veterans on your team, the fact that they already know one defense is an asset which you should not lightly discard. In other words, don't abandon last year's defense without very good reason if you have veteran players.

4

The right player for each position

Most youth coaches give me the impression that they see themselves as great molders of men. They believe they can teach and motivate almost **any** player to play a position well. That's what coaches do, isn't it?

No, actually.

Sure, we do **some** of that. As much as possible. But we youth coaches are more **finders** of talent than **creators** of it. We simply don't have the time—or the coaching talent—or the facilities—to turn mediocre players into great ones. Maybe no one does.

Case history

We had a bye during the 1991 season because Walnut Creek did not have a Jr. Pee Wee team. So we split our team into two roughly equally talented teams. One wore our **orange** home-game jerseys and the other wore our **white** away-game jerseys. The two teams played each other in a running-clock game.

Mind you they were all coached by me and the other coaches on our team. Both the orange and white teams used the 8-2-1 defense. How did they do on defense?

Although our **first**-string eleven had shut out the first-string offenses of the Napa, Fairfield, and Berkeley teams at that point in the season, neither the orange nor the white defense was able to stop their ragtag intra-squad opponent from scoring. The final score was two touchdowns to one. And this is against offenses consisting of players who had never played a down of offense mixed with second- and first-string offensive players.

Specialists

In each of the years I've been involved with youth football, other coaches have tried to create **separate** offensive and defensive teams. In other words, players would be assigned to one or the other team, but no one would play both ways.

Forget it.

In order to succeed defensively, the defensive coach must have access to virtually every player on the entire team. The success of your defense will be inversely proportional to the number of players you are prohibited from using on defense. In other words, the more players your head coach says you can**not** use on defense, the worse your defense will do.

The reasons coaches prefer the two separate teams approach are:

• That's the way it's done in some high schools and almost all college and pro teams and
• They are possessive about their boys and
• Like I said above, coaches fancy themselves great molders of men.

In 1991, the only player I was not permitted to use on defense was the first-string quarterback. As a result, my defensive stars in 1991 included two players who were barely allowed to play defense at all in 1990. We had a much poorer defensive record in 1990.

Virtually all youth football teams figure out as the season progresses that the separate offensive and defensive teams concept is hurting the team to an unacceptable degree. They find it out because they are losing games. But they have lost valuable time that could have been used to find out which players should go where.

The whole season

It took me **ten games** in 1991 to figure out which players should play where. At first, I made lots of changes. Then, as the season progressed, I made fewer and fewer changes. When we were in the post-season playoffs, I was only making about one personnel change for each game. After the last game in which we lost the league championship to Oakland, I felt I needed to make just one more change. It's possible that I would have made additional changes had the season lasted longer. But it seemed like I finally had it figured out.

Mind you that's after a whole season in which I had the **opportunity** to try, and **did** try, every player on the team except the main quarterback on defense. If I had been restricted in whom I could try early on, it would have taken **much longer** to figure out who belonged where.

Nature of the positions

Different positions require different characteristics.

Down linemen can be relatively **undisciplined** as long as they're not **so** undisciplined that they draw penalty flags, stand up, or don't go through the gap they're assigned. On my team, you'd be benched for that. It helps if linemen are big and strong. But one of my starters was not. Their weight should not fall in the bottom ten pounds of their weight class.

Ends need to be highly disciplined. They must take that "L"-shaped route to the ball carrier **every time**. The tendency is to want to get to the ball carrier as fast as possible. And the fastest way to get there is a **straight line**, not an "L." They must be willing to let someone **else** make the tackle of a ball carrier they might have tackled first if they had run full speed straight at the ball carrier.

I told my ends, "Your job is not to tackle the ball carrier. Your job is just to make sure the ball carrier is still back there when the down linemen and linebackers arrive."

Of course, my ends made lots of tackles. It's just that they'd better not let a ball carrier get around them because they were lunging out of control to try for a tackle.

Linebackers have to be the best athletes on the defense. They do everything. They attack the tight end and keep him at arm's length until they read the play. Then they slide off to the ball carrier's side and make the tackle. If it's a sweep, they are generally the defenders who should make the tackle right after the end causes the ball carrier to change direction or stutter step. And if the tight end or other receiver assigned to the linebacker goes out for a pass, the linebacker has to stay with him man-to-man.

Size is nice in a linebacker, but general athletic ability is more important.

Halfbacks need speed, good hands, and open-field tackling ability. They are primarily pass defenders and the second line of defense against the run. In that second-line-of-defense capacity, they two must cover the entire field from sideline to sideline. They have to be **disciplined** enough to stay with their man if he runs a pass route. But they generally are ball hawks once they're sure their man is not the intended receiver of a pass.

Halfbacks can be small.

Desire

All defensive players must have a powerful desire to get to the ball carrier. I don't know how to engender that. But I know how to find it. You'd better, too. Watch carefully and record what you see to find your eleven best tacklers.

Lots of observation

I wish you could tell who goes where by stop-watch times in 20-yard sprints or some such. But you can't. You just have to put people in the position in game or scrimmage conditions and see how they do.

Don't become locked into **first impressions**. Several boys we would have **cut** at the beginning of the season (if we had more than the league maximum 35) became **stars** on our defense. Other boys inexplicably go **down** in performance. Keep your eyes and mind open throughout the season. Some coaches seem to realize they originally picked the wrong boy for a position—but they cannot bring themselves to admit they made a mistake. To heck with that. Put the best eleven on the field.

Don't worry about what central casting would say. That is, don't fail to try a boy for a position just because he doesn't **look the part**. I had good performance from a defensive end who was very small but who had quick feet and good instincts—even though defensive ends are supposed to be big. And I mentioned a down lineman who was small but quite successful.

Feelings

Some coaches I've observed in football and other youth sports decide who's going to play what position and what percent of the game they're going to play based on the feelings of the players involved and their parents. That's an outrage.

No coach would ever **say** at the parents meeting or first team meeting,

> *"I decide who plays what position and who starts so I can hurt the fewest people's feelings. If you are better than another player—but his feelings might be hurt by my replacing him with you—I'll leave him in the position and you'll just have to stay second string or play another position. By the way, I also take into account whether the parents of each of you are happy. The squeaky parent's child gets the best position and playing time."*

No coach would ever **say** that. But many **do** exactly that.

Having to demote people is one of the unpleasant obligations of managers. Coaches are managers. Football coaches make mistakes like everybody else. In many cases, they make a mistake about who should play where and how much. When they discover that they have made a mistake, they **must** correct it immediately. That means demoting the previously overrated player and elevating the previously underrated player. That means hurting the feelings of the demoted player and possibly the feelings of his parents. Sorry, but it cannot be avoided.

If you don't have what it takes to make those hard decisions—continuously throughout the season—you shouldn't be a coach.

Coaches' sons

Your son is probably a player on your team. Most of your fellow coaches probably have sons on the team.

In my experience, parents, including coaches, vary in their ability to be **objective** about their sons. Some coaches are quite objective, others are somewhat objective, still others are blind to their son's many weaknesses as a player.

As defensive coach, you will have to fight with the unobjective about their son. Comes with the territory. If you let unobjective, squeaky-wheel coaches railroad you into playing their son in the wrong position or for the wrong amount of time, your team will suffer. Even the particular boy in question may suffer if he's not ready for the responsibilities thrust upon him.

To find out whether **you** are objective about your son, ask your fellow coaches. Check with them during coaches' meetings to make sure you aren't playing your son at the wrong position or giving him too much or too little playing time.

Note that it can go **both** ways. Most coaches are harder on their sons than they are on the other boys. Most coaches' sons tend to misbehave more at practice and games than their non-coach's son teammates, too.

Coaches' sons tend to be among the best athletes on the team. But some coaches are so concerned about appearances that they deny their son the chance to play in the position which is best for him and for the team. They are so concerned that people might think they are engaging in nepotism that they don't let their son get as much playing time as he deserves.

If there is any question in your mind that you are misplaying your son in either the favoritism or bending-over-backward-to-avoid-favoritism direction, ask your fellow coaches to decide on your son's position and playing time.

Stats

In Little League in 1991, my son was the best offensive player according to the Bill James Runs Created score we kept on each player. So I batted him in the top of the line up. We **thought** he was one of the best pitchers, too. But the stats we kept on the pitchers after each game showed he had the **worst** runs-given-up average. So after two pitching appearances, he did not pitch again the rest of the season. He was disappointed. But the stats were unambiguous. (In 1992, he was one of our best pitchers. So I may have relied too much on his first two outings the year before.)

That's why you should keep as many stats as you can when you coach. Stats aren't everything—especially in football. But you should check your own objectivity against them. And they make excellent convincers when you are trying to persuade players, parents, and fellow coaches of the correctness of your decisions.

The father's playing position

One of the ways the lack of objectivity manifests itself is regarding the son's fitness to play **the position the father played** when he was young. "I was a linebacker so my son will be a linebacker," may be the unspoken but powerful message of the father/coach. Basically, the answer is father did not **marry** a linebacker so it may be the genes the boy got from his **mother** are what make him better suited for split end. Whatever explanation you come up with, you can**not** play the kid at linebacker if he's not one of the two or three boys best suited for that position.

Every position ought to go to the most qualified boy. And living with the coach should **not** be a criterion. Even if there were some truth to such arguments as "I can give him extra practice at home," they are **unfair** to the other boys.

Nepotism can **destroy** a team. Nepotistic coaches who put their sons in important team roles in spite of obvious lack of qualification for the job create resentment among the other players, coaches, and non-coach parents. Players can develop a "Why bother?" attitude if the coach's son keeps nullifying their efforts with his ineptness. Or they will not compete for the position in question on the grounds that no one whose last name is different from the coach's has a chance.

Check the video

You have not seen the game or practice until you've seen the video. College and pro football coaches often respond to post-game media questions with, "I'll have to see the film." They aren't ducking the question. They've just learned from years of experience that you don't know what happened in a game until you examine the game video.

I guarantee you that you will be **amazed** by what the video reveals. You'll find boys you thought were great, not in the right place or not being aggressive. And you'll find boys you thought were weak players giving a good account of themselves.

We videoed **all** games. I also videoed some practice sessions at the beginning of the season. Until you've seen the video, you have not seen the game or practice.

Best defensive line; best secondary

In 1991, we had the best defensive down lineman in the league even though we hardly practiced that skill at all. Opposing coaches used to comment about them after the game. In 1992, we spent more time drilling our defensive down linemen than any other defensive activity. But no amount of practice corrected our weakness. We had a relatively weak front four in 1992.

In 1992, we had the best defensive secondary even though we practiced **not at all** on that skill. In 1993, we had the best tailback in the league. I never said a word to him about how to run. I just gave him the ball 25 times a game.

Conclusion: you are far more in the business of **finding** players than you are in the business of **coaching** them. If a player is not working out, spend more time looking for a replacement than trying to improve the one who's not working. In 1992, toward the end of the season, I started to put guys from glamour positions on the defensive line. I should have done it sooner. The best athletes can play any position. The weaker athletes can only play one or two positions. You have to put the weakest where they can contribute the most or do the least damage. The stronger athletes must do the jobs that remain.

5

Videotape

You **must** videotape your games and you should probably videotape at least some of your practices. If you can videotape your opponents when you scout them, do that, too. Our league rules prohibit use of any photographic or recording equipment when scouting.

Angle

When you videotape a scrimmage or game, the camera must be **as high as possible**. The directly-overhead Goodyear Blimp angle would be ideal. And I've wondered if we could persuade someone who owned a hot air balloon to use it to videotape our games from, say, above the track next to the field.

Another, perhaps more plausible, thought I had, was to get someone up on the light poles. Our high school, like many in the warmer parts of the U.S., plays its games on Thursday and Friday nights. To do that, they have a half dozen very tall light poles. A cameraman up on the light-servicing platform would have an excellent angle. Although I must admit I would not be very interested in either the dangerous climb or the uncomfortable perch. Maybe a remote-controlled camera could be put up there.

Whenever you get less than about a 40-degree angle between the camera and the ground, it's hard to see the line play.

Second angle

I recently went to a football game at Saint Mary's College in Moraga, California. I was interested to see that they had at least **two** video cameras going. (They also had a movie, not TV, camera at a third site.)

One was in the usual press box location. But the other was behind one of the goal posts. Furthermore, it was **very high**, about fifty feet. It was on a hydraulic scissor lift. The base had four wheels and screw-down supports. The operator stood on a steel platform with a waist-high steel guard rail. There was a control panel which could be used to raise, lower, and otherwise maneuver the platform.

The woman who was on the platform had a video camera which was powered by a long extension cord that simply dangled from the platform and ran to the snack bar building nearby. At half time and at game end, the woman lowered the platform to the ground.

I presume the end-zone camera was there to give the coaches **two** angles on each play. I've felt the need for that. Often, our offensive coaches would complain that a blocker ran right by a tackler without blocking him. And I keep wondering if the two players were really that close. Or did they just **look** that close because we had a **side** view. Maybe the end-zone angle would have revealed that the missed tackler was really twenty feet to the side of the blocker who seemed to run right past him.

Two cameras at each game might be more than even the most zealous youth coaches want to bother with. If so, you might try alternating games or halves. That is, video the first half from the press box area and the second from the end zone.

Ask at your parents' meeting if any parents have access to and would be willing to let the team make use of a cherry picker or other aid in getting a high camera angle. As a general rule, your league rules probably require you to offer your opponents **equal access** to any such perch.

Go to the press box

Most high school stadiums have press boxes. My first year as a youth football parent, I became self-appointed team videotaper. I discovered that I could admit myself to the press box at both home and away games by just acting as if I belonged there. I also discovered that virtually all press boxes have household type **electric outlets**. No need to run your camera on batteries. Just bring the battery charger/AC adapter which came with the camera and plug in.

You also need a **tripod**. Holding the camera on your shoulder is too tiring. Heck, just looking through the viewfinder throughout the game is tiring even when the camera is on a tripod.

Most press boxes have a fenced-in area on the roof for cameramen. If so, ask your videotaper to please use it. These are typically accessed by a **ladder** rather than stairs, so the videotaper's job description includes lugging body and camera equipment up the ladder. The person you ask to do it needs some strength and a healthy sense of balance. A senior citizen or unathletic person may not be able to get safely to the best vantage point.

Keep it on between plays

One of the parents who videotaped our games started and stopped the camera between plays. I don't like that approach. When you are trying to chart the game afterwards, you need to hear the public address announcer most of the time to understand all of what happened.

Not that PA announcers are infallible. They often credit the wrong players with runs, tackles, or fumble recoveries.

Keeping the camera on between plays also enables you to see the chain gang moving the down marker and the first-down chains. Those markers, in turn, let you see how many yards the field position changed on the play.

When the tape started and stopped at the beginning and end of each play, I had a great deal of difficulty figuring out what yard line the ball was on. Plus the camera operator often started the camera too late and we missed a play. Or there was a penalty but the announcement of it by the referee and PA announcer were left off the tape.

I asked our videotaper to state out loud the yard line, down, and yards to go between each play. The camera's built-in microphone will pick that up. Even better, the camera person ought to give a running narrative of who made the tackle, caused the penalty, etc. The more information, the better.

You can and probably should turn the tape recorder off during **time outs** and **half time**. (Although the cheerleaders and their parents like to see their half-time show at the post-game pizza party viewing of the game tape.)

Not too much close up

Parent videotapers also tend to focus narrowly on the linemen and ball carrier. Some even focus only on **their son**. Coaches also need to see what the split ends, flankers, and secondary are doing.

Generally, our tapes did **not** show those who were more than ten yards from the ball. You should instruct your videotaper to try to keep all players in the picture as much as possible. On kickoffs and punts, the videotaper really needs to zoom back to enable the coaches to see all the players.

Try having your videotaper sit in on a video evaluation session early in the season or in the preseason so he or she can see the problems caused by doing it incorrectly. Have them read this chapter, too.

Analyzing the tape

You can and should analyze the tape intensely. My approach was to run an opponent's offensive play, then, having seen where it went, I'd ask myself who should have stopped it. Then I'd run it again to see what the players who should have stopped it did on the play. And I'd jot down notes about who did well and who did poorly. At the first practice after the game, I'd go over my notes with the players.

I also watched the tapes more casually at the post-game pizza party and while riding my exercise bicycle. Sheer repetitions of watching reveal stuff you missed the first time or even the fifth time.

High school, college, and pro coaches watch videotapes incessantly. They call it "film," a carryover from the pre-videotape days. In his autobiography, Michigan's highly successful head coach Bo Schembechler says his house had more film than furniture. His wife, Millie, once told an audience,

> *Bo and I lead a normal life. When he comes home at night, I kneel down and kiss his Big Ten championship ring. And after dinner, if we get a few private moments, we go downstairs and look at film.*

We part-time, unpaid coaches can't afford to devote that much time to watching "film." But be advised that **real** coaches do watch lots and lots of "film." To the extent that you can do likewise, your team will be more successful.

Duplicating the tape

The tape ought to be duplicated as soon as possible after the game. Most of your coaches probably have the equipment to do it. (Many video cameras can be used as one VCR and your home VCR can be used as the other for duplicating.) And copies ought to be as widely distributed among your coaches as possible.

I have not done it, but I'd like to try the following: Each coach would be assigned to grade his share of players' performances. For example, on our team, which had 24 players, seven coaches, and an equipment manager, I'd ask each of the coaches and equipment manager to study the video tape and grade **three** players on each play. The grade would rate the player on how well he discharged his duties according to the written job descriptions discussed earlier in the book.

The coach should discuss the grades and comments with each player at the next practice. The grading sheets should be preserved for showing interested parents why their son plays where he plays or as little as he plays.

Here's George Allen's grading system from his book, *George Allen's Guide to Special Teams*:

Unassisted tackle	3 points
First hit on tackle	2
Assist on tackle	1
Block	2
Second-effort play	3
Big play	5
Hit of the game	5
Game breakers	10

Using the tape to coach

You should use the tape to **coach** your kids. They will sit still for about 15 minutes worth. We brought a VCR and TV to the stadium on occasional practice nights. We plugged it into the press box electric outlets, sat the kids in the stands in front of the press box, and showed them good and bad performance examples in the tape of the most recent game.

When we played a team for the second time in the season, we showed tape of our last game with that team as part of the preparation for the game. (Tape from the previous year is probably too out of date. The team may have all new coaches, mostly new players, or just a whole new approach.)

Frequently, players don't believe they are doing something until you show them on tape. For example, "I did **not** line up in the neutral zone! That ref was **crazy**!" Then you show the video which happened to be on the same yard line as the line of scrimmage and the player's helmet clearly crosses the point of the ball. "Oh." he says sheepishly.

John Madden tells the following story:

> "…*just as we started moving, [Gene Upshaw] got a holding penalty. When he came off the field, I chewed him out.*
>
> "'*I didn't hold him,' Gene said, 'believe me I didn't hold him.*
>
> "*Hearing that, I started yelling at the officials…*
>
> "*But the next day, as I watched the film, there it was, right out there for everybody to see. Gene had his arms wrapped around Ernie Holmes…*"

The video also gives them the **big picture**. They can see how their discharging their position's duties relates to the whole team's effort.

We tried taking the entire team to a meeting room for a two-hour all-video practice before our Oakland playoff game. We had stopped Oakland pretty good in the first game except for three touchdown plays which each went for about fifty yards. So we thought it would be good for the kids to see how well they played and that we only had to be three plays better to win.

Sounded good at the time. In fact, we learned that you cannot keep 24 eight- to eleven-year old boys quiet for two hours in front of even a big-screen TV featuring one of their games. We should have made a 15-minute tape to illustrate our point and shown it in the stadium in front of the press box the way we usually did.

At least one practice night of 15 minutes of video per week is probably the best amount of time to use video as a coaching tool. It could also be used in drills and scrimmage on an instant replay basis if you could set it up.

You should probably show the tape or selected excerpts to players in ten- or fifteen-minute shifts rather than show it to the whole team at the same time.

Tapes for the players

Players should be told they can get a tape of a game by bringing a blank tape to the coach in charge of video. Or maybe you can make an arrangement with a local video place. Leave them a master and authorization to duplicate it. Publicize it to your players and parents. Coaches could stop by to get their weekly copy.

Fund raising

I've never seen this done but it seems to me a team could raise funds by videotaping each game and selling copies of the tape to interested parents from both teams. You could duplicate the tape on site right after the game if you brought a second VCR and a bunch of blank tapes. Or you could just take orders and money and get the tapes to the parents later.

Awards banquet

We used our game videos to make a year-end **highlight tape**. We showed that at the season-ending awards dinner and sold copies to interested parents. Try to get a highlight of each kid in addition to team highlights. To make the tape a complete yearbook-style history of the team, you should try to videotape related but not game *per se* activities like practice rituals, cheerleaders' practice and game and competition performances, homecoming, fund raisers, parades, pregame warmups, weigh in, jamboree, caravan to away games, sign-painting parties, parents cheering, post-game snack bar visits, etc.

Recruiting

We have never used a particular video tape as a formal recruiting device. But my son **has** shown football game tapes to some soccer-playing friends he hoped to recruit. If you have a professional videotaper among your parents, that would be the best way to get a recruiting-quality tape made.

6

Scouting

You gotta scout.

When I suggested scouting in 1990, my fellow coaches dismissed it as impossible. As far as we knew, all Jr. Pee Wee games were played at 9:00 am on Saturday morning. Since we had to be at **our** game, how could we scout?

In 1991, my fellow coaches were more interested but, initially, we still wondered how we could overcome the fact that all Jr. Pee Wee games were played at the same time. I broached the subject of sharing scouting duties with one of our older Bears teams. We would scout their opponents who played in the afternoon if they would scout our opponents' morning games. But the coach of that team rejected the whole idea of scouting as "too much like professional football." His team won one game during the 1991 season.

High school

When I played football in high school, our weekly practice routine included some skill drills then scrimmage. Scrimmage was always our first-string offense against our second-string defense and our first-string defense against our second-string offense. The second string would play the role of the upcoming opponent. That is, our second-string defense would line up in the defensive formations of our upcoming opponent. And our second-string offense would run our upcoming opponent's formations and plays against our first-string defense. The team pretending to be the upcoming opponent is called the "scout team" because they use the scouting report as their playbook.

I don't know any other way to prepare for a game. I was flabbergasted when I found our 1990 Jr. Pee Wee team practicing entirely out of the Bears playbook. In other words, our offense ran Bears plays against our defense which only lined up in Bears defensive formations. Since we never play the Bears all season, I thought that was inadequate preparation to say the least.

First game, loss; second game, win

We only won three games on the field that year. And one was the **second** time we played that team that year. They beat us three touchdowns to one in the **first** game—all long passes down the middle. Then, when we were getting ready to play them the **second** time in an invitational bowl game, we were able to prepare very specifically to stop their passing game. And **this** time **we** won three touchdowns to one. There you have an excellent demonstration of the value of scouting.

Finding opportunities to scout

First off, reject the, "Scouting would be nice, but we can't because we all play at the same time" excuse. Where there's a will, there's a way.

Jamborees

First, there are the **jamborees**. In our league, teams gather in groups of three or four teams at various host fields for a preseason scrimmage. It's called a jamboree in our area. In 1991, we traveled to Benicia's field for a jamboree in which we scrimmaged Benicia, Manteca, and Walnut Creek. That was early Saturday morning on August 24th.

Obviously, that's an opportunity to scout the three opponents who attend the jamboree. We actually blew that opportunity to an extent because we did not yet have our scouting act down. As a result, we ended up with only sketchy notes about the opposing teams.

And our video operation was not yet squared away. I videotaped from directly behind our formations out on the field. And we had a mother in the stands. But she did not go to the press box elevation and her battery ran out during the scrimmage.

You need to make a concerted effort to thoroughly scout your jamboree opponents getting diagrams of each play.

As far as other jamborees taking place at the same time, not all your coaches need to be at the jamboree. One or two could skip it and attend another jamboree. When we made inquiries, we discovered that the other jamborees were not at the same time and date at all. Most were on Saturday **and** Sunday of the **following** weekend.

So on Saturday, August 31st, three other coaches and I scouted the Fairfield-Suisun Jamboree. We were not scheduled to play Fairfield-Suisun in the regular season and we did not meet them in the playoffs. But our opening game was against one of their jamboree teams: Napa. The other two were Tri-cities and River City. We were scheduled to play River City during the regular season and we thought we might end up playing Tri-Cities in the playoffs because they were in our conference. As it turned out, River Cities forfeited all their games because they didn't have enough players. It was their first year. And they didn't show up at the jamboree. So we scouted the other three teams to an extent.

On Sunday, September 1st, Oakland hosted a jamboree attended by the Fairfield Falcons and Vacaville teams. We were scheduled to play the Falcons and Oakland in our second and third games of the season. And we expected we would almost certainly play Vacaville for the conference championship if we got that far. (And that's exactly what happened.) So another coach and I scouted all three teams.

So by just attending three jamborees, we had scouted six of our eight regular season opponents and three **possible** post-season playoff opponents. The missing opponents were River City who forfeited their game against us and Berkeley. We did not scout Berkeley's jamboree because we figured we could scout them later.

Limitations of jamborees

Jamborees are **not** the best scouting opportunities. For one thing, there is **no kicking game**. They are controlled scrimmages with touchdowns but no kicks.

They are also **early** in the season. The more recent the scouting report is the better as we learned with Napa later in the playoffs.

Napa ran only a wishbone (with no triple option) in their jamboree and in their first game against us. Since we had played them twice, we did not bother to scout them in preparation for our playoff game with them. That was a mistake. They almost totally changed their offense for the playoff game. We only saw the wishbone a half dozen plays.

Jamborees don't count. As a result, the coaches quite properly do a lot of **experimenting** with plays, defenses, and players. For example, the Fairfield Falcons ran two quarterbacks in the jamboree: one, # 29, always kept the ball when he quarterbacked, the other always handed off or passed.

Boy, were we ready for that routine. We taught our defense to tee off on # 29 when he was at quarterback. The linebackers were supposed to blitz and the ends were supposed to contain deep because #29's end sweep was a deep bootleg.

Only problem was when we got to our Falcons **game** which was on September 22nd, # 29 **never took a snap**. Instead, he was their prime running back. We had assigned our best halfback to shadow the player who was the prime running back in the **jamboree**. But he only played a secondary role in the regular season game so at the half, we adjusted and reassigned our best half back to shadow # 29. We held the Falcons to minus 18 yards and scored a safety against them. But we would have done better had we not relied so heavily on the jamboree scouting report.

Other teams may not suspect that non-jamboree opponents are attending their jamborees to scout them. But they know that there are at least two or three upcoming opponents there. So I suspect coaches do not use their best stuff in jamborees because they don't want to show it to the jamboree opponents in a contest which doesn't count.

Sunday games

We played the Falcons on **Sunday**, not Saturday. How come? Because the Falcons shared their playing field with another team. So our assumption that all Jr. Pee Wee games in our league were at 9:00 am on Saturday was **incorrect**.

What did we do about it? First off, we used Saturday, September 21st to scout Berkeley, one of the two opponents we had not been able to scout at a jamboree. Turned out, the team they were playing on September 21st was the **other** team we had not been able to scout at a jamboree: River City.

I had to attend my other son's soccer game so another coach scouted the Berkeley-River City game. Unfortunately, River City only had three players so a controlled scrimmage was held between Berkeley and Berkeley with the three River City players blended in. So we got a pretty good, but less than ideal, look at Berkeley, our fourth game of the season. We learned they were a big **passing** team—a very valuable piece of information as we had learned against Tri-Cities the previous year.

Later in the season, we used the fact that some teams played Sunday games to get a second look at Manteca and Vacaville. Manteca had to share a field, too.

And finally, in the playoffs, games were held on Saturday **and** Sunday. I suspect this is done specifically to make scouting possible. Whatever the reason, that's how it worked out. We played Napa in our first playoff game at our field on **Saturday** morning, November 2nd. On **Sunday**, three of us traveled to Vacaville to see them blow away Benicia 31-0 in their first playoff game. That was the **third** time we had scouted Vacaville.

The following Saturday, we had off because our game against Vacaville was on Sunday in Manteca. So six of our coaches, five of our players, and one wife scouted the Oakland-Fairfield Falcons playoff game which Oakland won 7-0. That made them Delta Conference champions and set them up to play the winners of the Valley Conference Championship game between us and Vacaville. On Sunday, we beat Vacaville 6-0 to win the Valley Conference Championship and the right to play Oakland for the Western League Championship the following weekend.

At one point during the Vacaville playoff game, we wondered if Oakland had come all the way out to Manteca to scout us. Or did they figure because they beat us 18-0 and they beat Vacaville, 32-7 during the regular season they didn't need to bother.

We turned and checked the stands. And there they were. Two guys sitting quietly by themselves writing on clipboards. One had his purple-and-yellow Oakland Dynamites starter jacket on the bench in front of him. At the playoff level, we always saw scouts from our upcoming opponents at our games. And they saw us at theirs.

Different game times

Every Jr. Pee Wee game I've been to in five years has been the first game in the morning—except one. Woodland had us play in the afternoon in 1990. So don't assume that **all** games at your level are played at the same time at all fields in your league.

Scout during games

Suppose you investigate the game times and dates of your opponents and there is one or more who simply always plays at the same time as you. You **still** have to scout them.

You may be able to get a coach from one of your **sister teams** to trade scouting assignments with you the way I tried unsuccessfully to do. For example, let's say you coach Midgets (the highest level) and they usually play at 4:00 PM on Saturday as in our league. You could probably persuade a Jr. Pee Wee coach to scout an upcoming opponent's Midget game in return for your scouting a Jr. Pee Wee game. Then you scout at 9:00 am on the appointed day while your Jr. Pee Wee associate is coaching his game. Then, at 4:00 PM that same day, he scouts the Midget game while you coach at your game.

Another alternative is to recruit a **non-parent**. Parents are generally out because they want to watch their kid play.

For example, there may be a **former coach** who lost his job because of team politics or a Woody Hayes kind of incident. (Hayes was the highly respected, highly successful coach of Ohio State for most of his 28-year coaching career. He was fired the day after he punched an opposing player who made an interception in the 1978 Gator Bowl.)

Football coaching is **addictive**. Former coaches are generally lost without their weekly football fix. I suspect those who could get over any hard feelings they might harbor toward the association that fired them might be delighted to get back in the game as a scout.

If the hard feelings are too strong for that, you might see if a fired coach from a **neighboring** team is willing to scout. In his case, the hard feelings would be going the other direction.

And the fact that he is not nearby should not be a problem when you consider that all scouting is done at fields **other than** your own. In fact, the geographically most desirable scout would be one who lived in the center of all the league's teams other than yours.

If you have an oversupply of coaches in your association, you could make the coaching career ladder start with scouting assignments. That is, before you can coach, you have to pay your dues by scouting.

If you have an injured player who cannot play, perhaps he and his dad will be willing to help the team by scouting during the games he has to miss.

If worse comes to worst and your only scouts are your own coaches, take turns—like serving on guard duty in the military.

But you must scout.

Our 1991 scouting schedule

Here, in tabular form, is how our scouting schedule ended up:

Date and day	Opponent	When scouted
9/7 Saturday	Napa	Fairfield-Suisun jamboree on 9/1
9/15 Sunday	Fairfield Falcons	Oakland jamboree on 9/2
9/21 Saturday	Oakland	Oakland jamboree on 9/2
9/28 Saturday	Berkeley	Berkeley-River City game Saturday 9/14
10/5 Saturday	Walnut Creek	Benicia Jamboree, they forfeited 10/5
10/12 Saturday	Benicia	1. Benicia jamboree and 2. Richmond-Benicia game played in Richmond on Sunday 10/6
10/19 Saturday	Manteca	1. Benicia jamboree and 2. Manteca-Vacaville game played in Manteca on Sunday 10/6
10/26 Saturday	Richmond	Richmond-Benicia game played in Richmond on Sunday, 10/6
11/2 Saturday	Napa	1. Fairfield-Suisun jamboree on 9/1 and 2. in our first game with them on 9/7
11/10 Sunday	Vacaville	1. Oakland jamboree on 9/2, 2. Manteca-Vacaville game played on Sunday 10/6 in Manteca, and 3. Benicia-Vacaville playoff game played in Vacaville on Sunday, 11/3
11/16 Saturday	Oakland	1. Oakland jamboree, 2. our first game with them on 9/21, and 3. the Fairfield Falcons-Oakland playoff game played on Saturday 11/9 in Concord.

Scouting schedule

You should make a scouting schedule as soon as you get your league game schedule. At the first coaches' meeting after you get that league schedule, figure out how you can cover **all** your opponents. Remember, the best scouting reports are:

- fresh (recent)
- regular games rather than jamborees
- done by your coaches rather than non-coaches.

Look for days to scout by checking for:

- jamborees on other days than yours
- game days which are different from yours
- game times which are different from yours
- byes in your schedule either by design or because of forfeit by opponent.

Finding the scouting date, time, and site

You need to find out the exact location, date, and time of each game played by your upcoming opponents before you play them. If your league automatically gives all that information to you, good. Ours didn't. We had to track down details by phone. All we knew was who was playing whom on what weekend. We were not told if the game was Saturday or Sunday, what time kickoff was, or the location.

As soon as possible, find out the dates and times of the games with scouting potential for you. That is, the games played by your upcoming opponents before they play you.

Then assign coaches to scout each game.

Make sure you get the address of the game site or at least the name of the institution at which it will be played. Our games were all at high schools, junior high schools, or colleges. Those are rather prominent landmarks which are even listed on most maps. And half the customers in any convenience store you stop at will know where the school you're looking for is if all you know is its name.

If you can, get **directions**. We generally did that by calling the president of the association we were visiting before the game. Yes, we worried about them sending us on a wild-goose chase. But it never happened.

If you do not even know the name of the school where the game is being played, you'd better leave **early** and visit every high school, junior high school, college, and public park in town, in that order.

Don't make any assumptions about the day or time. I got directions to Richmond from a Richmond official. But I neglected to confirm that the game was on **Saturday**. It wasn't. I had to come back on Sunday and unnecessarily missed part of our Saturday intra-squad Orange-White game because of my erroneous assumption.

Don't make any assumptions about the place either. When we played Walnut Creek in 1989, it was at a Walnut Creek High School. In 1991, I assumed they played at the same school. Wrong. They weren't even playing in Walnut Creek. They were playing in Concord, a neighboring town!

Scouting team

Try hard to get at least **two** coaches on each scouting assignment. The more the merrier. It's hard for one man to see and write down everything. (In the California Youth Football league, we aren't allowed to use video, film, or audio equipment when scouting—only pencil, paper, clipboard, and binoculars.)

When we scouted Oakland for the playoffs, we had six scouts and each was assigned a specific position or positions to watch on each play. Nevertheless, I and my two helpers missed a tackle-eligible play which Oakland ran. I saw the play but not the tight end dropping back. Fortunately, our offensive scouts sitting nearby noticed it and came over to tell me. We practiced the response to the tackle-eligible play until the boys understood it the following week. As far as I know, Oakland did not use the play in the subsequent game.

Scouting blank forms

I designed the blank scouting form on the next page. Professional scouts may have better forms. On the other hand, since they can use video, maybe they don't.

When you scout, you want to get down **every** offensive play and every defensive play. To do that, you must watch the **entire** game. And you must chart **every** play. The one you miss could be the one that beats you—or the one that would have let you win.

The great gold nugget find in a scouting report is a **one-play formation**. Those usually only happen once a game. So they could well happen when you're not looking if you only scout part of the game. By scouting every play, you see their favorite play, second favorite, etc. And you can see their down-and-distance tendencies. If there is a pattern in how they call plays in response to external situations, you can teach it to your players and thereby give them a tremendous advantage.

My blank forms contain the basic offensive players which must be in every scrimmage play: center, guards, and tackles. The quarterback, running backs, ends, and flankers are left off because they can line up in different places.

There's also room for the situation and result of the play.

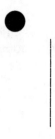

Date: _____

@

_____

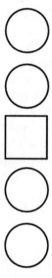

I made these blank diagrams with Aldus Super Paint on a Macintosh computer. You do as well by hand or with a typewriter. There are a maximum of 50 to 90 plays per youth game so you need that many play sheets for each game you scout.

Put the sheets in a loose-leaf binder. By binding the pages, you insure they stay in the right order and don't blow around in the wind. The order is important because you can spot patterns in the opposing team's play calling. You should also have pages in the back which show a full football field. Use them to diagram **kicking** plays. Kicking plays are beyond the scope of this book. I cover special teams as well as offense and defense in my book, *Coaching Youth Football*.

As the offense breaks its huddle, quickly jot down the positions of the remaining six players. Dots are quicker than Os and they're adequate. Use a felt-tipped pen.

Mark the numbers of the **important players**. Try to see and note the **line splits**. You need to look from the end zone to tell what the line splits are. Note **unusual** ways of lining up like offensive ends or backs who line up in a two-point stance. Note pre-snap **motion**. At least once, move close enough to hear the particular snap count the quarterback uses. Does he say, "Down!" or "Ready!" or "Team!" Is his count rhythmic or does he deliberately vary the time between counts to try to draw the defense off sides? We used to send players, generally our sons, who accompanied us, down near the field and behind the end zone to check the line splits and to hear the cadence.

Draw lines indicating who moved where when the ball was snapped. Mark the final ball carrier with a filled-in circle. Mark the path of a pitched or passed ball with dotted lines. Here's a filled out sheet.

You only have time to write dots for each player and a line showing the path of the ball carrier at the game. When you get home, put big circles like the ones preprinted on the form for each player. Also add blocking assignments for each player. The scout play diagrams become the script for your scout team during practice the week before you play that team. The scout team coach stands at the line of scrimmage between plays and holds the scout team binder up so the scout team players can see the next play. They each get their assignment then go execute the play.

I'd like to know who the opponent's bench warmers are but I never could figure out how to do it. I was too busy just trying to get the plays down. You'd need extra scouts and have to assign one to do just that I suspect.

Other things to look for:

• shifts
• types of offensive blocks used
•

Here's a filled-out scouting report diagram followed by a general information form I developed to be completed during lulls in the scrimmage or game. Put it at the front of your scouting book.

Date: 9/20/96

Vallejo @ Saints

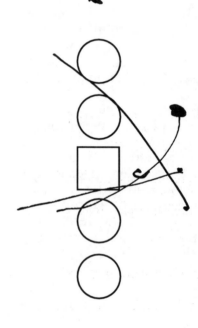

Scouting general information

Team: _____ Age/weight level: JPW   PW   JM   M

Date: _____ Scout: _____

How many players on the team being scouted? _____

What offensive cadence do they use? (E.g., "Ready Set Hut Hut")

_____

What do they usually go on? (e.g., first hut): _____

How far is each lineman's foot from his neighbor? (You must go to the end zone angle to

get this.) _____

	On offense	On defense
Which players are in two-point stance?	_____	_____
Three-point stance?	_____	_____
Four-point stance?	_____	_____
What are the stars' numbers?	_____	_____
What are the 6-play players' numbers?	_____	_____

Special teams:

Where on 40-yard line did they kick off from?_____

Where did the kick off land? Yard line? _____Where on yard line?_____

How far behind long snapper is punter? _____

Is punter off set or directly behind long snapper?   _____

Which direction does punter step when he punts? _____

When punter's foot hit ball, how far behind offensive line was he? _____

When punter's foot hit ball, which offensive lineman was he behind? _____

Did they kick their PATs?   yes   no

What type kickoff return did they run?_____

What type punt return did they run?   _____

7

Analyzing scouting reports

OK. Now you've got a scouting report done by you or an associate. How do you analyze it?

Diagram every play

I produced an opponent's playsheet each week for the players and other coaches. That was simply a diagram of each of the upcoming opponent's plays. This would not be a diagram of each play of the game that was scouted. Rather it was our condensed version of the top-secret playbook the opponent presumably handed out to their players.

It also showed where **our** players lined up against each of the opponent's offensive formations and it had miscellaneous notes about the opponent's offense. In most cases, the scouting report filled two sides of an 8 1/2 x 11 sheet of paper. As with other diagrams, I usually produced it on my Macintosh with the MacDraw program.

Analyzing the report

You simply go through the scouting report play by play and reproduce it more neatly.

Since the opponent's play diagram is the piece of paper the scout team coach uses in scrimmages to show the scout team how to mimic the upcoming opponent, it needs notes about which players are in a two-point stance and so forth. If the opponent has a dangerous star player, you will probably want to put one of your scout team players in a jersey with the same number during scrimmage. So the opponent's play diagram has to indicate where that player is in each play.

Special rules

If the opponent does a play in which lesser-known rules are pertinent, note that on the report. For example, Manteca ran a screen pass in which the ball went **backwards**. This is a **lateral**. So I made a note on the Manteca playsheet that this was a lateral and that meant that if the lateral was batted down, dropped, or overthrown, it was a **live ball**, not an incomplete pass, and that our players should pick it up and run it for a touchdown. Tackle-eligible plays are another example of those where I made a note about the rule on the scouting report.

Multiple formations

As a defensive coach, I **loved** to play teams that had lots of formations. I guess the offensive coaches in question thought defenses would be **confused** by different formations. Not ours.

As you saw in the job descriptions we handed out, our defensive players only had to learn three or four rules about where they line up in response to different offensive formations. For example, our cornerback lined up two yards in front of the widest receiver other than the tight end and went in motion with him if he moved before the snap. The offense could learn 30 different formations with the cornerback's man in 30 different places and our guy would simply go to a spot two yards in front of him—in response to each of those 30 formations.

The reason I liked multiple formation offenses is that the more formations they have, the fewer plays they run from each formation. Napa, for example, was at one extreme at the beginning of the season. They only had **one** formation, the wishbone, and nobody ever went in motion. So you knew **nothing** about what Napa was going to do until they snapped the ball and the players started moving. I'd like my kids to know sooner than that what the play is.

Manteca's screen lateral

At the other end of the spectrum were teams like Manteca and Benicia. They frequently had a formation from which they only ran one or two plays. Think about that.

Manteca had a screen lateral as I mentioned above. They lined three guys out wide to the right and the quarterback quickly wheeled around and threw to the rearmost guy. That was the **only** play they ran out of that three-guys-split-out-wide-to-the-right formation.

We noted on the scouting report that this was the **only** play they ran out of that formation. We told our players it was a **lateral** and that any loose ball was live. We reminded them they could **pick it up** and run for a touchdown. I said on the scouting report, "Yell 'screen!' when they line up in this formation."

I made a flip chart of tell-tale formations including that screen and I went around quizzing the players during practice that week and in the pre-game period. I would walk up to a player, show him the play on the flip chart and ask, "What's this?" The boy would study it and excitedly yell, "Screen!" "Right. How about this one?" I'd say showing him the next diagram and he'd yell, "Sweep!" and so on. The boys enjoyed the little flip-chart quizzes. And they darned well knew what those formations meant when the other team showed them in games.

We also **practiced** defending against those plays the week before the game. As the scout team broke the huddle and came to the line of scrimmage, I'd be yelling at the defense, "OK, what have we got?" They'd study the formation and start yelling, "Screen! Screen!" or whatever. Then we'd have the scout team run the play over and over as often as time permitted until we could defense it well.

For some reason, we never recovered or picked up the ball in practice against that Manteca screen. The scout team which was playing the role of Manteca always recovered it. And darned if the same thing didn't happen in the actual game. Manteca came out in that formation. Our players and coaches yelled, "Screen! Screen!" They threw it, missed it, and Manteca recovered it. Here are three pages of 1991 Manteca scouting report and the one-page 1992 Fairfield Falcons scouting report.

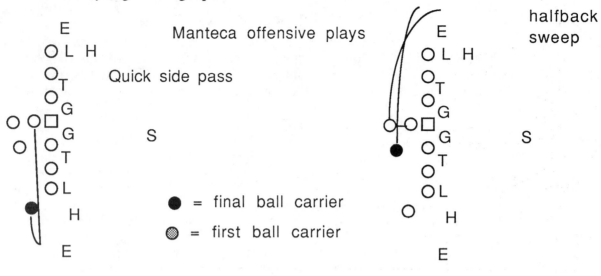

Manteca offensive plays

Quick side pass

halfback
sweep

● = final ball carrier

◉ = first ball carrier

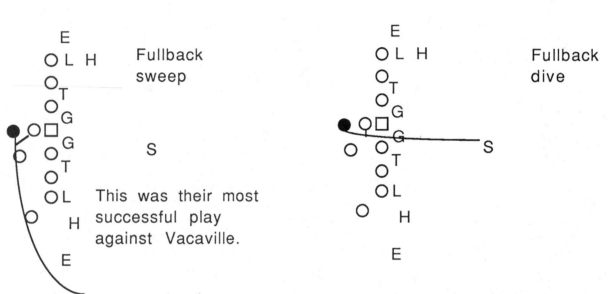

Fullback
sweep

Fullback
dive

This was their most
successful play
against Vacaville.

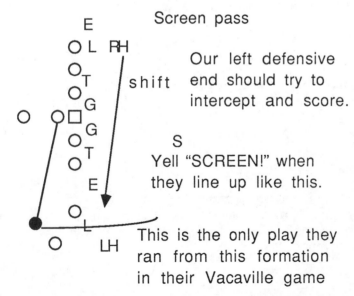

Screen pass

shift

Our left defensive
end should try to
intercept and score.

Yell "SCREEN!" when
they line up like this.

This is the only play they
ran from this formation
in their Vacaville game

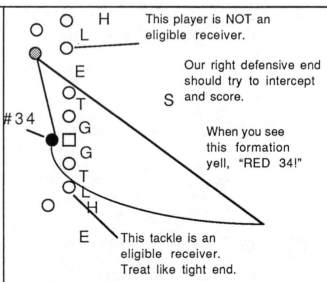

This player is NOT an
eligible receiver.

Our right defensive end
should try to intercept
and score.

When you see
this formation
yell, "RED 34!"

#34

This tackle is an
eligible receiver.
Treat like tight end.

Linemen: Don't let #34 out of backfield when
they line up in this formation. Tackle or block him.

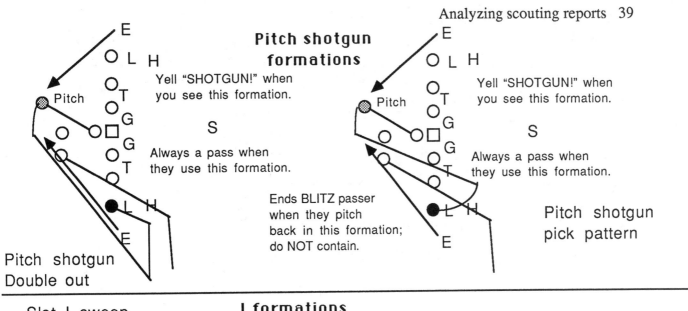

Pitch shotgun formations

Yell "SHOTGUN!" when you see this formation.

Pitch

Always a pass when they use this formation.

Ends BLITZ passer when they pitch back in this formation; do NOT contain.

Yell "SHOTGUN!" when you see this formation.

Pitch

Always a pass when they use this formation.

Pitch shotgun pick pattern

Pitch shotgun Double out

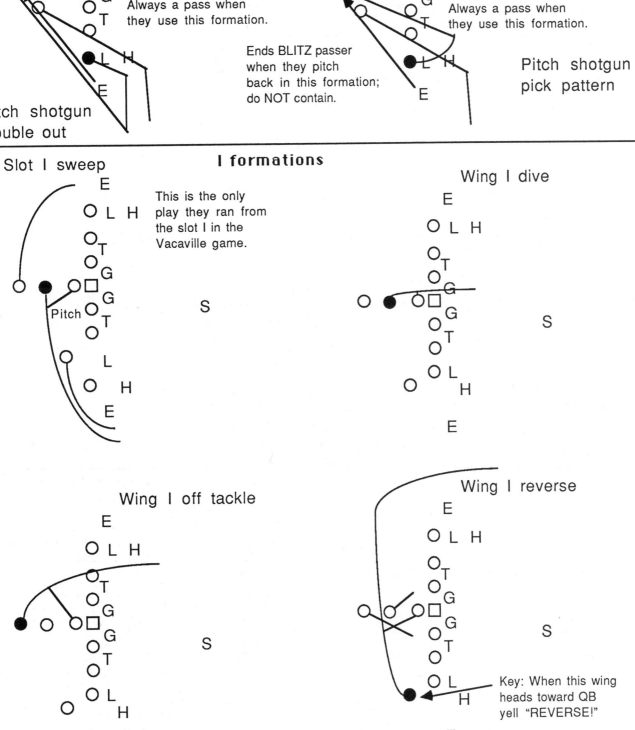

I formations

Slot I sweep

This is the only play they ran from the slot I in the Vacaville game.

Pitch

S

Wing I dive

E

S

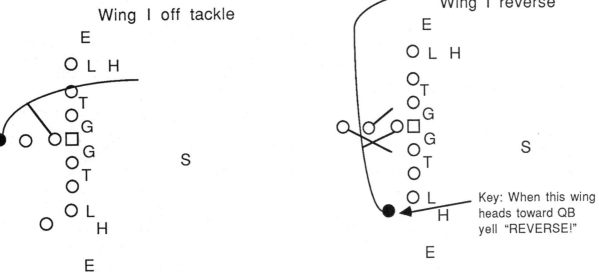

Wing I off tackle

S

Wing I reverse

S

Key: When this wing heads toward QB yell "REVERSE!"

Wing I post pass

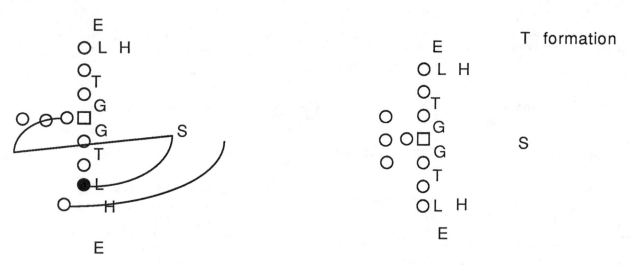

T formation

T formation: Manteca has a straight T formation with two tight ends. From that formation, they run the usual dives, off tackles, and sweeps.

Manteca gains most of its yards on sweeps. They get 3 to 5 yards up the middle.

Keys:
- 3 eligible receivers on one side means screen pass. Yell "SCREEN PASS!" One of our halfbacks must shift to other side. End try to intercept.
- Wing in slot means sweep to that side. Yell "SLOT SWEEP!"
- Wing heading toward center means reverse. Yell "REVERSE!"
- One back deeper than two others who are side-by-side means the pitch shotgun. Yell "SHOTGUN!" and look for a pass. Ends BLITZ passer.
- 4 players wide on one side means pass to halfback followed by him passing back to QB downfield. Yell "RED 34!" End try to intercept. Guards attack by air. Keep #34 (QB) in backfield by legal tackle or blocks.

Falcons offense

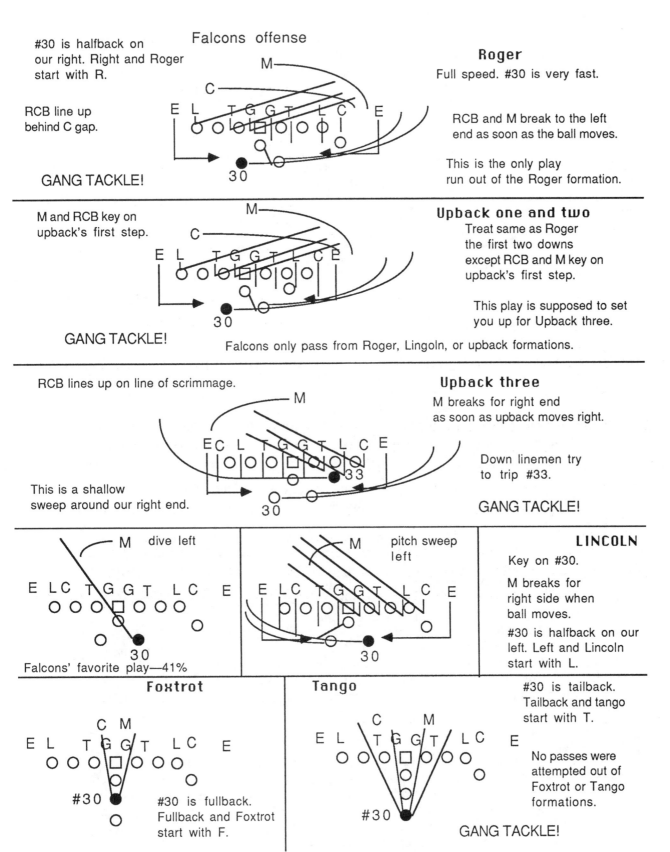

#30 is halfback on our right. Right and Roger start with R.

RCB line up behind C gap.

GANG TACKLE!

Roger

Full speed. #30 is very fast.

RCB and M break to the left end as soon as the ball moves.

This is the only play run out of the Roger formation.

M and RCB key on upback's first step.

GANG TACKLE!

Upback one and two

Treat same as Roger the first two downs except RCB and M key on upback's first step.

This play is supposed to set you up for Upback three.

Falcons only pass from Roger, Lingoln, or upback formations.

RCB lines up on line of scrimmage.

This is a shallow sweep around our right end.

Upback three

M breaks for right end as soon as upback moves right.

Down linemen try to trip #33.

GANG TACKLE!

M dive left

Falcons' favorite play—41%

M pitch sweep left

LINCOLN

Key on #30.

M breaks for right side when ball moves.

#30 is halfback on our left. Left and Lincoln start with L.

Foxtrot

#30 is fullback. Fullback and Foxtrot start with F.

Tango

#30 is tailback. Tailback and tango start with T.

No passes were attempted out of Foxtrot or Tango formations.

GANG TACKLE!

Always keep your head up when you block or tackle.

At the top of the first page of the Manteca scouting report, you see four rather normal plays all run out of the same formation. I had little to say about them on the report.

But at the **bottom** of the first page are Manteca's two **one-play** formations. Note how many comments there are to help our players make the most of this "intelligence bonus." I would think the Manteca coaches would have nightmares if they knew such a document was being studied and practiced by our team all week before their game with us.

The scouting reports reproduced in this book are the actual reports we gave to our players. These are not a neater, improved version done just for this book.

We beat Manteca 31-0, our biggest victory margin of the season. On defense, we held them to minus 28 yards and no first downs. I think that says something about complexity. We had the simplest defense in the league. And Manteca had the most complex offense of the ones we saw. Talentwise, we probably were stronger—but not 31 points stronger.

Note on the second page of the Manteca scouting report the keys and yelling instructions. We wanted our players not only to recognize the formation but to alert their teammates as well. Also, we suspect there is a little psychological effect on the opponent when they come out in one of their razzle-dazzle play formations and the defense starts acting like they've just run into an old friend.

The "pitch shotgun?"

I didn't know what to call Manteca's crooked T formation with the left halfback behind the other backs. But in practice, the quarterback always pitched to that left halfback and he threw a pass. So I concluded that the Manteca coaches apparently wanted to have a shotgun formation, but they didn't have a center who could snap the ball reliably to a shotgun quarterback. So I called it the "pitch shotgun."

(It's interesting to note that Manteca did not have a **punting** game either. We presume that's because they had no long snapper. We saw that they had no punting game when we scouted them. We told our players that during practices before the Manteca game. When Manteca had fourth and long early in the game, we yelled out at our players. "They don't have a punt! They don't have a punt!" A Manteca mother who was working the chain gang on our side of the field heard us and said, "That's right, but how did **you** know?" She thought a traitor had told us.)

Whatever you call the crooked T or pitch shotgun, our kids knew that whenever they saw Manteca's left halfback lined up a bit behind the other backs to yell, "Shotgun!" and prepare for a pass. The defensive backs and linebackers got mentally into their man-to-man coverage mode and our entire line pinned their ears back in preparation for an all-out assault on the left halfback. As I recall, the only pass Manteca completed all day was a look-in to the left tight end for a gain of about two feet.

In the I-formation diagrams, you again see the **one-play formation** mistake. Manteca normally had a wingback on one side when they used the I. But when they wanted to **sweep** out of it, they **split out** the tight end and made the wingback a **slotback**. Think about that. They're going to do a sweep, which is their best play. But before they start the play, they telegraph to us exactly what play it is and which side it's going to. So much for the element of surprise.

The wing I

The wing I diagrams illustrates a formation which tells our players that one of **four** plays is coming. The dive, off tackle, post pass, or reverse. Since the dive and off tackle are quite different from the reverse, all of which are quite different from the post pass, the wing I is a Manteca formation which didn't give us much useful information. But Manteca had to **telegraph** the **reverse** immediately after the snap by having the wing move in a different direction than he moves in any other play.

Our linemen and halfbacks are worried about all 4 wing-I plays until the snap. Then the wing takes a step sideways and our halfback yells, "Reverse!" That alerts our down linemen that they can stop worrying about the post pass, dive, or off tackle and go full bore for the reverse. Furthermore, it alerts our ends that the play is a reverse going to the side opposite where the wing lined up. That tells our left defensive end to pursue through the backfield and our right defensive end to go into a come-to-Papa mode as he turns left toward the quarterback at the depth he practiced that week when we ran this play.

Just **telling** the players this in a scouting report is not enough. You have to **practice** it during the week. In this case, have the wing take one step to the inside and stop while the halfback yells, "Reverse!" Do that several times in both directions so both halfbacks learn. Then have the scout team run the play over and over so the defense gets used to the Pavlovian sequence of:

1. wing steps toward middle
2. halfback yells, "Reverse!"
3. defense tackles a wing running sideways three yards behind the line of scrimmage.

Manteca, also had a T-formation series. But the plays they ran were not unusual in any way—or telegraphed in any way—so we gave the T short shrift in the playsheet.

The keys described on the third sheet are also a description of the five flip charts I used to quiz the players in our preparation for the Manteca game. I gave them that flip-chart quiz over and over up until one minute or so before our kickoff team took the field.

Player keys

I was a bit weak on picking up player keys in 1991. By player keys I mean that some teams put their star players in different positions for different plays. For example, Oakland had a star who wore number 34. To an extent, we could figure out where the play was going by where he lined up. When he was at wing, there was a good chance it was a pass to him. When he was in the backfield, it was often a hand off to him.

To make sure you pick up on player keys, try to note the **player numbers** of the backs when you scout. Then, when you analyze the raw scouting reports the weekend before you play that team, try to find patterns. Try to find who the most frequently used ball carrier is. Who is the favorite receiver?

Vallejo's scrambler

Spotting player keys was important in our 1992 victory over Vallejo. For example, we noticed that when their #3 was at quarterback, he always dropped back as if to throw a long pass—which he could do—but he preferred to **scramble** and run.

We taught our kids this and instructed our ends to be careful to approach him from the side **under control**. Every time he came out in the quarterback position, I yelled, "Scramble! Scramble!" The Vallejo coaches could hear me because my megaphone was aimed at them as well as at my defenders. We kept #3 from escaping time and again.

Finally, the Vallejo coaches figured they'd fool us. They put #3 at quarterback, but had him run a **quarterback sneak**. Apparently, they thought we were overplaying the scramble. I don't know how you do that. And they thought they'd fool our kids with the sneak. He gained about two feet on the play. Our guards were doing the same old boring explode-low-through-the-A-gap and met him instantly. We beat Vallejo 13-6 in the greatest Bears Jr. Pee Wee game I've ever seen.

The predictable—and unstoppable Falcons

The 1992 Falcons were another team that moved a player around to different spots in their formation. Their great running back was Gregory Reed (no relation) #30. We saw he was moving around at the game we scouted. But we did not recognize the pattern **at** the game. When I got home and analyzed all their plays, I cracked the code. You can see the result in the fourth scouting report.

The Falcons had nothing **but** one- and two-play formations when you took note of the location of #30. The fact that we still could not stop them shows how good a back Reed was.

They also made two changes between their Suisun game, which we scouted, and our game. They switched sides so our game was a mirror image of the Suisun game. That fouled us up more than it should have. And they put three down linemen on one side of the center and two on the other.

If #30 had not been so talented—and we had not made the mistake of telling the Falcons that we scouted the Suisun game—we probably would have stopped them cold with this kind of scouting report. This was the most predictable offense I've encountered in two years. And I mean the **worst kind** of predictability: the **formation** told you where the ball was going. But even with that tremendous handicap, #30 still scored 12 points against us.

If Reed were on my team and I coached offense, I'd run an I or single wing formation with him at tailback and never use a second formation. I'd darned well get him the ball on almost every play. But the **formation** would tell the opposition **nothing** about where he was going with it.

Distributing the scouting reports

When I got raw scouting diagrams from another coach or did them myself I would file them in a scouting folder. Then, when the Sunday before the opponent in question arrived, I would take those scouting diagrams out of the folder and use them to create a formal, neat, one- to three-page playsheet for the players and coaches.

I would analyze whether they favored their right or their left. (Contrary to widespread belief, I never found a team that was not almost precisely 50/50 when it came to which side they ran to.) I would calculate the percentage of times each play was used. I did not calculate down-and-distance tendencies because there are so few plays in a youth football game that you don't have enough data. You might only have two third and longs so you really cannot draw conclusions.

I would give the other coaches their scouting report at the coaches meeting on Sunday or Monday night. Then we would give each defensive player a copy at the end of the week's first practice which was almost always Tuesday night.

The value of scouting

After not having any scouting at all my first year as a coach—and sorely missing it—I tended to **over**value the scouting reports when I finally got them at the beginning of the 1991 season. I made lots of defensive changes each week at the beginning of the season to take advantage of the scouting reports. But by the end of the season, I did not get so excited about them.

In general, the value of a scouting report is directly proportional to the **unusualness** of the opposing team's offense. If they run a straight T formation with two tight ends and they do nothing but dives, off tackles, sweeps, and drop-back passes, the scouting report really won't have you doing anything you shouldn't have prepared for during the **preseason** when you had **no** scouting reports.

You're also looking for **keys**—indicators in either the offensive **formation** or the **location** of key players or the **initial movements** of key offensive players—of where the play is going. The fewer different formations the offense runs, the harder it is to find pre-snap keys.

Even if you can't find pre-snap keys, just knowing the opposing team's best plays and best players will help you. You can spend more practice time that week working on defending against those plays.

8

Substitution schedule

On Friday night before each game, I made two substitution schedules: one for a close game and one to use if we had a two-touchdown lead or our opponent had a three-touchdown lead late in the game. The substitution schedule shows who plays in which position for each of the first 40 defensive plays. Generally, 40 defensive plays was the most we'd see in a game—and then only in a game in which we were doing badly.

The purpose of the substitution schedule was to make sure our minimum-play players got their minimum number of plays and to put them where they could contribute the most or hurt the least.

Minimum-play players

At an early coaches' meeting, we assigned each player on the team to either offense or defense for the purpose of getting their mandatory minimum number of plays. The offense and defense each ended up with about four such players. As stated elsewhere in the book, our league rules at the time required us to give each player **six** plays (now ten).

No more than one at a time

In the 1990 season, we once got behind in our substitutions of six-play players as we called them. So we put two in at the same time—next to each other on the defensive line.

Big mistake. The opponent ran a dive that went 70 yards for a touchdown right through them. We resolved to never again put two six-play players in the game at the same time unless we had a good lead.

24 plays

If you have four six-play players and you don't want any two in the game at the same time, it will take you 24 defensive plays to complete your mandatory play requirements.

We had entire games where the opponent only got in 19 offensive plays. Generally speaking, when your team is doing well, the other team will get fewer offensive plays—in the 20 to 25 range in my experience. Even mighty Oakland only got to run four plays against us in the entire first quarter of their first game with us. Of course, the fact that they scored a 60-yard touchdown on the first play from scrimmage made them not **need** many plays.

But the point is, if you need 24 plays to get your minimum play guys in, you have to start with the very first play from scrimmage. For those of you not familiar with youth football, each team is required to supply two mandatory play monitors. These are usually volunteer parents taken from the stands just before the game.

One from each team stands on each side of the field. That is, a representative from each team stands on each team's sidelines. They usually stand together and chat when not doing their job. The mandatory play monitors from other teams who were on **our** sideline often expressed amazement that we started putting our minimum play guys in on the first play. And they were similarly amazed in some games when we had completed our mandatory play requirements at the beginning of the second quarter.

Other teams seemed to wait to put their six-play players in until the game was safely in hand or surely lost. Then they would put them in **as a group**. I have nightmares about having to do such a thing in the second half of a close game. I want them in **one at a time**, and to make sure I finish at that rate, I have to start on the very first play from scrimmage.

Two on, two off

The no-more-than-one-minimum-play-guy-at-a-time rule means that two guys go on the field and two come off on each play. Each pair of substitutes contains one starting player and one minimum-play player. The starter is going in to replace the minimum-play player who took his spot on the last play. The minimum-play guy is going in to replace a starter for one play.

Note on the substitution schedule below that the two columns labelled Sub # 1 and Sub #2 state who's going in for whom. It is from those two columns that you work during the game. I presume the mandatory-play monitor also uses those columns to see that the subs are going in as planned.

As the opposing offense is in or breaking their huddle, you yell out the **next** two subs from the schedule. For example, "66 and 41, you're in next play!" Then when the referee blows the play dead, you remind the two players, "66 and 41, get in there!"

Once you confirm that they are going in, you look at the two sub columns and alert the next two players—one of whom, the starter, is just coming off the field. "67 and 35, next defensive play!"

Go over it with the players beforehand

Show each player the substitution schedule **before** the game. The conversation goes like this:

To a starter: "Bob, you're going to play right tackle today. And you're L2 on the kickoff team. Jim is going to be replacing you at right tackle every fourth play. His first play will be the third play of the game. OK?" (Showing him the schedule as you talk)

To a minimum-play player: "Jim, you're going to be at right tackle today every fourth play. Your first play is the third play of the game." (Showing him the schedule as you talk)

Write on their hands

My sons are on a swim team in the summer. The swim team coaches write each swimmer's events on the back of their hands in felt-tipped pen.

In football, my players would often ask, "What position?" when I told them it was their turn to go in during a game. Or they would go onto the field and not know who they were replacing.

So I started writing their position on the back of their hands or arm before each game. My fellow coaches laughed at first. Later the offensive coordinator starting writing his own reminders on his guys' hands.

My only criterion is, "Does it work?"

It does.

Write the defense and kickoff team positions, if he's on the kickoff team, on the player's hand. A player's hand might say, "D   LT   K   R1" which means he's the left tackle on defense and his kickoff position is the first player in from the right sideline.

Twelve players on the field

Twelve players on the field is usually a **15-yard penalty**. That's true if the twelfth player participates in the play. It's called, "Illegal participation."

If he's running off the field when the center snaps the ball, it's only a five-yard penalty. And in our league, they simply never called it if the kid was running off the field.

Fifteen yards is a lot. And illegal participation is a stupid penalty. It's also a **coach's** penalty in most cases.

In the 1990 season, we got penalized for illegal participation in each of the first three games. I resolved that would not happen again in 1991. But it did—also in the first three games—even though we actually practiced sending substitutes in during the preseason. In 1992, we finally got our act together to the point that we did not have a 12-men-on-the-field penalty at all. (Although we **did** play a number of plays with only 10 men on the field.)

You really have to have your act together. That includes using a written substitution schedule for each play until your minimum-play guys have all completed their plays. It also includes having your field captain count players before each play. If he has other than eleven, he's to call **time out** or yell the appropriate orders if there are no time outs left.

You must have only one coach in charge of substitutes. And I found it had to be me. Once, when I had an assistant handling substitutions, I looked out and saw only **three** down linemen. Our 8-2-1 was supposed to have **four**. So I quickly told a fourth to go in.

Turned out there were **already** four. One was standing up. If I had been handling substitutions, I would have known that. As far as delegating the chore, I found that didn't work because I as head offensive coach would feel the need to get involved in a substitution decision like the one I just described. The offensive coach thought I would not have **time** to handle substitutions. But I really didn't have anything else to do since we didn't call defensive plays. (We only had one defense.)

In our first 1991 game, a minimum-play **defensive** player stayed in the game after a change of possession and became the twelfth man on an **offensive** play. If I had it made it more clear that he was only going in for one play at a time, that probably would **not** have happened.

Ten players on the field

Ten players on the field won't cost you a penalty. But it may cost you the game.

It happens when a player assumes he's supposed to come out but does not wait for his substitute to relieve him. Tell the players the **planned** substitution schedule. But you must also train them to remain at their post until their sub relieves them in person. The sub may forget—or be hurt—or have completed all his mandatory plays.

You can also get ten players on the field if a player gets **injured**. At the time of the injury, you get a sub in because the game stops while people administer to the injured player. But on the next **change of possession** or **special-team play** in which the injured player is supposed to participate, you are likely to forget.

For example, say your left linebacker gets hurt. No problem, you send in the injury sub for the linebacker position. Then your team intercepts a pass and runs it back for a touchdown. The defense comes off the field, the offense gets the extra point and you yell, "Kickoff team!"

But you forget that the injured linebacker is **also** R3 on the kickoff team. The sub who went in for the linebacker on defense sits down for the kickoff because he's not on the kickoff team. Says so right on his hand. Or maybe he **is** on the kickoff team. And he's exactly where the letters on his hand say he should be. But **nobody's** at R3.

Again, the solution is to have the kicker count the players every time before he kicks. We **always** had the kicker count them—even in practice—so it became a part of his kicking routine.

Mandatory play monitors

You have to **brief** your mandatory play monitors before each game—especially if they have not done it before or not done it recently.

In our first 1991 game, we failed to brief our mandatory play monitor. We expected that game to be easy and it was. So I gave each player a **whole quarter** rather than just six plays. Late in the game, the mandatory play monitors on our side informed us that several players only had **one play** so far. These were players who had played a whole quarter!

I was steaming. I didn't say anything improper. I just protested firmly that they **had** played a quarter. I showed them my computerized substitution schedule. I invited them to ask the boys in question. They adamantly maintained, "We didn't see them go in and if we didn't see them, they didn't go in."

They further suggested that it was more likely that **we** were **lying** than that **they** had **not been paying attention**. We still didn't lose our cool but our facial expressions and body language inspired one of the mandatory play guys to say out loud that he was considering punching me in the nose after the game.

I told our head coach the situation and reminded him that one of **our** parents was supposed to be half of this two-man, mandatory-play-monitoring team. Turned out one of them **was** one of our parents. From the way they were acting, I thought they were **both** from the opposing side and were deliberately trying to sabotage our team.

Anyway, we had to put these players in **again**. In some cases, we had to put defensive players in on offense and vice versa to comply with the rules by the end of the game.

Had that been a close game, we could have **lost** because of our failure to brief our mandatory play monitor as to the importance of his job and the need to pay attention on every play. Plus, I learned to give our mandatory play monitor a copy of my substitution schedule. Try to get the same parent to be the mandatory play monitor for each game. One of ours said he enjoyed doing it because, "It's the best seat in the house."

Injury subs

Youth football has fewer injuries per capita than some other youth sports like soccer and gymnastics. But it is almost certain than one or more of your players will have to come out of the game with a bump or bruise for at least a few plays.

That is **not** the time to start thinking about who should take his place. Think about it the night before the game when you are making your substitution schedule. Note that at the bottom of my substitution schedule, there are injury subs for each category of defensive position. Note further, that they are listed in order. The top one goes in for the first injury, the next one for the second.

Kickoff team

I was in charge of the kickoff team as well as the regular defense. So I also had the kickoff team line up and an injury sub for the kicker and for a tackler on my substitution schedule. I'll discuss the kickoff team in a later book.

Here's an example of my close-game substitution schedule:

Top Secret Game Plan. Do NOT show to opponent's Mandatory Play Monitor.															
Defensive Substitution Schedule for 11/16															
Play	LHB	LE	LLB	LT	LG	S	RG	RT	RLB	RE	RHB	Sub #1	Sub #2	Play	Yds.
1	25	78	31	67	52	20	70	85	68	26	99				
2	25	78	31	67	77	20	70	92	68	26	99	77 for 52	92 for 85		
3	25	78	31	67	52	35	70	92	68	26	99	52 for 77	35 for 20		
4	25	78	31	67	52	20	70	92	88	26	99	88 for 68	20 for 35		
5	25	78	31	67	52	20	70	85	68	26	99	85 for 92	68 for 88		
6	25	78	31	67	77	20	70	92	68	26	99	77 for 52	92 for 85		
7	25	78	31	67	52	35	70	92	68	26	99	52 for 77	35 for 20		
8	25	78	88	67	52	20	70	92	68	26	99	88 for 31	20 for 35		
9	25	78	31	67	52	20	70	85	68	26	99	85 for 92	31 for 88		
10	25	78	31	67	77	20	70	92	68	26	99	77 for 52	92 for 85		
11	25	78	31	67	52	35	70	92	68	26	99	52 for 77	35 for 20		
12	25	78	31	67	52	20	70	92	68	26	88	88 for 99	20 for 35		
13	25	78	31	67	52	20	70	85	68	26	99	85 for 92	99 for 88		
14	25	78	31	67	77	20	70	92	68	26	99	77 for 52	92 for 85		
15	25	78	31	67	52	35	70	92	68	26	99	52 for 77	35 for 20		
16	88	78	31	67	52	20	70	92	68	26	99	20 for 35	88 for 25		
17	25	78	31	67	52	20	70	85	68	26	99	25 for 88	85 for 92		
18	25	78	31	67	77	20	70	92	68	26	99	77 for 52	92 for 85		
19	25	78	31	67	52	35	70	92	68	26	99	52 for 77	35 for 20		
20	25	78	31	67	52	20	70	92	68	26	88	20 for 35	88 for 99		
21	25	78	31	67	52	20	70	85	68	26	99	85 for 92	99 for 88		
22	25	78	31	67	77	20	70	92	68	26	99	77 for 52	92 for 85		
23	25	78	31	67	52	35	70	92	68	26	99	52 for 77	35 for 20		
24	88	78	31	67	52	20	70	92	68	26	99	88 for 25	20 for 35		
25	25	78	31	67	52	20	70	92	68	26	99		25 for 88		
26	25	78	31	67	52	20	70	92	68	26	99				
27	25	78	31	67	52	20	70	92	68	26	99				
28	25	78	31	67	52	20	70	92	68	26	99				
29	25	78	31	67	52	20	70	92	68	26	99				
30	25	78	31	67	52	20	70	92	68	26	99				
31	25	78	31	67	52	20	70	92	68	26	99				
32	25	78	31	67	52	20	70	92	68	26	99				
33	25	78	31	67	52	20	70	92	68	26	99				
34	25	78	31	67	52	20	70	92	68	26	99				
35	25	78	31	67	52	20	70	92	68	26	99				
36	25	78	31	67	52	20	70	92	68	26	99				
37	25	78	31	67	52	20	70	92	68	26	99				
38	25	78	31	67	52	20	70	92	68	26	99				
39	25	78	31	67	52	20	70	92	68	26	99				
40	25	78	31	67	52	20	70	92	68	26	99				

Injury subs		E		LB		GT		S		HB					
		20		25		91		68		27					
		68		99		60		32		32					

Kickoff	LE	LFT	L3	L2	L1	K	R1	R2	R3	RFT	RE				
	26	99	68	25	78	31	67	27	92	70	78				
sub	32					26									

The left column labelled "Play" refers to the sequence of the game. Play 1 is the first play (from scrimmage) of the game and so on.

The next eleven columns are the defensive positions. Below those headings, you can see the jersey number of the player playing in that position on each of the first 40 plays.

Then come the Sub #1 and Sub #2 columns showing the two players going in and the two players going out at the beginning of that play.

The play and yards columns are for keeping track of the progress of the game. I'll discuss those in another chapter.

You can see the injury subs listed for each category of position below the 40-play schedule. The top one of each pair goes in first.

Note that some of the injury subs are already playing other positions. When the injury sub is already playing, you have to replace him with **his** injury sub. For example, if #20 gets hurt at safety, you move the right linebacker, #68 to safety. That means you have to move #25 to right linebacker from his left halfback spot. And #27 comes off the bench to replace #25 at left half back.

That's complicated. But with injuries you generally have a long time to get organized while the medical technician talks to the injured player out on the field.

Computer spreadsheet program

I did my substitution schedules on a computer spreadsheet program. If the six-play guys always go into the same position, you only need to do the first four plays manually. Then you tell the computer to repeat that sequence of four, including all columns from LHB to Sub #2, from play 5 to play 24. The main reason for doing it on the computer is that you can tell the computer to repeat recurring patterns with one or two keystrokes.

You could almost as easily design a blank version of my substitution schedule. Fill it out by hand each week. Put your starters in pencil across the play number 1 line. Then write one sub in on each play line. Wherever there's no number written, the first play starter plays in that position on that play.

Six-play guys in bold

Note that I've put my six-play guys in **bold-face type**. That's to help me and the mandatory play monitor see where they go and when. The six-play guys on this substitution schedule are #88, #77, #35, and #85. The latter three go in every fourth play at the same position. #88 is a player who is very small and who is soon spotted by the opponents as somebody to pick on. Because of that, I put him at **four different** positions so that by the time the other team notices where he is, he's gone. And if they figure out the every-four-plays sequence on the other six-play players, and try to anticipate #88's return to a position, they will be disappointed. (In 1992, # 88 was a no-kidding star of the team.)

Don't get too cute

It occurred to our head coach that we should always bring the **weakest** starter off the field when we substitute. In theory, that leaves the strongest ten players on the field all the time. Substituting the way I do often causes one of our **top** players to leave the field for a play.

But upon reflection, I decided trying to shift players around like the injury sub routine I described above was too confusing and likely to result in a position being completely uncovered.

Another problem with the weakest starter leaving for every six-play player is that the weakest sub then may **never** get on the field himself. He could become a player in need of **his** six plays, too.

The only way you could get away with the weakest player coming off every time is if he and the other minimum play players all played the **same position**. And that's probably not a good idea because the other team's offense routinely probes the entire defense for weak spots at the beginning of the game. If they find one, they attack it again and again.

Big-point-spread substitution schedule

When we got a big lead, I relaxed my no-two-minimum-play-players-in-at-the-same-time rule. I would have the minimum play players and the starters share their position by each going in for two plays at a time. I would also have offensive players whom I wanted to train or try out for defense share positions with starting defensive players.

Not just charity

The big-point-spread substitution schedule is not just an act of charity toward players who don't get much playing time. It is an important opportunity to train and evaluate backup players. Indeed, you will almost certainly find when you review the video of a big-point-spread game that a backup player performed better than your starter.

Depth is very important. I believe our 1991 defensive down linemen were the best in the league. But the amazing thing was two of them could be injured and we'd **still** have the best defensive down linemen in the league. That's because I had two spares who got extensive playing time. Matter of fact, both had been first string and had either been moved to start at another defensive position or they were only reluctantly moved to the bench. But both were excellent, experienced down linemen.

Actually, you could have injured **all four** of my down linemen and the four substitutes would **still** probably be the best down linemen in the league—although we'd start getting dangerously weak at **other** defensive positions because we'd be switching linebackers and halfbacks to the down linemen positions they'd played in previous years.

Finally, you want to give your youngest players as much playing time as possible to build for next year—to keep them on the team and to give them experience and confidence.

Running up the score

It's against the rules in our league to continue to run up the score after you get a certain lead. One of the steps you are supposed to take to prevent it is to substitute freely.

In our game against Manteca, the score hit 31-0 even though I immediately switched to the two-touchdown lead substitution schedule when it was 12-0. In fact, I had a semi-two-touchdown-lead substitution schedule going from the first play of the game. That is, I had some medium-level players sharing positions every other play in addition to the six-play guys going in every fourth play at other positions.

In that game, we eventually had everybody and his brother playing everywhere. Offensive linemen were playing running back. Offensive split ends were playing defensive line. It was *Amateur Hour* and *Star Search* rolled into one. At one point, I was yelling to experienced defensive players on the field, "Hey, Billy, tell George how to play cornerback after this play!"

The Manteca team still did not get a first down. Maybe they had their six-play and defensive guys in on offense, too. In any event, Manteca will no doubt have stronger teams in years to come.

Hurry-up offense

What if the opponent runs a hurry-up, no huddle offense?

We never encountered it.

In 1993, we ran a warp-speed no-huddle for entire games until the last game of the season. We ran 70 to 80 plays a game, about double the normal number.

If the opponents are **quick** with their no-huddle offense, they can prevent you from getting your subs in on schedule. As a result, the same six-play player will stay in for each of those hurry-up plays. If the other team doesn't notice him, that shouldn't be too much of a problem. And they are **less** likely to notice him because they have no huddle in which to discuss it.

If the other team takes their time when the clock is stopped—after incomplete passes, running out of bounds, moving the chains, etc.,—you can make your substitutions then. In that case, treat each unbroken **series** as a play on the substitution schedule. Play number one becomes series number one; play number two, series number two; and so forth. Only remember that the six-play player on the field should get credit for more than one play per series.

Few good defenders

In 1991, I had a very weak minimum play player. As stated above, I hid him successfully from the opposing team by putting him at a different position every time he went in. That worked. In 1993, I needed to do the opposite. But I did not realize it until the season was over.

In 1993, I had the opposite problem. I only had one defensive veteran. I generally had him play the middle linebacker position in my 10-1. The problem was that the opposing offense would probe and find weak points in my defense because of all the rookies. I should have told my one veteran, Will Sykes, to never play the same defensive position two plays in a row. That is, he would be authorized to trade places with a teammate every play. On play #1 he might tap the left linebacker on the butt and say, "Play middle for this play." On play #2, he'd tap the right cornerback on the butt and say, "Play middle on this play."

The result would be the offense would never find a weak point that stayed weak. They might run off tackle right and gain yards. But if they did it again and again, they'd eventually be stopped when Sykes was playing at that hole. In fact, he could probably learn to anticipate their plays from tendencies and the success of the previous play and so forth. In that case, his instruction would be, "Play the position where you think the next play will go."

If the opposing team ever figured out that he was moving around, they could audible out of any play to his position. Then we would have to have him shift at the last second on so forth. The bottom line is you need to move around both extremely weak players and extremely strong players, if you have them, so the offense cannot find a play that consistently works.

9

Game-day preparation

Youth football practice time is tightly controlled. In our league and the others I'm familiar with it's two hours a night three nights a week. However, there is no rule that I'm aware of on **pre-game** activities. So there is a temptation to try to get a lot accomplished during that time.

However, we tried it one year. And it seemed **not** to work. Basically, we had too much time on our hands with too many boys who were antsy to play the game.

An hour and a half early

Our games started at 9:00 am usually. Our team newsletter told us to be at the game site an hour and a half earlier. That's probably about right.

The only mandatory pre-game activities are weigh-in and stretching. Unfortunately, weigh-in was always a bit disorganized in our league. And we spent a lot of time waiting for it to happen.

When we were allowed in the locker room, I went around visiting with each of my defensive players individually. At that time, I would write their position on their hands and go over their place in the substitution schedule with them. I would also review with them, often using a flip-chart quiz, the opposing team's offensive keys. That is, the formations which indicated they were about to do a certain play and the initial movements of key players after the snap which indicated which way the play was going. If we coaches were not allowed in the locker room, I would accomplish my individual visits tasks during the miscellaneous time before the game. For example, while waiting to go into the locker room for weigh-in; with the lighter, already-dressed players as they waited for the heavier players to emerge from the locker room, while milling around waiting for stretching or player introductions, even in between exercises.

Equipment

At **home** games, if a player forgets equipment, you can probably either have a relative get it from his home or get a replacement from your equipment locker. But at **away** games, missing equipment can be a real problem.

This is really the equipment manager's job. But as defensive coach, you need to be concerned that your players are ready equipment wise.

Before they leave home, the boys should gather their equipment into their equipment bags using a checklist. Here's a suggested one:

- home game jersey
- away game jersey
- football shoes
- helmet (make sure all internal pads are intact)
- teeth protector
- chin strap
- shoulder pads
- girdle
- tail-bone pad
- two hip pads
- game pants
- belt
- lace for front of pants
- two thigh pads
- two knee pads
- game socks
- second pair of socks in case the first pair gets wet from dew or wet weather
- jock
- under-shoulder-pads shirt

Optional:

- forearm pads
- down-linemen gloves
- receiver gloves
- neck roll
- extreme weather gear
- shin guards
- rib pads
- elbow pads

At our first 1992 game, which was not only away but far away, one of our players discovered that his equipment was in another family car which had been left home. Fortunately for him, another player was too heavy and couldn't play. But the equipmentless player did not get in until the second half as a result.

Because of the possibility of equipment being forgotten or becoming unserviceable during the game, the equipment manager needs to have two full sets of player equipment. He should also have additional inventory of smaller items like teeth protectors and chin straps.

Travel in uniform

The best way to reduce the possibility that someone will forget their equipment is to tell them to get dressed for the game in their homes. We did that twice at the end of the season for the purpose of getting extra practice time before the game. It caused no problems—

except players forgetting all or part of their street clothes—no shoes other than football shoes, no street pants. Forgetting one's street clothes can cause inconvenience after the game. But from the perspective of a defensive coach, I much prefer the boy forgetting all or part of his **street** clothes to forgetting all or part of his **football** equipment.

I know it's traditional to put your equipment on in the locker room before the game. To heck with tradition. Whatever works. They can take off their equipment and change to street clothes in the locker room **after** the game if they want the "locker-room experience."

Stretching

You need to have the players stretch and shake out the cob webs. But you do not need any strenuous calisthenics that will tire the boys out. Calisthenics are generally the province of the head coach. But to the extent that you have input, you should resist any exercises which will produce fatigue.

Full-speed hitting

On the other hand, I believe your pre-game warm-up **must** include full-speed hitting. We noticed early in the season that our opponents' best drives against us usually occurred on the first drive of the game. In our two games with Oakland, they scored on that first drive. And since we never scored against them, that one score would have been enough to win the game.

We concluded that our boys simply were not mentally ready to play until after five or six plays. OK. So we made sure thereafter that those first five or six plays **did not count**. That is, we ran those first five or six plays against **our own team**.

We tried to have three or four players go against each other in mini-scrimmages. That worked great in practice. But for some reason, it flopped as a pre-game drill. The kids weren't hitting hard enough.

So we had the first-string offense run five or six plays against the rest of the team and the first-string defense defend five or six offensive plays run by the remaining players. And we coaches circulated around the scrimmage exhorting the players to get fired up and hit hard. Our two extra players (we had 24 in 1992) rotated in.

Go-on-the-ball drill

Defensive linemen jumping offside is a perennial problem. And it is intolerable. In many of our games, we held the opponent's offense to negative yards or small positive yardage on the day. Given those miserly total yardage's, a player who jumps offside may, with that single lapse of concentration, become the opponent's leading ground gainer for the day.

To help prevent jumping offside, you should give your defensive linemen (including linebackers in the 8-2-1) practice going on the ball. That is, have someone call the opponent's cadence and snap the ball with the defensive linemen going on the ball rather than the count. The coach or player who calls the cadence should deliberately use long counts and inflection to try to get the defense to jump offside. Try to get in about ten snaps before kickoff.

Man-to-man-coverage drill

If you have time, it would be good to give your pass defenders some practice covering receivers man-to-man. I was rarely able to do this before a game because the offense always took most of my defensive backfield for offensive drills.

The drill is simply a coach or quarterback sending a receiver out on a pass pattern with a defender lining up two yards in front of him then staying with him when he goes out. I found it's often better to do this drill with no ball. In man-to-man coverage, the defender is supposed to be looking at the receiver, not the quarterback. When you actually have a ball in the drill, the defender tends to watch the quarterback. That's bad. With no ball, the object becomes to stay with the receiver—and that's exactly what you want.

During the drill, you could also have the safeties work on their staying-behind-all-receivers technique.

Opponent's plays and formations

Before kickoff, you should go over the opponent's playsheet. Create a playsheet with **no defensive positions marked** on it. Then use it to quiz your players. "Where do you line up when they come out in this formation?" "What do you do when they run this play?" Make sure each player knows the right answer to those two questions for each of the opponent's plays.

Kickoff assignment

With each member of the kickoff team and kickoff team injury subs, go over the player's position and job description.

Field captains

Review with your field captain and his substitute the captain's responsibilities.

• Count the players before every play
• When to call time (wrong number of players on the field, strange offensive formation)
• clock management (If we're ahead, call time just before other team ready to snap; if we're behind, call time immediately.)
• Penalty-decision guidelines.
  Look at defensive coach. If he's not paying attention:
    • We do not take points off the board
    • We want the ball if that's one of the choices.
    • Don't decline a penalty unless they lost as many yards or more yards on the play as the penalty would cost them.
• Take charge and correct problems you see.
• Go over the substitution schedule so he knows where the six-play players will be and when.
• Keep team fired up

Psyche up

Perhaps the most important thing that has to happen during pre-game activities is that the team must get into the proper frame of mind to play football. Football is an aggressive collision sport and most boys are not normally in an aggressive, collision frame of mind.

We got our boys into that frame of mind partly with the full-speed hitting and partly by having them yell in unison.

Each week, we tried to have a theme. For example, the first week, our head coach would yell, "Who are we?" and the boys would answer, "Bears!" Then he'd yell, "What are we?" and the boys would answer, "Champions!"

For the first Oakland game, I decided the only way our Clydesdale-speed players could stop Oakland's thoroughbred-speed players would be to hit them in the backfield before they got up a head of steam. So I came up with this routine:

Coach: "What're we gonna **do**?"

Players: "At**tack**!"

Coach: "What're we gonna **get**?"

Players: "A **sack**!"

We did that all week during practice and during pre-game time. I think that worked about as well as it could. Unfortunately, it wasn't enough to overcome Oakland's superior speed and blocking and tackling technique. Although Oakland people told us afterward that they were surprised at how tough the game was. They only gained 15 yards in the first half after scoring on the first play from scrimmage. They did not score again until the fourth quarter when they got two touchdowns.

More about psyche up in a chapter on that subject.

Self-talk

Most players have bad habits regarding tackling technique or job description responsibilities. You should identify each player's **biggest** bad habit and get him to talk to himself about it between plays.

The self-talk should be positive rather than negative. For example, a player who has a habit of putting his head down when he tackles or explodes off the line should tell himself, "Head up! Head up!" A player who tends to leave his feet too soon should remind himself, "Stay on your feet! Stay on your feet!" A safety who tends to let receivers get behind him should say, "Keep everybody in front! Keep everybody in front!" And So on.

You **don't** want **negative** self-talk because the mind tends to focus on the image of the words, not the negative imperative. For example, "Don't leave your feet!" puts the image of leaving your feet in your mind. That's exactly the **opposite** of what you want. The key word "don't" is an abstraction which your mind cannot picture.

Choreography

Most teams use their pre-game calisthenics time to put on a show for the fans and the other team. They go through elaborately choreographed clapping, yelling, and thigh-pad-slapping rituals—like the New York Giants might do if they were asked to replace the Rockettes for a performance.

I'm half an expert on such shows. That's because I graduated from West Point and marched in hundreds of parades there. We didn't slap our thighs or clap our hands. But we **did** slap our **rifles** when we did order arms, right shoulder arms, and all that stuff. Same kind of thing. If I have any say over calisthenics, I'd like to crisp them up a bit—the way we were trained to do them at West Point. I don't like anything related to the football team to be done sloppily. I fear it will carry over into execution on the field.

But I don't like putting on a show for spectators or opposing players—other than the show of playing well during the game. Pre-game rituals including calisthenics and yelling should be directed toward our own players. They should be businesslike and aimed at preparing our team for the game, not impressing the fans or intimidating the opposing team.

Indeed, California Youth Football rules say,

14.13   **Behavior from the sidelines**: No individual, be it coach or player, in the sideline area shall make verbal exchanges with personnel from the opposing team.

14.131   All verbal remarks from the sideline during a game can only be directed at one's own team. Remarks should be limited to coaching instructions and positive reinforcement and cheers for the efforts of one's own team.

Those rules don't explicitly prohibit players on the field from participating in a noisy ritual intended to intimidate the opposing players. But such rituals clearly violate the spirit of the rule. Rules or not, show off rituals are a waste of time and a distraction from the business at hand.

Pre-game checklist

Here's a checklist of things to take care of on game day before kickoff:

• check each player's equipment
• go over each defensive player's position assignment(s) for the game
• go over the substitution schedule with each defensive player
• go over the opponent's plays and formations and with each defensive player
• go over kickoff position and job description with each kickoff team member
• give each defensive player some self-talk to recite to himself between plays
• review duties with field captain and backup
• stretching
• running
• full-speed scrimmage
• brief mandatory play monitor
• go-on-the-ball drill
• man-to-man-coverage drill
• locate comfortable, private spot for half time meeting and alternate in case the other team takes that spot

Checkoff roster

You should have lots of team rosters for various purposes. One should have the above pre-game checklist on it along with each player's number. As you checked each player off during the pre-game, you would mark his line on the roster. Here's a sample.

	20	25	26	31	32	35	52	60	67	68	70	77	78	85	88	91	92	99
Equipment																		
Position																		
Sub schedule																		
Playsheet																		
Kickoff																		
Self-talk																		
Field captain																		

10

Tracking plays

You don't really know what happened in a game until you see the video. But you aren't going to see the video until **after** the game. And that's too late to make adjustments. So you have to try to track the game while it's going on.

You should have an assistant track the plays by marking up a point-of-attack success chart. I tried unsuccessfully to do both that and run the game. There wasn't enough time.

Draw a line representing every offensive play. The chart below represents the offensive team going toward the top of the page. Each horizontal line represents five yards. Every time they run the ball, draw a vertical line representing how many yards they gained or lost. Start the vertical line where the ball carrier crosses the line of scrimmage.

Sample series

Here's a narrative description of a series and then I'll give you the marked up point-of-attack success chart.

Play # 1   dive right for 2, tackle by our left guard and right halfback
Play # 2   sweep right for 7, tackle by our left halfback
Play # 3   dive left for 2, tackle by our right guard and right tackle
Play # 4   out pattern to our left linebacker's man for 5, tackle by left linebacker
Play # 5   sweep left for -4, tackle by our right end and right linebacker
Play # 6   post pass incomplete
Play # 7   punt, sacked for -10 by right guard

Point of Attack Success Chart

You may wonder why this is so sketchy. Try it in a game. Try it with a televised pro or college game or a tape of one of your youth games. You have to write down the information very fast. This is about as much as you can do.

Analyzing your tracking

In addition to marking down what's happening, the assistant coach who does that must continually analyze his notes and visit with the defensive coordinator. In the above series, I'd want the assistant to come to me and show me the tracking sheet as soon as the defense leaves the field. After this series, he should say something like this to me:

Assistant: "Jack, 78 got beat on that sweep for 7. They completed a pass to 31's man but he was right on him. It was just a good pass. Not enough pressure."
Defensive coach: "What'd 78 do on the sweep?"
Assistant: "I'm not sure."
Defensive coach: "OK. Leave him in. But keep an eye on him."

Actually, we don't refer to players by number. We use their first names. Using last names, which is common in football, strikes me as too grown up and military. But using numbers would not be a bad idea because that's the way the substitution schedule is set up.

Adjustment schedule

In addition to close-game and big-point-spread substitution schedules, I make up an adjustment schedule the night before the game. That lists personnel and X's and O's changes to be made during the game if things don't go well.

First, personnel. You never know when one of your players is going to have a bad day. It may be his health or the way he matches up with the guy across from him. Or it may be the weather affects him more than it affects another player. Some guys get down when the game is not going well. Whatever the reason, you must have an open mind regarding every player on the team.

If the play tracking indicates somebody's not getting the job done, replace him. Remember that in the heat of battle you often misanalyze the play. So don't replace anyone until you or an assistant has focused on him and actually seen him screw up.

Second, X's and O's. I generally don't change my defensive alignment during a game. One reason is it may confuse the players. But again, you must have an open mind.

If an offensive play works consistently against your defense in a game, it may be either your personnel or your alignment that's causing the problem. But don't start thinking about making adjustments during the game. Think them through the night before.

Here's a sample personnel adjustment schedule.

If this player is getting beat		change
LHB	25	switch with 31
LE	78	20 to LE, 78 to LG, 52 to bench, 32 to S
LLB	31	switch with 25
LT	67	switch with 91
LG	52	switch with 91
RG	70	78 to RG, 20 to LE, 70 to bench, 32 to S
RT	92	switch with 91
RLB	68	switch with 25
RE	26	switch with 20
RHB	99	switch with 27

This adjustment schedule puts injury subs into the game in some cases as if the player who is getting beat were injured. In other cases, the coach had to pick between two well-qualified players for a position. If one gets beat, he tries the other there. In other cases, a player who is proven effective at one position is moved to another because he is needed more there. But if the player at his old position is repeatedly getting beat, move the proven player back to his old position. And so forth.

Here's a sample alignment adjustment schedule:

We're getting beat by	change
Sweeps	Have the cornerbacks line up a yard outside the linebacker instead of directly behind him
Dives	Tell the safety to move into five yards from the ball instead of eight
Off tackle	Have the cornerbacks line up behind our tackles and/or have the defensive ends slide along the line of scrimmage instead of penetrating
Short passes	Cornerbacks bump their man at line of scrimmage
Long passes	Blitz the linebackers
Reverses	Have the cornerbacks pursue through the backfield like the end
Shotgun	Blitz the ends

Again, don't be too quick to make these changes. If you change, players may get confused about their responsibilities and leave a gap in the defense. Also, everybody makes mistakes. You don't want to change a defense that works 95% of the time just because a player blew his assignment once. Change your alignment or responsibilities only in response to patterns of **repeated** failures.

Experiment time

Another thing you might want to do in a big-point-spread game is experiment with a radically different defensive alignment.

In 1991, I often toyed with the idea of a 10-1. There really is such a defense and I have some literature on it. In fact, the Kent State University coach, Trevor J. Rees, who wrote it says his team used it **everywhere** on the field, not just in goal-line stands. In retrospect, I wish I had tried it during the three 1991 games when our lead was at least three touchdowns. (In 1992, one of our cornerbacks moved up to the line of scrimmage on his own before the snap. By the time we discovered it two games later, we had also noticed that his side did far better than the side where the cornerback was **behind** the linebacker. So we told the other cornerback to move up on the line, also. They retained their pass defense responsibilities. They were simply in better position to discharge their more frequent run-defense duties. Believe it or not, our pass defense seemed even **better** with the 10-1 than it was with the 8-2-1.)

11

Penalty avoidance

I am a great admirer of the books, *The Hidden Game of Baseball* by John Thorn and Pete Palmer and *The Hidden Game of Football* by Bob Carroll, Pete Palmer, and John Thorn. Those books reexamine the statistics and logic behind the many standard decisions coaches make.

For example, going for it on fourth and one is considered a gamble if you are deep in your own territory. But Carroll, Thorn, and Palmer say that if you analyze the results of teams going for it on fourth and one and related statistics, you find that you should **always** go for it on fourth and one. The reason is the probability of making it is high and the consequences of failure are not as bad as you think. Over the long run, a team that goes for it on fourth and one will score more points than a team that punts.

Penalties don't matter?

But on page 116 of *The Hidden Game of Football*, they say something which strikes me as illogical,

> *...for the most part, we don't see any clear connection between avoiding penalties and winning.*

What about our 1990 game against Woodland? They scored two touchdowns on kickoff returns. Both were called back on clipping penalties. They never scored again. The game ended in a 0-0 tie and **we** won it in overtime 7-0.

What about the 1991 Big Game between California and Stanford? Cal was the favorite. But they drew eleven penalties and ended up losing.

What about the 1992 Fairfield Falcons versus Suisun Junior Pee Wee game? Suisun scored late in the game to tie it at 19. Then, when they lined up at the three-yard line for the extra point, a Suisun player lined up in the neutral zone. After the penalty, they were on the **eight**-yard line. They passed. It was incomplete. They lost the game in double overtime.

I suspect the conclusion of the *Hidden Game* guys stems from the fact that the pro teams they studied generally had roughly equal penalty rates. In youth football, where you have many rookies and uneven coaching, some teams can have far more penalties— especially at the beginning of the season. At the end of the season, the penalties seem about the same because the players have been trained by the referees, if not by their coaches.

You can really steal a march on your first several opponents by training your kids during the preseason to **not** draw penalty flags.

Youth versus pro football

Unfortunately, the conclusions drawn by the authors of *The Hidden Game of Football* may not be valid for youth football because of the great differences between the pro game they analyze and the youth game. For example, I've never seen a field goal attempted at the Jr. Pee Wee level. And pros have a built-in penalty-avoidance mechanism from years of organized football playing.

Draw a flag, take a seat

For our 1991 Manteca and Richmond games, I told our players that anyone who drew a penalty flag would instantaneously become a six-play player for that game. That is, if he has already gotten his six plays, he's done for the day. If he also plays on offense, he's done for the day on defense. If he's a starter and commits his infraction on his second play, he gets four more then he's done.

Did that work as a deterrent? The only penalty in the Richmond game was five guys jumped offside on one play. So many that I had to renege on my threat and let them all stay. In the Manteca game, there were no defensive penalties at all. None.

So, the threat to take a player out of the game for a penalty may have worked as a deterrent in two games. But suppose one of my strongest players drew a flag in an important, close game? Is pulling him for the day in the best interest of the team?

It might be.

It depends on three variables.

- Who is the replacement player and how much difference is there in the two players?
- Was the penalty part of a recurring pattern of penalties by that player or was it his first one of the season?
- Did the penalty give the other team a first down or dramatically increase the probability that they would get a first down or touchdown?

The Hidden Game authors created the following scoring table for yards gained on a play in the three different down situations:

Points	1st down	2nd down	3rd or 4th down
-4	turnover	turnover	turnover
-1	-3 or more	-3 or more	-3 or more
0	less than 40%	less than 60%	less than 100%
1	40% to 79%	60% to 79%	100%
2	80%	80%	————
3*	11+ yards	11+ yards	11+ yards
4*	21+ yards	21+ yards	21+ yards
5*	41+ yards	41+ yards	41+ yards

* subtract one point if not a first down

You want your defensive players to produce the largest negative point total. That's *Hidden Game* points, not scoreboard points. And you use this table to evaluate your players' performance.

A player who jumps offside when the situation is first and ten would have one positive point assessed against him because the 5-yard penalty takes the offensive team more than 40% toward their goal of a first down. (See line four of the table.) If he tackled a ball carrier for a three-yard loss, he'd get minus one point (line two). And if he caused a turnover (as opposed to just being lucky enough to fall on a ball caused by someone else), he'd get minus four points.

So evaluate your players according to the table and play the best eleven. Our worst penalty boys tended to either jump offside once a game or face mask once a game. Encroachment is worth up to two positive points depending on the situation. Face mask is worth up to three positive points depending on the situation.

If you assign points according to that table for tackles, missed tackles, penalties drawn, and so forth, the boys whose penalties are significantly hurting the team will move down the depth chart appropriately (i.e., become second or third string). The table also is forgiving if the penalty comes in, say, a third and twenty-five situation. Even a face mask penalty in that situation will not get the offense a first down.

Although a 15-yard penalty in **any** situation **does** change field position significantly. Seems like a player who moves the ball 15 yards toward the opponent's goal ought to be downgraded even though it wasn't enough for a first down.

I suggest you keep two statistics on your defensive players: *Hidden Game* points and yards given up. Yards given up is easy to assess on penalties. Just ask the referee who drew the penalty and assess the yards to that player. Yards given up on plays with no penalties is more subjective. Your video graders have to assess blame. If a play goes for seven yards, all seven have to be allocated to appropriate defensive players.

The main point is that some "good" players draw more than their share of penalties. Casey Stengel once said,

> *I don't like them guys what get one run with their bat and give up two with their glove.*

Similarly, you shouldn't like those guys who tackle the ball carrier for a two-yard loss on one play then draw a face-mask penalty on the next play. A less skillful player who would have tackled the ball carrier for a zero-yard gain, instead of a two-yard loss, seven times still leaves you better off than the more skillful player's one face-mask penalty. Actually, the player I'm calling more skillful really isn't—because penalty avoidance is one of the skills a good player has.

Given the down-over aspect of most penalties, you'd rather have a player who allows three five-yard gains through his hole than one who commits one face-mask penalty.

Penalty avoidance plan

- Teach your boys the rules.
- Enforce the rules in practice (I and many of our other coaches have a penalty flag in my pocket at practice. I threw it so much that the players showered me with penalty flags at our awards banquet one year. They also gave me a mounted yellow flag signed by all the players.)
- Tell your boys that they are constantly being evaluated to see who should be playing where and that drawing penalties lowers their rating.
- If a boy's rating is such that he's first-string but will be second-string if he gives up, say, three *Hidden Game* points, tell him that he will lose his job if he gives up those points in this game. Same applies to his replacement.

In other words, the proper way to threaten players about penalties is to relate it to their position on the depth chart. If they are number one at their position by a large margin, even a 15-yard penalty should not cost them their job. But if they are number one by only a small margin, tell them about their borderline situation and urge them to concentrate so they do not draw a flag.

Encroachment/illegal procedure syndrome

In my four years watching youth football games, I have observed a strange but consistent phenomenon: virtually all encroachment penalties against the defense are followed on the next play by illegal procedure penalties against the offense and vice versa. Darnedest thing.

I believe I have come up with the solution. Urge them to "Go on the ball! Don't give it back by jumping offsides!" as they are waiting for the snap on the next play after an illegal procedure penalty. I did that in 1992 and it worked every time.

Long run/clipping syndrome

Another syndrome is the incidence of clipping penalties during long runs. My impression is that most youth football runs of more than 20 yards are called back for clipping. As a defense coach, you are only concerned about that on runs after interceptions and picked up fumbles. Again, I have found that just yelling a reminder to the players fixes the problem. When one of our guys is on a long run, I yell, "No clipping! No clipping!" Since I have a loud voice and I have a megaphone at games, they get the message. It seems to work.

We even did a drill one year in which we taught our players to pursue a ball carrier at full speed even if they have no hope of catching him on the theory that such frantic pursuit might draw a clip and clipping penalty on the other team. And that **worked** in games. If your players do **not** frantically pursue a hoplessly gone ball carier, the offensive players will not attempt to block them and you will not get the clipping penalty you need.

I believe we were one of the least-penalized teams in the California Youth Football League, if not **the** least penalized team, in 1991 and 1992 because of the extra effort we made in that department.

13

Scoring on defense

One statistic I am especially proud of with the defenses I've coached is the number of points they scored. For example, 32 points in ten games or 3.2 points per game in 1991. We did it with:

2 interception touchdowns
2 picked-up fumble runs
4 safeties.

In contrast, our opponents' defenses, including the mighty Oakland, only scored six points in ten games for an average of $6 \div 10 = .6$ points per game. Oakland's defense scored zero points against us. The six were scored by a Fairfield Falcons defender who stole the ball from our halfback in the fourth quarter and ran 70 yards with it to win the game (which was 2-0 in our favor up to that point).

As I mentioned in the scouting chapter, we scouted our opponents 19 times in games and controlled scrimmages. In those 19 scouting observations we never saw a defense score a point. If you just count the games, we scouted six games other than those we played in. So the total points we saw scored by our opponents was actually six out of sixteen games, not ten. And that gives an average of $6 \div 16 = .38$ points per game. Our 3.2 points per game were $3.2 \div .38 = 8.42$ times better than our opponents' average.

In 1992, we scored 22 points in eleven games or two points per game on average. We did that with:

1 interception touchdown
2 picked-up fumble runs
2 safeties.

Napa interception

First credit for the 1991 Napa interception and touchdown run back goes to the boy who made the catch. He had to leap high and to his right rear to get it. And he had to run about 40 yards.

Now as to the reason you bought this book, the **coaching** aspect. Coaching may deserve significant credit for that particular interception and run back.

When we scouted the jamboree at which Napa played, they ran a pass play that we called the "Quick flat pass" in the Napa playsheet we handed out to the players. Here's the actual diagram we made and gave to our players:

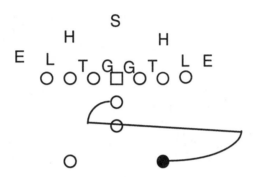

As anyone familiar with football can see, this is a **dangerous** play for the offense. If it is intercepted, a touchdown is very likely because the intercepting defender is already behind or even with the deepest offensive player.

I drew my players' attention to this play in a **chalk talk** at the practice field. That is, I diagrammed it on a 2' x 3' white board. Then we coaches demonstrated the play while the players watched from a down-on-one-knee semi-circle. We had a player play the role of defensive end and try to intercept and go for six.

He complained that we were so tall that the pass was too high for him. So I re-demonstrated the play acting as the Napa quarterback, only this time I got down on my knees. That worked. The end intercepted and took off. We then had the scout team throw that pass against each of our defensive ends.

Normally, the only thing I want the defensive end to do on a pass play is sack the quarterback. But since this was a quick pass, the end was not likely to get to the quarterback in time. So I told them, "Look, you don't normally have pass responsibility. But if, when you're squaring in to tackle the quarterback on this play you happen to see a pass going over your head, reach up and grab it. Then run it into the end zone."

And that's exactly what happened. Napa ran their quick flat pass to their right. Our left defensive end saw it about to pass overhead. He jumped up and grabbed it and ran it in for a touchdown. That was an excellent example of scouting intelligence being converted to specific instruction and rehearsal, then being converted to six points for the defense in a game.

The Napa pitch

In 1991, Napa lined up in a **wishbone** formation on offense—but they did **not** run the option play for which the wishbone is famous. Rather they ran a designed deep pitch to the halfbacks.

In their jamboree, they missed the connection on that pitch more than they made it. Their quarterback's pitches were constantly flopping around on the ground like beached bass. As the defensive coach, I was salivating as I watched those missed pitches at the jamboree.

To take advantage of that scoring opportunity, we practiced picking up missed pitches and running with them. Previously, we had taught our boys how to fall on a fumble. (You end up on your side in the fetal position but with your head up to avoid neck injury, holding the ball with both hands and arms against your belly.) But, in the case of these pitches, we told the boys that picking the ball up and running with it was better than falling on it.

And we literally created a drill in which we lined players up Napa style, had the quarterback pitch to the halfback, who deliberately muffed the pitch. Our defensive player would be approaching the intended receiver as this happened then he would scoop up the ball and go.

No pitches

As it turned out, that practice paid no dividends in the Napa game. Napa's coaches saw the same thing I did at the jamboree and eliminated the deep pitch from their repertoire.

But our practice in preparation for Napa apparently paid **delayed** dividends. We picked up a fumble and ran it for a touchdown in both the Benicia and Richmond games in 1991. In 1992, we did the same in the Napa and Manteca games. The main thing is to eliminate the always-fall-on-the-ball mentality.

Most coaches believe their players should always fall on a loose ball because they believe it's more certain of getting possession. I disagree. We told our players to pick it up and run if they could, falling on it only if they had to to prevent the offense from getting it back.

Depends on your offense

Part of my thinking was because of our offense. In 1991, our offense scored only 10.8 points per game and only scored more than one touchdown in three of our ten games. So we looked for points anywhere we could get them. Had we had a powerful offense, My thinking might have been, "Just fall on it so our offense can do their magic."

No fumbles lost because of attempt to pick up

We did not lose any fumble recoveries at all as a result of our teaching our kids to pick it up and run when they could in 1991 and 1992. They instinctively chose to fall on the ball when that was the proper choice. If anything, they still favored the fall-on-it approach too much in spite of our drilling them on pick-ups. We made a second effort (through a one-boy-scoop-up-a-loose-ball drill) to encourage pick-ups rather than fall-ons the week before the final Oakland playoff game in 1991. In 1992, picking up fumbles was standard in our approach. We drilled it a couple of times. When somebody forgot and fell on a ball in scrimmage, I made a big deal out of it. In 1993, trying to pick it up may have cost us one fumble recovery. But there is no question that we are ahead over the three-year period with four touchdowns and about 100 yards gained before tackles against only one lost possession.

In 1994, when I started coaching high school football, I told my team that if they tried to pick it up and run as much as possible, we would probably get two touchdowns as a result during the season. And that's exactly what happened. We got one touchdown in the first game and one in the third game. We could have gotten two more in a later game. The opposing long snapper snapped the ball over the punter's head twice deep in their own territory. Both times, our punt return team fell on the ball. I was not the coach of that unit. I have found that you have to practice picking up bad punt snaps and blocked punts to get it into the players' heads. The coach in charge of that unit did not practice picking up those balls.

Benicia interception touchdown

The Benicia interception touchdown was **not** the result of scouting. And it was not as difficult a catch. The defender caught it on the run and made a good run to the end zone. But there was really no offensive receiver in the impact area to fight for the ball.

Most of the credit goes to the left defensive end who pressured the quarterback into passing badly. This was a **different** left defensive end than the boy who made the Napa interception. This defensive end had extremely quick feet. That enabled him to stay with the quarterback as he tried to get away. By the time the quarterback threw the ball, the end had hold of his shirt and was starting to swing him around.

Youth quarterbacks do not like to eat the ball. As a result, they often throw it when they should not. The Benicia quarterback only threw twice in that game. We intercepted both of them. And both times our defensive ends were putting extreme pressure on the quarterback. In the 1992 Vacaville playoff game, the same defensive end put great pressure on the quarterback and we got our only touchdown interception runback of that year.

If there is a lesson it is that you may want to put your quick players at defensive end rather than in the defensive secondary where they traditionally go. Because youth football players tend to be bad pass blockers, youth quarterbacks tend to leave their pitiful pockets too soon, and youth quarterbacks tend to throw when they should eat the ball. So just as wearing a hat on a cold day can help keep your feet warm, so can putting quick players at defensive end help your defensive backs make interceptions.

Safeties

"Push 'em back, push 'em back, Waaaay back!" goes the well-known cheer.

We did. Four times we pushed 'em as far back as we could—right into their own end zone in 1991. In 1992, we did it twice. In 1993, we had the eventual league champions on their own six-inch line at the half.

There's no trick to that. Just hard-chargin' defense.

We got the first one in our second game. And after that taste of "blood," we had a defensive **red zone mentality**. That is, when our defense had the opponent's team inside the opponent's twenty-yard line, our defense started thinking safety. Our coaches and parents started **chanting** "Safety!"

We believed that when the opposing offense had the ball inside their twenty, we were very likely to get a safety.

In the 1991 Richmond game, our offense had the ball first and ten on Richmond's eleven-yard line. Then we got a first down at the one. But Richmond mounted a heroic goal-line stand and pushed our offense back out to about the five. We lost the ball on downs.

That was the **good** news for Richmond. The **bad** news was that the San Ramon Bears Jr. Pee Wee **defense** was now coming onto the field (mostly the same boys, actually). And facing our defense in that field position ranked right up there with spitting into the wind and drawing on the Lone Ranger as things you didn't want to do in 1991. Our defense took just two plays to do what the offense had been unable to do—they punched the ball into the end zone for a score—a safety.

Do you really want a safety?

As proud as I was about our six safeties, I wonder if we would not have been smarter to let the ball carrier get to the one before we tackled him. In the Richmond game, the score right before we got our safety was 13-6. We **lost** the game 13-8.

If we had let the ball carrier get to the one, then tackled him, we could have forced them to punt. It's tough to punt from the one. There are only eleven yards to the back of the end zone. Punters like a little more elbow room. In addition, the punter and center are extremely **nervous** when they are snapping the ball ten or eleven yards across the end zone. The potential for disaster is great and the number of youth football players who are cucumber cool in such situations is extremely limited.

A punt from the end zone is very likely to be blocked or dropped. Fall on an opposing **ball carrier** in the opponent's end zone and you only get **two** points. But fall on the **ball** in the opponent's end zone and you get **six** points.

It might be wise to train your players to prefer one-yard line tackles to safeties in late-game situations where they will not give your team the lead.

Pucker time drill

One drill which occurs to me for that purpose would be to have your players choose up sides and take turns trying to get the ball out of a first and ten from their own one yard line. Set up a special rule that if the offense gets the ball beyond the twenty, the defense becomes the offense and must start their own drive from their own one. However, if the defense can force a turnover **inside** the twenty, they go on offense from the point of recovery (if they didn't just pick it up and run it in). In this special game, touchdowns are the only scores that count—you get **zero** points for a safety. In fact, if you score a safety, you immediately become the offense and start out on your own one. The team that scores the most points gets out of end-of-practice wind sprints.

This game should teach the defense that it's OK to let a ball carrier **run** out of the end zone—as long as he doesn't get far after he leaves. But it's **not** OK to let a ball carrier in the end zone **pass** the ball. Don't sack the guy. Such passes should be batted—and the batted ball caught on the fly if possible. Since the offensive team knows the defense will not tackle them in the end zone, they will try to scramble around back there looking for receivers.

Give this game a code name like "Pucker Time!" Then use that name in late-game situations where two points won't give you the lead to remind your players to avoid the safety and set up the touchdown instead.

Blocked punts

Blocked punts are the **ideal** time to pick up the ball and run instead of falling on it. In fact, falling on a blocked punt is flat out stupid—unless it was touched by a receiving team player after it had gone **more than two yards** beyond the line of scrimmage.

You fall on a ball to prevent the other team from getting it. But when the ball in question is a blocked punt, there is **little need** to fall on it. It doesn't matter which team falls on it. It's still the receiving team's ball. So don't fall on it—pick it up and run. (There **is** the danger that the punting team can pick up the ball and run for a first down, touchdown, or at least better field position before turning it over to your team.)

You should practice blocking punts and picking them up as well. Have the scout team deliberately punt the ball into the backside of a lineman to simulate it being blocked. And have the defense concentrate on picking up the blocked punt and running with it.

We called this a "golden opportunity" in the week before our 1991 Oakland playoff game. When Oakland had to punt during the game, I yelled "Golden opportunity!" to the defense to remind them to look for the blocked punt and pick it up and run. We practiced it many times the week before the game.

No luck in the game though. They got off all three punts.

In 1992, we blocked a Napa punt, picked it up and ran it into the end zone for a quick six points right at the end of Napa's first drive. After that demoralizing start, they lost 27-7 and the game was not as close as the score suggests because we put a bunch of subs in when it was 27-0.

Backward passes

I already mentioned Manteca's backward pass. Most teams have such a play. Or they may inadvertently turn an intended forward pass into a backward pass when the flow of the play does not go as planned.

Rule 2-22-5 defines a backward pass as "a pass thrown parallel with or toward the passer's end line." The passer's end line means the back of the end zone behind the goal line which they are defending.

This is another golden opportunity to score. Remember, if a backward pass is batted, muffed, or overthrown, it is a **live** ball, **not** an incomplete pass. We practiced picking this one up and running with it, too. But we never succeeded in a game. (In 1992, we dropped such a pass when we were on **offense**, picked it up, and ran it for a 50-yard touchdown on the first scrimmage play of the game. The opposing team from Richmond figured it was an incomplete pass and pulled up even though there was no whistle. We went on to beat them 19-6 after that unexpected start.)

Ball stealing

We held the Fairfield Falcons to minus 18 yards in 1991. But we lost the game because the Falcons stole the ball and ran it back for the winning score. They couldn't even score the extra point afterward. But they didn't need to. They won 6-2.

It was obvious that the Falcons coaches had taught ball stealing. We scouted the Falcons-Oakland playoff game the week before we played Oakland. In that 7-0 loss, the Falcons repeatedly tried to steal the ball—unsuccessfully. Oakland hung on to both the ball and the victory.

In our next game after the Falcons beat us in 1991, one of our players tried to imitate the Falcons ball-stealing trick. The result was an Oakland ball carrier, whom he could have easily tackled, got by him and scored a touchdown. It was called back on an irrelevant penalty. The exact same thing also happened in 1992 with the same result.

Your defense should practice ball stealing. But they should be told that it is **poor tackling technique**. As such, it should **only** be used in desperate situations when you need a touchdown to win and there is not enough time left to force a punt or turnover on downs.

We practiced it in 1992 and successfully stole several balls in games. But we taught the kids to do it **only** when the ball carrier was already stopped by a teammate. Our drill was to have a ball carrier with a defensive player wrapped around his legs. The **second** defender would then approach the ball carrier from behind and push the ball out. In the actual games, the strippers just went up to the ball carrier and took it. In the game videos, you'd simply see an opposing ball carrier get caught up in a group of our players. Then, without the ball ever popping loose, you'd see our guy running the other way with the ball. We stole the ball three times in the 1992 Napa game. We never scored or ever got a big gain. But we **did** get the ball for our offense.

13

Pass defense

Everybody who sees my 10-1 says, "What about the pass?" As I've said earlier in the book, we had virtually no problem with passes. Let me discuss the details of how to stop the pass.

You stop the pass with three things:

• pressure on the passer
• block the receivers from releasing on their routes
• covering the receivers once they are in their routes.

My approach to defense favors the first two. But you must always do all three.

Pass rush

The correct method of rushing and tackling the passer is described in the chapter on tackling.

Plugging receivers

I never spent much time thinking about the technique of blocking receivers to keep them on the line until I got to high school coaching. Blocking receivers to delay their running their pass routes is common in high school and it can be raised to a high skill.

The technique is called "bump-and-run." You hear that phrase a lot in NFL broadcasts.

The rule

In the NFL, defenders can only bump the receiver for the first five yards or some such. Many youth coaches assume that NFL rules and youth rules are the same. Not that one. Youth teams use the high school rule which is,

Rule 9
Section 2 Illegal use of hands and holding
Art. 3 The defensive player shall not:
e. Contact an eligible receiver who is no longer a potential blocker.

The Case book published by the same National Federation that publishes the high school rule book says, you cannot block a receiver if he

...is not attempting to block or has gone past or is moving away...

My interpretation of the rule is that you can attack the receiver on the snap and you can keep attacking until he escapes or the ball is in the air. Once he gets away from you, you can**not** keep blocking him. You can assume the receiver is attempting to block you at the snap because blocks happen too fast to make any other assumption.

The stance

Face the receiver at a 45-degree angle on his inside shoulder. You should be as close to the neutral zone as you can legally be. Get into the proverbial "good football position." That is, your feet are shoulder-width apart, knees are bent to almost a quarter squat, head up, back straight, elbows in, hands open in front of your chest facing the receiver.

Focus your eyes on the receiver. Do not try to see the ball move.

Outside release only

You want to force the receiver to release outside. If he tries to release inside, you block him with your hands. This screws up the youth pass I fear most, the look-in or slant-in.

On the snap

When the receiver starts to move forward or toward the defender, the defender hits the receiver in the middle of the chest with his outside hand. Try to drive the receiver down the line of scrimmage toward the center. If the receiver releases **outside**, there is no need for contact.

Do **not** step toward the receiver to make the hit. Let the receiver come to you. Take your first step with the foot closest to the direction the receiver is trying to go. That is, if he tries to release inside, take your first step with your inside foot.

If the receiver is a tight end, I think you should step up and attack him on the snap. He is far more likely to be blocking than a wide receiver. And waiting passively for that to happen can put you flat on your back.

Stay with him

The defender must stay between the receiver and the goal line you are defending. In his book, *Play Football the NFL Way*, Tom Bass says, "...we want the defensive player to maintain a position where his belt buckle is slightly ahead of the inside hip of the receiver. He should be a foot away from the receiver to the inside, so that the receiver cannot lean into him and push off." Keep your hands up so you can fend him off if he comes toward you.

Once the receiver gets into his route, watch his eyes. Do not try to look back at the quarterback. The receiver's eyes will tell when the ball is coming. They widen. He will also bring his hands up as the ball approaches. And if you have lost proper position on the receiver, forget about the receiver's eyes or the ball. Just catch back up. The ball cannot score a touchdown by itself. But the receiver can. You must stay with him.

Drill with no ball

You should drill this with**out** a ball most of the time. The ball is a distraction. The defender is supposed to focus on the receiver and only look for the ball when the receiver looks for it. Ignoring the ball, as you must do when in man coverage, is an unnatural act. Practice without the ball to get your players used to the total focus on the receiver.

Initial moves at half speed

Practice the initial moves at the line of scrimmage at half speed—that is, the stance and initial step and hand movement. Do the same on for the receiver's pass routes the first several times you defend them.

Videos

You should get training videos on football techniques. The catalogs listed in the back of this book offer videos titled:

- *Defensive Backs Run/Pass Schemes* by Don James, U. of Washington
- *Defensive Backs* by Paul Jette, TCU
- *Defensive Backs* by Gene Stallings, U. of Alabama
- *Colorado Bunp and Run* by G. Brown
- *Championship Defensive Secondary* by B. Oliver, Clemson

and others with similar titles. Training videos are excellent for novice coaches. They generally show state-of-the-art techniques. Youth coaches frequently base their teaching on what they learned years ago in high school or college. In many cases, their memory is faulty and/or the techniques in question are out of date.

Breakaway belt

A device which I suspect would be great for teaching man-to-man coverage is the Breakaway Belt. It's offered in the Speed City catalog (800-255-9930).

For $13.95, you get two belts with long tails that have matching Velcro ends. The receiver and defender each put one on. Then they are connected. The receiver tries to break the connection. The defender tries to stay close enough to maintain it.

Crossing receivers

One of the standard tricks for defeating man coverage is to have two receivers cross. In most cases, they are trying to run a pick, like in basketball. Picks are illegal in football. But the infraction is rarely called.

The standard antidote is for the defenders to trade men before they collide. Assign one of the defensive backs on each side to call "Switch!" when necessary. And practice this. It's tricky.

"Pass!" "Air!"

You must train your players, including the ones on the bench, to yell,

"Pass!" when the quarterback shows pass
"Air!" when the ball leaves the passer's hand
"Oskie!" if and when it is intercepted.

They get lazy about this and must be punished in practice when they are not loud enough. I had my high school kids doing some pushups when they failed to yell loud enough. Hearing the word "Air!" helps the defender tell when to look for the ball.

Fly to the ball

Once the ball is in the air, everybody must go to the ball at full speed. That includes linemen, ends, linebackers, and defenders from the other side of the field. If a defender has been beat, he must get unbeat, even when the ball is in the air. Looking back slows you up.

Motion

When your man goes in motion, you must go with him. Indeed, motion is often used to ascertain whether you are in man or not.

It is more difficult to bump a receiver who is in motion. It's also more different to cover him. In a 1995 Dallas-49ers game, the 49ers often put wide receiver Jerry Rice in motion to make it harder or impossible for Deion Sanders or other Dallas defensive backs to cover him. The 49ers won the games.

The fade

The offensive antidote to bump-and-run coverage is the fade route. In that, the receiver releases outside and runs full speed down the field or to the corner when the end zone is close. The passer throws the ball in a high arc over the outside shoulder of the receiver. When it's accurate, it cannot be intercepted because the receiver's body is between the ball and the defender. But it can be caught.

How do you stop it? The answer is too subtle for a book. Rather I would recall the words of the winningest Texas high school coach, Gordon Wood,

A defense can stop any play, if it sees it enough times in practice.

So if you want your defenders to learn how to stop the fade, let them do it a zillion times in practice.

Elapsed time

In general, if a passer does not get rid of the ball in **three seconds**, he is sacked. Furthermore, every tenth of a second that transpires between the snap and the release of the ball increase the probability of an incompletion or interception.

Your line should work on their pass rush to try to make the elapsed time until sack **as short as possible**. At the same time, your pass defenders should work on delaying the receivers for as long as possible.

Stopwatch drill

Players like competitive drills. One that I found helpful for teaching delaying receivers as well as receiver release is done as follows:

Put one player at a spot and tell him to get to the limit of a 10-yard semi-circle as fast as he can. Line another player up on him and tell him to delay the first player as long as possible. Start the drill with a snap of the ball and time how long it takes the one player to get to the edge of the semi-circle. The shorter the time, the better for the evader; the longer the time, the better for the delayer.

This teaches receiver release and defender delay of the receiver which is the subject of this chapter. The same idea also can be used to teach pass rush versus pass blocking. Keep track of both players' time and run a championship to see who is the best at each skill. Go through several iterations in which players are never matched up with the same opponent twice. Make sure the best on each side get to go against the best on the other side. Otherwise, the best may simply be a player who drew a weak opponent.

The results of this tournament should be a factor in deciding who starts at cornerback and linebacker.

Pass interference

You must hold a quickie clinic at the beginning of your season to explain pass interference (Rule 7-5-10 and 11). Then you must flag and punish anyone who commits it during practice. The penalty for defensive pass interference is one of the most severe in football: 15 yards from the previous spot and automatic first down. Intentional pass interference, which I've never seen called, is for penalized an additional 15 yards. A player who chronically draws penalty flags, especially pass interference, should be benched.

You should know that there is no pass interference if a forward pass does **not cross the neutral zone** (Rule 7-5-7), nor is there a prohibition against ineligible receivers being down field or any pass-type restrictions on blocking by either team.

One-armed DBs

Defensive backs (free safeties and cornerbacks) have a laudable fight-for-the-ball mentality. But they frequently play as if they only have one arm. In many cases, they should be **intercepting** the ball instead of batting it down. But they have such a deeply ingrained bat-it-down mentality that they settle for the bat down too often.

Coaches should push constantly for interceptions. Going for the interception is less of a gamble than many seem to think. For one thing, a missed interception deflects the ball most of the time.

Everything's a gamble

True, a DB who goes for the interception sometimes misses and the pass is completed. But the exact same thing happens when you try to bat the ball. Whenever a DB does anything near a receiver, he is gambling. There's even a gamble with **tackling**—the pass interference call. Trying to intercept the ball is the best way to avoid a pass interference call. With a bat down, you have one arm free to commit pass interference. "Idle hands are the devil's workshop" is especially true in bat-the-ball situations. With a tackle, timing is the gamble.

The only time you bat a ball is when it is at the extreme limit of your reach. That's about a six-inch wide band at about a three-foot radius from your breast bone. If it's **inside** that band, you can **intercept** it. If it's **outside** that band, you can't bat it **or** intercept it. The other time when you should bat the ball is when it is **third or fourth down** and you are likely to get better field position from the bat down. You have to practice that third- or fourth-down bat down a little to get it into the defender's minds.

Participate in receivers drills

Your offensive pass receivers should do catching drills daily. Your defensive backs should join them. Remember, **they both have the same job description once the ball is in the air.** You must drill **out** of the defenders the notion that receivers catch and defenders bat.

Oskie!

When an interception is made, the defense, players on the field and bench, should yell, Oskie!" Don't ask me why. It's standard in football. (Although some teams yell, "Fire!" I prefer Oskie because fire has two other important meanings: a command to shoot and the sounding of an alarm at a conflagration.) Upon hearing Oskie, the defense must switch to offense being careful to avoid clipping. You need to practice interceptions and the defense's response to them with a scout offense on the field.

Swing pass

In man-to-man coverage, some defensive back is assigned to the each running back. In a swing pass, which has become very popular in college and the NFL, a back runs sideways out of the backfield and catches a pass behind the line of scrimmage. Frequently, he delays leaving. Often, that's because their job description says, block any blitzing defenders on your side and if no one comes, go out on a swing route.

This pass can be very dangerous if the defensive back assigned to cover the receiver loses track of him. You need to have your scout offense run this play until your players defend it correctly.

Pass defense practice script
- Inside pass rush
- Contain pass rush
- Tackling technique for tackling passer
- Stripping technique
- Bump and run
- Covering receivers on all likely routes
- Switching man responsibilities when receivers cross
- Yelling "Pass!", "Air!", and "Oskie!"
- Switching to offensive mood upon take away
- Picking up fumble and running with it
- Fly to the ball
- Where to line up versus all offensive formations
- How to adjust to motion
- Fight for the ball
- Tip drill
- Catching fundamentals

Try it, you'll like it
The first reaction to my 10-1 is always, "What about the pass?" I have explained the theory in this chapter. But let me also reassure you that I generally did not have a problem stopping the pass. I can only recall three games in five years where my teams were beat by passes. In one case, we got a same season rematch and shut down that team's passing game as well as winning the game. Another team that got a same season rematch with us decided to do more passing the second time and we beat them worse as a result.

The pass will always be dangerous to football offensive coordinators at all levels. But there is no evidence to support the notion that reducing the number of rushers improves pass defense. If you watch top college and pro defenses, you will see that some succeed at pass defense by emphasizing the rush and bumping receivers as I advocate. Others succeed with nickel and dime packages. I have found that overall defense at the youth level—that is stopping both the run and the pass—is most successful when the defense emphasizes the pass rush and plugging receivers accompanied by man coverage. Dropping more defenders into pass coverage than the number of quick (on or near the line of scrimmage and not behind down linemen) receivers in the offensive alignment weakens the run defense and provides no guarantee of a compensating strengthening of the defense against the pass. The youth leagues in which I coached kept no stats on pass and run defense. But I suspect that if stats had been compiled, my defense would have been number one against the pass. That is, it appeared to me that we got more interceptions and sacks than any other teams I saw.

14

Psyche up

I became a good football player the day I figured out that you have to be psyched up to play football. It happened between plays during a practice scrimmage. I was playing right defensive end for my high school's scout team. I had been doing badly all season. Every time I missed a tackle, I assumed it was because my **technique** was incorrect. I kept fiddling with my technique, but made no progress.

Then I got mad at myself. My thoughts went something like this:

> *"You know, Reed, you thought you were going to be a good football player. But you stink. Ball carriers are constantly breaking your tackles. And blockers block you easily."*

I went on like that for some long seconds then I decided,

> *"To heck with technique. This time, when the ball is hiked, I'm going to attack like a stark raving maniac. If anybody tries to get in my way, I'll run over them!"*

Anyone close enough to see probably would have noticed that my eyes had narrowed, my nostrils were flaring, I was breathing faster. I was seething with an artificial rage toward my own poor play as well as toward the other team and their ball carrier.

When the ball moved, I exploded across the line and sacked the quarterback on about the second step of his intended drop back. I don't know what the guy who was supposed to block me did. He probably watched me go by and wondered, "What got into him?"

On the next play, the quarterback tried to roll out on my side. I sacked him again.

From that moment on, I was a completely different and much better player. The defensive coach started calling me, "Tiger Reed." Unfortunately, the **head** coach reacted by getting mad at the first-string offense for letting a second-stringer like me get the quarterback. He never figured out that I had changed as a player.

'Getting religion'

I used to do a radio program on real estate with the late Tom Harmon. Harmon won the Heisman Trophy in 1940 as a halfback for the University of Michigan. One day at lunch, I told him of my above-described transformation in high school football. He smiled knowingly and said, "That's called 'getting religion.'" He added that his wife had asked why he wasn't helping their son, Mark, when the boy first began to play football. Tom told her, "I can't accomplish anything with him until he 'gets religion.'" (Mark "got religion" and starred in football for UCLA before becoming a TV and movie star and *People Magazine's* "Sexiest Man on Earth.")

In his book, *Total Impact*, All-Pro defensive back Ronnie Lott says, "A good football player is somebody who is technically sound. If I were only concerned with technique, however, I would still be kicking tumbleweeds in Rialto."

At another point, Lott says of the Chicago Bears' Walter Payton, "The Bears had a fourth-and-one on their 40 and Payton carried the ball into the line. Our 325-pound nose tackle, Michael Carter, smacked into Payton, knocking him back a yard. Payton's feet kept pumping. That wasn't leg strength. It was rage."

What's permissible in youth football

Clearly, "game face" and powerful emotions are part of emerging successfully from football collisions at the high school and higher levels of football. So I assumed that we youth coaches were supposed to teach our players the same "method acting" types of techniques.

Wrong.

It is considered improper in youth football to use many of the psyche-up techniques that are standard at the higher levels. For example, California Youth Football rules say,

> *14.132 Coaches, players or other personnel along the sidelines should never encourage their own players to engage in aggressive behavior against the opposing team. Outbursts such as 'stick him,' 'bust him,' 'hit him,' etc., are strictly forbidden.*

In his book, *A Parent's Guide to Coaching Youth Football*, John P. McCarthy, Jr. says,

> *I get sickened by the way some coaches preach violence to the kids, screaming, 'Kill him, go out there and hurt someone!' I know that they are usually just trying to psych a kid up, but I can't see how such guidance is good for young boys. I understand that it's an emotional game, but parents need to ensure that their child gets a correct perspective.*

Our approach

Keeping in mind the CYF guidelines and that we're dealing with 8- to 11-year old boys, not the San Francisco 49ers, we psyched our boys with cheers that we discussed as to youth football propriety at our coaches meetings.

For the first two weeks of the season, we used the cheer I described earlier:

Coach: "Who are we?"

Players: "Bears!"

Coach: "What are we?"

Players: "Champions."

This was our head coach's routine. I was not especially fond of it for three reasons:

• Saying we are Bears does not have any particular emotional charge. After all, the San Ramon Bears do not have a well-known, proud tradition like Notre Dame or some such. Our 8-3 official record in 1991 was the best record any San Ramon Bears team ever had. So yelling that we are Bears simply states a fact.

• Saying we are champions is a bit presumptuous. True, our returning veterans had won the division championship the previous year. But most of our players were rookies. And we were now in a new season.

• The words "Bears" and "champions" are soft-sounding, abstract words. They do not get the blood moving nor do they conjure up appropriate mind pictures. I prefer cheers that have words with K and T sounds. Those sounds resemble the crack of a whip and strike me as more conducive to the hard-hitting state of mind football players seek.

For our third game of the season against Oakland, I came up with this cheer:

Coach: "What're we gonna do?"

Players: "Attack!"

Coach: "What're we gonna get?"

Players: "A sack!"

Here you have the hard, whip-crakcing K sound at the end of each player answer. The words "attack" and "sack" also conjure up images of a hard-charging player sacking the quarterback or other ball carrier for a loss.

'Minus 50'

In preparation for the Benicia game, I tried setting a **goal**. We had held Napa to 32 yards, Fairfield to minus 18, and Berkeley to minus 36. Benicia seemed weaker than those teams. Also, they had a couple of deep-in-their-own-backfield running plays and their quarterback had a tendency to run backward to avoid pressure. So I told the defense our goal for the Benicia game was to hold them to minus 50 yards. The week's cheer was:

Coach: How many yards is Benicia gonna get?"

Players: "Minus 50!"

In the event, we held Benicia to minus 100 yards or so if you count the number of yards we moved the ball after intercepting two passes and picking up a fumble. Not counting those yards gained by defensive players carrying the ball, we only held them to minus one. The end zone got in the way of our minus fifty goal twice. We got two safeties.

How to cheer

There is a certain way to do these cheers. For one thing, we wanted them to be extremely **loud**. Sheer volume seems to get the players' mental state where it needed to be.

It's the old psychological theory that if you **behave** the way you want to **feel**, you will eventually start to **feel** the way you are **behaving**. Loud yells **appear** to be indications of passionate feeling. Therefore, they tend to **produce** passionate feeling.

The other thing we insisted on in cheers is **crispness**. The words are to be yelled in unison. They are to be enunciated properly. They are not to be slurred.

For example, in preparation for our 1991 Vacaville game, we changed the answer to the question, "What're we gonna do?" from "Attack!" to "Attack! Attack! Attack!" At first, the players tended to be out of synch so the answer was all jumbled up. We made them do it over until they got it right. I had to act as an orchestra conductor waving a magic marker to get them together.

Not too complex

You have to keep these themes **very simple**. In 1990, we played Vacaville during the regular season and lost 12-0. But our boys had really been in a fog that day. We noticed it in the pre-game warm-up and told them so.

So when we discovered we were playing Vacaville again for the conference championship, I chose the following theme.

> "The first time we played these guys, we were not our normal selves. And we lost. But Vacaville doesn't know that. They think the team they played was the real Bears. And they're coming back expecting to play the same team.
>
> "Actually, what we did without intending to is we set them up. We made them think we're a weak team that they can beat by two touchdowns.
>
> "Pro athletes do that a lot. For example, Ricky Henderson sometimes pretends he hurt his leg to set up the other team. Then he steals second. His limping is the set up; his stealing second is the kill.
>
> "And that's the way it's going to be with us and Vacaville. The first game was the set up; the second game is going to be the kill.
>
> Coach: "What was the first game?"
>
> Players: (Tentative blank looks)
>
> Coach: "When I ask 'What was the first game?' you say, 'The set up!' When I ask what is the next game, you say 'The kill!'"

Gradually, they said the answers I wanted. But I learned from their questions that they did not understand the whole idea. It was too complicated. We lost to Vacaville 18-0 in the 1990 playoff game

'Win one for The Fort'

A little **humor** can work to loosen the boys up. During the 1991 season, our local paper said Ron Fortle had caught a pass for an extra point in our Benicia game. We had no one named Ron Fortle on the team. We didn't even have anyone whose name remotely resembled Ron Fortle. No Fortle is listed in our local phone book. No one associated with the team has ever heard of Ron Fortle.

So we decided to make a joke of it. Before our Vacaville playoff game, one of our themes for the week was, "Win one for The Fort." We imagined that "The Fort" would be Ron's nickname. Or at least that's what worked best as a takeoff on Notre Dame's "Win one for The Gipper" legend.

We had the boys cheering:

Coach: "Who are we gonna win it for?"

Players: "The Fort!"

We made huge signs saying,

"Win one for The Fort"

"San Ramon Bears declare November 9, 1991 Ron Fortle Day."

Those signs were hung prominently at the Manteca stadium where we played Vacaville. "Win one for the Fort" was painted on at least one car window for the caravan from San Ramon to Manteca. This inside joke seemed to give us a small psychological edge over our opponents—not unlike the psychological lift prisoners of war get by running inside jokes against their guards. We won 6-0.

'In the box'

In the Oakland playoff game, I had a yell based on our defensive **strategy** for the game.

The strategic theory was that Oakland's running backs were much too fast for us to catch. So we had to stop them **before** they got going. Here's the handout I gave the boys that week.

The defensive plan for Saturday's game against Oakland is to keep Oakland's ball carriers in The Box. The Box is a three-sided rectangle between our defensive ends and in front of our linemen and linebackers. It looks like this:

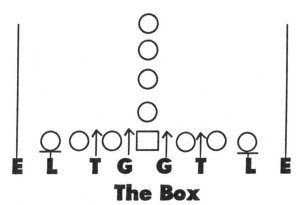

The Box

When they get outside The Box, Oakland's fast runners are dangerous. But as long as they're inside The Box, they are nothing special. If we keep them in The Box, we will win.

The other box

Actually, there are **two** boxes we'd like to keep Oakland's runners in. The other box is the one drawn in white powder around each team's **bench**. If we can keep Oakland's offense off the field entirely—and inside that bench box—we will win.

How do we keep Oakland's offense off the field entirely? By scoring every time we get the ball then kicking on sides kicks which we recover. We probably cannot score every time we get the ball or recover every on-sides kick. But we will try. Here are the ways we will use to minimize the number of plays Oakland's offense runs:

• **On-sides kicks.** All our kick offs on Saturday will be on-sides kicks to our left. Our kick-off team must do their best to get the ball AFTER it goes at least ten yards AND touches the ground OR after a member of the Oakland team TOUCHES it. If we touch it **before** it goes ten yards and touches the ground or touches an Oakland player, it's a **five-yard penalty** against us. But remember that Oakland can not only touch it anywhere they want, they can pick it up and run for a touchdown. Tri-Cities picked up an on-sides kick in the Midget game and ran it back for a touchdown. Try to get the ball but make sure no Oakland player gets it and runs with it. The rules say we (kicking team) cannot pick up a kickoff and run with it, so just fall on it.

• **Call time outs at last second.** The offense is allowed to take **25 seconds** between when the whistle blows ending the last play and when they must snap the ball for the next play. If they take longer, there is a delay of game penalty. So we should call time out when 24 seconds have elapsed when we're on **offense** and just before Oakland is ready to snap the ball when we're on **defense.** If you call time out before the 24th second on offense or before the Oakland quarterback is ready to take the snap, you waste a chance to reduce the number of plays the Oakland offense gets to run.

• **Stay in bounds.** When a runner of ours is close to the sideline, he should stay in bounds. If he goes out of bounds, he stops the clock. If he stays in bounds, the clock keeps running while we huddle. We want the clock to keep running so Oakland will get fewer chances to break loose.

• **Incomplete passes.** Incomplete passes have the advantage of putting the ball back to the line of scrimmage rather than where the quarterback was sacked. But they have the **disadvantage** of stopping the clock. So if the passer can do it, it would be better for him to fight his way back to the line of scrimmage than to intentionally throw an incomplete pass.

Make first downs. Every time we make a first down, we keep Oakland's offense off the field for another four downs. That's why we still want **complete** passes and out-of-bounds runs that get first downs.

• **Stop Oakland from getting first downs.** Every time we stop Oakland from getting a first down, their offense has to go to the bench box. They can't score from there.

The corresponding yell was:

Coach: "Where are we gonna keep 'em?"

Players: "In the box!"

Now that's got a nice hard K sound. (X = KS) But "The Box" is an abstract word that is only indirectly related to the actual physical act I wanted the players to perform, that is, tackle the ball carrier very soon after the snap. Maybe a less abstract, more directly related word picture would have been:

Coach: "How far is Oakland's ball carrier gonna get?"

Players: "One step!"

'Let's shock the world!'

Another thing I tried to do to prepare for the second Oakland game was use Stanford's 1990 upset of number one-ranked Notre Dame as an inspiration. Stanford was unranked at the time. And they were 17 1/2-point underdogs to Notre Dame.

In our league, Oakland was ranked number one in the standings for their division and they had to be a consensus number one in the entire league since they were undefeated and only allowed seven points all year.

In addition, I figured since we lost to them 18-0 in the first Oakland-Bears game, we had to be 18-point underdogs—almost the same point spread as Stanford-Notre Dame.

I had read somewhere that the Stanford players started a chant of "Let's shock the world!" during the week they prepared for their 1990 Notre Dame game.

So I told the Bears players the story of the 1990 Stanford-Notre Dame game (which Stanford won 36-31) and tried to start the same chant on the first day of our practice the week before the Oakland playoff game.

Coach: "What's our slogan?"

Players: "Let's shock the world!"

It didn't work. I don't mean we lost the game. We **did** lose 25-0. But I don't think the "Let's shock the world!" yell ever meant anything to the players. It was just something Coach Reed said to yell. They never seemed to buy into it.

I still think the whole idea of trying to use the Stanford-Notre Dame game as inspiration was good for our Oakland playoff game. I just didn't figure out the right way to present it.

Growling

When they first come out for football, virtually all rookies need remedial aggressiveness training. They simply are not accustomed to running into another boy full speed. They don't trust their equipment or their technique to protect them. What we are asking them to do seems insane.

We have the veterans demonstrate full-speed tackles and blocks to prove that it can be done and that you do not shatter into a million pieces if you hit someone hard. But still, fierce football collisions are an acquired taste.

One thing that seems to help is to have the players **growl** just before the snap in practice scrimmage or in drills.

We are Bears, remember? And bears growl. Telling the **mouth** to make a fierce noise seems to have the effect of making the **mind** get more fierce. At first, the boys are uncomfortable with the growl. It seems silly. They growl tentatively and softly. But we insist they do it over if they don't growl loudly enough. After a few plays, they start getting into the spirit of it and initiating the growl themselves.

Stale cheers

That "Who are we?/What are we?" yell has been used by San Ramon Bears Junior Pee Wee coaches for at least three years now. I don't think any cheer ought to be used for more than **one week**. They get stale. When they get stale, they become meaningless. And they do more harm than good.

At West Point, before I got there, the Army football team once came from behind to win in a fourth quarter seemingly in response to a spontaneous chant by the Corps of Cadets: "Fourth quarter's ours! Fourth quarter's ours!"

Great. The problem is the Corps of Cadets continued to yell, "Fourth quarter's ours!" in **every** game when we got to the fourth quarter and we were losing or only ahead by a few points. Inevitably, the chant was used in games when the fourth quarter turned out **not** to be ours. In spite of complaining letters to the editor of the school paper, they were still yelling it when I graduated. And I would not be surprised to learn that they are chanting, "Fourth quarter's ours!" to this day.

I just watched the 1991 Army-Navy game today. And I saw a cadet on the sidelines dressed as A-Man. When we were cadets, the Batman TV series was a big hit. A-Man was a takeoff on Batman. The Military Academy Band would play the Batman TV show theme song as A-Man cavorted on the sidelines. We would clap in unison. It was all very clever and charged us up.

But that was 25 years ago. And the guy is still there! It has been said that West Point is a place with 194 years of tradition unmarked by progress. If you look up stale psyche-up ideas in the Football Dictionary, A-man's picture would be next to the definition—and "Fourth quarter's ours!" would follow the "e.g."

One of our coaches really liked the Attack/A sack cheer and wanted to keep using it. I refused because 1. We lost the game in question 18-0 and, 2. I knew it would lose its power if used again.

Tradition

A long history of success is the one exception to the don't-use-stale-cheers rule. Notre Dame's coach would be nuts if he didn't use "Win one for the Gipper" at least as a wall slogan. He would also be nuts if he did not call upon his team to live up to the record of great Fightin' Irish teams of the past.

In our league, the Oakland Dynamites have a tremendous long-term record. If I were their coach, I'd be sure to hold that record up to the rookies to make them acutely aware of the tradition they have joined and are expected to carry on, if not enhance.

Make sure you really have such a tradition before you do that, though. My high school coach tried to make a big deal out of the great Collingdale tradition (not the real school name.)

A Collingdale football coach of the past had a very successful career and his teams had been called "The Golden Eleven" by a local sports writer. The coach tried to convince us, therefore, that, "...putting on a Collingdale football uniform was like putting on a New York Yankee or Notre Dame uniform." Nice try. But it was simply unpersuasive.

Tears

The most dramatic psyche-up result I ever saw was in my senior year of high school. Every Friday night, we players would go to the gym and the coaches would talk to us or play inspirational recordings in the locker room. Our games were Saturday afternoon.

Our toughest game of the season was to be against Haddonfield. As I recall we were four-touchdown underdogs. (My high school team went five and three that year if I remember correctly.) Friday night before the Haddonfield game, our school's wrestling coach was the speaker.

This guy was toughness personified. He had been an alternate on the U.S. Olympic wrestling team. He looked like he ate nails for breakfast. If you only heard his voice and never saw his face, you'd still think he ate nails for breakfast. He was not a football coach.

The theme of his talk was what a great head coach we had. He told us how he had seen head coaches in college take away an injured football player's scholarship and discard the player as if he were a burned-out light bulb. And our coach, he said, was such a great guy who really cared about us and so forth.

But it wasn't **what** he said as much as **how** he said it. As he spoke, this toughest guy we had ever seen began to cry. By the end, tears were streaming down his face and he was sobbing.

Wow!

We were stunned and deeply moved. We filed out silently and went home. Someone who arrived after the speech might have thought we had just been told one of our teammates had died.

The next day Collingdale demolished Haddonfield 27-0. I distinctly remember the team's mood during the game. It was quiet and businesslike. There was no rah rah. The team was just intently focused and determined. Everyone had on what has since come to be called a game face.

The newspapers called it the upset of the season in the league. Haddonfield didn't know what hit them. And if we had told them it was a sobbing wrestling coach, they probably would not have understood. Maybe you had to be there.

The effect wore off. Collingdale was mortal again the following week.

I've often wondered if the tears were contrived, if the wrestling coach offered to perform that act every four years for whomever was the current football coach. If they **were** contrived, give the man an Oscar.

I doubt contrived tears would work for other than a great actor. But I know those which are perceived as real can work a miracle in the right circumstances. My advice would be to let the tears come if they're coming in a pre-game talk. But don't fake it.

Anger at the players

Another psyche-up technique which was used against us at Collingdale High was the coach getting angry at the players. Our head coach had previously been head coach at Petersboro (not the real name). On Monday the week before the Petersboro game, the team captains decided to write the words "Win it for the coach" on adhesive tape on everyone's helmet. And we chanted "For the coach" during the week.

Come half time however, we were **behind** by two touchdowns. After making us wait longer than usual in the locker room, the head coach finally came in and said,

> *"Win it for the coach! Win it for the coach. If this is the way you play when you're winning it for me, forget it. I don't want my name associated with what you're doing out there!"*

His voice was dripping with sarcasm when he said, "Win it for the coach!" And he was mad as hell when he said the rest. And that was **all** he said. He stalked out of the locker room after those few words instead of the usual discussion of adjustments to make in the second half and so forth. We sat there with our heads down feeling like jerks.

Then some of the team leaders started yelling, "We can do it! We can do it!"

"We can do it!" was a chant we had heard about on a Bob Richards recording the coach had played for us at a Friday night meeting earlier in the season. Bob Richards was an Olympic decathlon gold medal winner and a minister. He made his living in part by doing highly inspirational, sports-based speeches. One was about a little college whose football team started yelling, "We can do it!" like they were possessed and almost beat a heavily favored, much bigger opponent as a result.

We turned ourselves into shrieking banshees yelling, "We can do it!" and pounding each other on the shoulder pads. We exploded out of the locker room and bounced onto the playing field like popping corn in heat. We came from behind to beat Petersboro in the second half. The students in the stands were amazed. They all wanted to know what the coach had said to us in the locker room. "Not much," we told them.

Phony anger

Unfortunately, the coach tried that anger routine again at half time in the last game of the season. But this time, it was obvious to all of us that his anger was contrived to inspire another Peterboro-like comeback. He was trying to manipulate us for the benefit of **his** win-loss record. We didn't appreciate that. We finished the game as we finished the half—behind.

You'd better be careful with the anger-at-the-players routine. As with crying, you can't be phony. Not only will it fail for that game, but you will have lost credibility in general with the players. Also, you can sour the players on the whole program or even on football in general.

Youth football, unlike high school football, does **not** involve either the professional careers of a coaching staff or the self image of a student body, booster club, and alumni association. Youth football is a volunteer organization designed to provide kids with an opportunity to play a wholesome game with other children and to learn good citizenship habits. So anger is something which should be be used only in very limited quantities.

The most disastrous example of a coach overdoing the anger routine was Lew Alcindor's high school basketball coach. The team was doing badly in a playoff game at the half. To try to fire Alcindor up, his white coach called him a "nigger." Alcindor was speechless and beside himself with anger. Playing well was the last thing on his mind.

That resulted in an immediate, complete, permanent break with that coach. Alcindor, as you probably know, later changed his name to Kareem Abdul-Jabbar and went on to star in the NBA where his coaches presumably fired him up without resorting to racial slurs.

Ups and downs

Here are some words of wisdom from legendary coach Vince Lombardi:

> *To be a good coach, you have to be the opposite of what you feel. When your team is going bad, you want to get on their ass but that's when everybody else is on their ass. That's when you need to pat 'em on the back, to tell 'em to just keep working hard enough to win and everything will be all right. Converseley, if everything is going good, you don't have to pat 'em on the back because everybody else is. That's when you have to be tough.*

Not everybody is Knute Rockne

I can't sing. At West Point, they made everybody try out for the Glee Club. I washed out in about 20 seconds. I also can't tell a joke on purpose—although I frequently make people laugh by accident from the way I phrase things.

The talent to do various things was not distributed equally to everyone at birth. Just because the board of your youth football program chose you to be a football coach does not mean you are a good inspirational speaker. My observation is that many youth football coaches can**not** fire up their players. They try. But their efforts fall flat like a song sung by one who cannot sing or a joke told by a non-comedian.

There is a good chance that you are such a person. You can find out by objectively watching the reaction of your players to your psyche-up efforts. Since most of us have trouble being objective about ourselves, a better way may be to discuss the matter at coaches meetings just as you should discuss nepotism. For example:

> Coach: *"Hey guys, I need to know if I have whatever it takes to fire up the boys. Tell me straight. Are my attempts at playing Knute Rockne going over like lead balloons?"*

As a general rule, every seven-man coaching staff probably has one or two coaches who ought to leave the inspirational speeches and cheerleading to others on the staff. And the others ought to tell those two who they are to avoid efforts which are ineffective at best and counterproductive at worst.

Player personalities

Coaches sometimes demand that players and fellow coaches behave in a certain way before and after games. How people behave off the playing field is really none of the coach's business. John Madden learned this lesson when he coached the Raiders. He tended to be highly serious before games. And when he caught players joking around, he yelled at them and essentially demanded that they behave the way he behaved before the game. In fact, some players naturally behaved the same way as Madden, but many others did not.

One of his players, Blair Sheldon, came into his office and said,

> *Coach, there are all different kinds of personalities in that locker room before a game. Everybody wants to win the same way but there are different ways of preparing to win. Some guys take a nap, some guys go to the bathroom, some throw up, some listen to music. Some, like me, tell jokes. We're not all the same.*

Recorded speeches

I already mentioned the Bob Richards speeches. I've been trying to track them down—without success. They were excellent. I would highly recommend good recorded speeches which you have previewed before playing them for your players. Recorded inspirational speeches were the main thing our coaches gave us at our night-before-the-game meetings.

When to play them is more of a problem for youth football coaches than it was for my high school coach. Any time spent in team meetings is considered practice time—at least in our league. So the only way you can have a meeting to play inspirational recordings is to take it away from practice time.

Pre-game time is often less restricted. If you have a separate locker room from the visitors, you could play the recording while your players dress for the game. If the game is an away game, you can play inspirational recordings on the team bus, if you have one. We don't. If players travel individually or in several vans, you could give a cassette to each driver and have them play it on the car cassette player or on a portable boom box.

Football music

My high school coach always had football marching songs and "You gotta be a football hero" playing in the locker room when we were dressing for a game. I bought a couple cassettes of football fight songs one season but, not being the head coach, I could never get them played.

Other songs which are not football songs *per se* can nevertheless be highly inspirational like "The Impossible Dream," "We are the Champions of the World," "One Moment in Time," "Only the Strong Survive," "Chariots of Fire," "Rocky," etc.

You can play them before and after the weigh in, on the team bus, etc.

Our high school coach also had them playing over the public address system at our stadium before kick off. That'll psyche up the other team, too.

The best song would be one that you write just for your team. We've thought about doing that but never got around to it. You'd pick an existing, rousing tune and compose new words to it to fit your team.

I hasten to add that such an activity might infringe on the **copyrights** of the owners of the song you are using. For example, last I heard, former Beatle Paul McCartney owned the rights to the famous football fight song "On Wisconsin."

It's not the end of the world if the copyright is owned by someone. You can contact the copyright owners through ASCAP and ask how much, if anything, they would charge to permit you to perform your version of their song at your games and other activities. In general, they try to price the right to use their stuff cheaply enough to **encourage** its use, **not** prevent it. There is no money in **stopping** people from singing a song.

If dealing with copyrights sounds like too much, use a song which is in the **public domain** (no one owns a copyright on the song so everyone is free to use it) either because its copyright **expired**, like "Old Folks at Home (Swanee River)" or because it was **never** copyrighted to begin with, like "Yellow Rose of Texas." Be careful here, too. Some songs which you may **think** are in the public domain are, in fact, copyrighted, like "Happy Birthday to You" or "For He's a Jolly Good Fellow." That's why they don't sing "Happy Birthday to You" at kids' parties in restaurant chains like Chuck E. Cheese.

Hearing songs can be inspirational. **Singing** rousing songs is even more inspirational. If you can get a team fight song or adopt your high school's or some such, have your kids sing it once a week at practice or as they march into the gym on game day or whenever it works.

I have to make a comment here about the Star Spangled Banner. They play it before each Jr. Pee Wee game in our league becaues we are the first game of the day. Virtually all teams used the Whitney Houston version from the 1991 Desert Storm Superbowl. I hate that version. Whitney Houston is a great singer—and her performance at the Desert Storm Superbowl was very moving in the context of the tribute to the troops involved in Desert Storm.

But the national anthem was not meant to be sung by night-club singers who stylize it and make it a tribute to their own ego more than a tribute to the "nation for which it stands;" who pronounce words like "free" and "brave" as if they had five syllables. Apparently, all the singers who believed the Star Spangled Banner should be sung straight have passed away since Jose Feliciano first did his controversial stylized version in the World Series. The sylized versions, in addition to trivializing the anthem and what it represents, also take forever to finish. Please just play a version performed by a military or college marching band. As far as I know, there are no stylized strictly instrumental versions.

Bands

When I first attended a youth football game, I was amazed at how much like high school football the operation was. There were professional referees, uniformed coaches, cheerleaders, a public address announcer, and electric scoreboard, a snack bar, adult linesmen, etc. In contrast, Little League and soccer games rarely have any of those things. There is, however, one thing which is present at high school football games but missing from the youth football games I've attended—a **band**.

Seems to me we ought to have a band. Perhaps the high school band would be willing to play at a youth football game at least once during the season. When I attended a Saint Mary's College football game in Moraga, California this past fall, I was surprised to see that the band which played for Saint Mary's that day at least was the California High School Band. California High School is the San Ramon, California high school at which our San Ramon Bears youth football program plays its home games. Our youth football program exists, in part, to improve the California High School football program.

Or maybe a junior high or elementary school band would play at your games. Some areas have youth bands, orchestras, and drum and bugle corps which are not affiliated with any school. Maybe they'd appreciate an audience to play for.

We tried to simulate a band with a boom box and the University of California fight song on cassette. That worked pretty well. But a live band would be better.

One word of caution, many **youth** bands are dreadful. Or to put it more delicately, they play in a way that only a band parent could love. You're better off with**out** a band than to have one which sounds terrible.

Keeping the players loose

Players can be **too** fired up, too tense. One of the most famous attempts to loosen players up before a game was San Francisco 49ers coach Bill Walsh's 1981 Superbowl bellhop stunt.

Walsh had to come to Pontiac, Michigan separately from the team. He arrived before the 49ers and paid a hotel bellhop $20 to let him wear the bellhop's uniform. When the 49ers bus arrived, Walsh kept grabbing at the 49er players' luggage.

This was an enormous hit with the media—a supposed perfect pitch move by the "Genius" coach which contributed to his team's victory over the Bengals in Superbowl XVI. In fact, it appears from the several books I've read by and about the 49ers that the bellhop stunt largely flopped. Many players did not recognize Walsh in the bellhop uniform, were downright annoyed by the persistent bellhop who wouldn't take no for an answer, and only heard it was Walsh later.

In general, I think light humor and kidding around is probably all you need to avoid excess tension. Elaborate stunts like the bellhop maneuver often fall flat. Plus I think kids are less likely to get up tight than adult coaches and players.

In 1990, our players always struck me as intimidated by our opponents—before they even laid eyes on them. In 1991, the opposite seemed true. Our guys were always loose and confident. **Other** teams seemed intimidated by **us** in the locker room. Part of the reason was we had some big guys in 1991. Several teams asked our Jr. Pee Wee players if they were Pee Wees—which is a 15-pound heavier weight class.

I suspect our 1991 looseness was partly due to:

• the great success we had at our jamboree
• the particular kids we had in 1991
• scouting and practice against the scout team.

By the time we got to a game in 1991, our players had already played the "opponents" three times in our three weekday practices. Our players had studied the opponent's playsheets. We knew who their best backs were. We knew what their favorite play was. Except for our playoff opponents, no one seemed to scout us. So Saturday games had an element of old hat to our players. But our opponents were usually seeing us for the first time and were wide-eyed with uncertainty.

Don't peak too early

If you play your games on Saturday morning, there's not a lot of point to getting your players sky high on Tuesday night. Or ever Thursday night for that matter. There's not even much point in getting them sky high at 8:45 if the game is at 10:00.

You want them fired up at **kickoff** time.

Demand a proper cheer and a modicum of loudness during the weekday practices. Torque it up a little during the pre-game calisthenics. Torque it up more at kickoff minus 15 minutes. Finally, have them waking the dead in your sideline huddle just before kickoff.

Second half

You'd better make sure your team is similarly fired up for the second half. Benicia was. And our offense was unable to score a point against them in the second half. Same thing happened when I scouted the Benicia-Richmond game. Richmond scored 13 in the first half. Benicia came out fired up after the half and shut Richmond out in the second half.

Treat the last several minutes before the end of half time the same way you treat the last several minutes before the original kickoff. Have your players waking the dead with their yelling just before they take the field.

Football as war

To psyche up their players, a lot of football coaches tell them football is war and use combat battle cries for inspiration. An NFL video I have has the Houston Oilers wearing army helmets and yelling, "Hit the beach!"

In his book, *Total Impact*, Ronnie Lott says he constantly used the phrase, "Take no prisoners!" when psyching himself up.

In addition to playing and coaching a little football, I studied war at West Point and participated in one—Vietnam.

It is true that there are tactical and strategic similarities between war and football. Military officers could learn much from football coaches and vice versa. Principles of war like surprise and mass are also valid on the football field. The war dances which indians did before battle resemble football pep rallies.

However, to say that football **is** war only shows how ignorant the speaker is of what war is. There are many war veterans who have also played football—the most notable recent example is Rocky Bleier of the Steelers. I would be surprised if Rocky Bleier ever said, "Football is war," after he was wounded in Vietnam.

So don't tell your kids that football is war. Football is a game—a rough game to be sure—but it's **only** a game. The injuries are rarely serious—especially at the youth level. Real war is body bags and unspeakable maiming.

Football is largely a game of **skill**. War is largely a game of **chance** at the level of the individual soldier. A coach who tells his kids that, "Football is war," may unwittingly be recruiting a boy for future military service for the wrong reasons. To tell a boy that, "Football is war," is also to tell him that, "War is football," which it most certainly is not.

There's nothing wrong with serving in the military. But it ought to be done out of a sense of duty—not because an impressionable young man believes his older, wiser football coach was telling him that war, like a football game, is exciting fun.

We coaches also should not trivialize the sacrifice that dead and wounded war veterans have made—or the risk that current military personnel face—by equating it to what goes on in a football game.

'Take no prisoners'

Ronnie Lott, as I said, is very big on the line, "Take no prisoners!" So are a lot of other football coaches and players. I've heard it on an NFL video. The Eastbay mail order sporting goods company offers a t-shirt which says "The Big D, defense, Take no prisoners."

They should all eliminate that particular phrase from their repertoire.

I realize that, when used in the context of football, "Take no prisoners!" is simply a metaphor which means vaguely to play really hard. There's nothing wrong with playing really hard. That's exactly what your players should do and you need to find words to inspire them to do that.

But not those words.

Used in the context from whence it came—combat—the phrase, "Take no prisoners!" is an admonition to commit **murder**.

You get prisoners in combat by accepting the surrender of enemy soldiers. Accepting surrender is **required** by the Third Geneva Convention, to which the United States is a signatory. There **have** been instances where military units took no prisoners—like Malmedy and My Lai. The alternative to taking prisoners is to **kill** those who try to become pisoners. An enemy soldier waves a white flag and comes out with his hands up. If you take no prisoners, you shoot him.

In addition to violating the Geneva Convention, it also violates one of the Ten Commandments and the U.S. Uniform Code of Military Justice (Army Regulation 350-216, 5/28/70). If you shoot a would-be prisoner, you should be court martialed. And if a witness reports it to an honest officer, you will be.

General Douglas MacArthur once said the following about the usefulness of sports in training military leaders. It is often quoted and is carved on the wall of the gym at West Point,

> *Upon the fields of friendly strife,*
> *Are sown the seeds*
> *That, upon other fields, on other days,*
> *Will bear the fruits of victory.*

Our youth football games and practices take place on "fields of friendly strife." Our players are highly impressionable. It is not inconceivable that one of our players might someday find himself in a foxhole searching for guidance. And that he might find it in words his football coach told him years before.

We should not, in our zeal to psyche up boys for a game, sow in our players' minds a seed like "Take no prisoners" which, upon other fields, on other days, may bear the fruits of atrocity.

Psyche up can win games—or lose them

Your players all have to get religion to be successful. Furthermore, your team needs to be psyched up for each half of each game. The team that is most psyched up will generally win. Furthermore, a weak, psyched up team can beat an otherwise superior, flat team. We lost one Richmond game partly because the Richmond coaches were better prepared for the cold rain and partly because the Richmond players were more psyched up for the game than our players were—in spite of the fact that we were clearly two-touchdown favorites.

15

Practice schedule

Three purposes

Practice has three purposes:

- teach individual fundamentals
- teach position job descriptions (including cooperation with adjacent teammates)
- evaluation.

Big picture schedule

Your season has two major segments:

- preseason
- during season.

The difference from a practice standpoint is that you have **no scouting report** to focus your scrimmage work on during the **pre**season.

Your season has two other segments:

- **before** players are assigned to positions
- **after** players are assigned to positions.

Before players are assigned to positions, you teach every player every individual fundamental and you evaluate every player at every position. It is relatively easy to organize practice at this point because everybody gets equal time at everything. You typically set up multiple stations and rotate groups of players from station to station. At each station, the players stand in line waiting their turn to do the drill or evaluation in question.

Every player, every coach, every minute

All practice time should be scheduled according to the principle of:

- every player
- every coach
- every minute.

By that I mean your practice schedule must say where every player is and where every coach is at every minute of the practice and it must say what those players and coaches will be doing every minute of the practice.

The common deviation from that principle is:

- give me my favorite first-string players
- I'll work on X with them
- give me one helper coach
- everybody else go with Coach Y
- I don't care what the other coaches and players do.

This is maddening. It results in coaches standing around chatting with each other oblivious to the practice. It creates a group of outcast players. The "everybody else" group of players is typically a miscellaneous mixture of positions which are hard to integrate into a cohesive drill. On our 24-boy squad, "everybody else" was usually a couple defensive linemen, a couple defensive backs, and a defensive end.

I could make up interesting drills for them for awhile. But try doing it night after night for months.

Basic evaluations

You need to do at least the following evaluations of everybody:

- 20-yard dash (time with stopwatch)
- head-on tackling
- side tackling
- pass catching ability
- agility (stopwatch).

Do these the first day or the first week of practice. Also, set up a procedure whereby latecomers to the team go through these tests. We tested our players the first week. But many players joined the team later than that. I often wondered how they'd do on the tests. You should have a profile sheet on each player showing their test scores, age, and weight. Latecomers should be taken aside by a coach who tests them individually and fills out their sheets as was done with the rest of the team the first week.

Tackling standard

Tackling is the most fundamental of all defensive techniques. You need to have some standard which you want everyone to achieve. I did not think of it as a standard at the beginning of the season, but I did at the end.

Ours was:

Head-on tackle
- head on ball (but always off to the side; no spearing)

• head up
• shoulder on belt buckle
• feet shoulder width apart
• back straight
• butt below shoulders
• hands grabbing top of back of thighs
• lift off the ground

Side tackle
• head on front side of ball carrier
• head up
• shoulder on thigh
• back straight
• arms wrapped tightly around legs
• lift off the ground.

In each case the tackler is to stay on his feet and drive through the ball carrier lifting him off the ground.

Perfection

You must make your players tackle over and over in stop-action, slow motion, half-speed, three-quarters speed, full speed, whatever it takes to get them to do it perfectly. Keep doing it in slower and slower slow motion from shorter and shorter distances apart until they get it perfect. Then gradually speed it up and spread them farther apart. Always go back to a slower speed and shorter distance if they are doing it wrong at the speed and distance you are using.

One of the goals of your tackling drills is to get every single defensive player up to the tackling standard as quickly as possible.

Some of your veterans will already be up to the standard on day one. You need to identify who is and who is not as soon as possible so you can assign the substandard tacklers to remedial tackling and the standard ones to position drills.

Here's where you can get pictures of good tackles

You need photographs of correct tackling technique. I will not provide them in this book because that has already been done better than I can do it in the following books:

• *A Parent's Guide to Coaching Football* by John P. McCarthy, Jr.
• *Youth League Football Coaching and Playing* by Jack Bicknell
• *Sports Illustrated Football Winning Defense* by Bud Wilkinson
• *Play Football the NFL Way* by Tom Bass.

Also, moving pictures are probably even better. I recommend ESPN's *Teaching Kids Football* with Bo Schembechler or the *Pop Warner Video Football Handbook*. I do not recommend NFL films for tackling technique. Some contain a few tackles which show good technique. But most demonstrate what, for kids, would be terrible technique. The book authors I just mentioned and Bo Schembechler are far better qualified than I to tell you what correct tackling technique should look like. All I will try to do is relate the difficulties I had teaching boys the technique and how we achieved the limited success we had.

Fumble recovery

Teach fumble recovery as soon as your kids get into pads. Most coaches seem to teach only **falling on the ball**. As I said in the scoring-on-defense chapter, you should also teach **picking it up and running with it**.

I estimate it will take you about three or four repetitions to teach your players the proper way to fall on a ball. They should end up in the fetal position on their side with the ball tight against their belly and covered by both arms. The **chin should be away from the chest** to avoid a neck injury caused by another player crashing into a helmet of a player who has his head down. You probably do not have to revisit the skill of falling on the ball the rest of the season. One brief session should be enough.

Competitive fumble recovery drill

Competition livens up almost any drill. The players get more intense. They work much harder. They have more fun. And competitive drills resemble your weekly football games more in that the games are, of course, competitive.

The common competitive fumble recovery drill is to have two lines of players. The coach tosses the ball out and the first player in each line tries to get it. The toss is a **mistake** in a competitive drill. If you're going to have two boys compete for the ball, place it **motionless** on the ground equidistant from each boy. Otherwise, the winner is too often determined by the bounce the ball takes and the kids will quit competing if it doesn't bounce their way. Placing it on the ground equidistant from the competing players makes the competition fair.

Write down how each boy does in the competition for evaluation purposes and because the boys want their success recorded. You could organize the competition like a little single-elimination tournament. That will enable you to rank the entire team as to their ability to recover fumbles. The winners will take pride and confidence from their accomplishment. The losers will, hopefully, resolve to work harder. I guarantee the non-top players will clamor for a rematch whenever you hold a competitive drill. How many times do football players clamor for a drill?

Make sure you also toss the ball so it's bouncing around in **non**competitive fumble recovery and pick-up-and-run drills. The boys have to learn to deal with bouncing balls, too, because that's often what the ball does in a game situation.

The feedback loop

Suppose that you were not running a football team. Rather you were just running a place-kicking team. In your preseason, it would not be hard to decide what to work on. You'd come up with the formation you wanted to use and you'd teach each player where he lined up in that formation. Then you'd practice the four skills a place-kicking team needs to master:

- the long snap
- the hold
- the kick
- blocking.

OK, now suppose that you have your place-kicking jamboree. You check the video afterwards and find that your line held, your snaps were good, but your holder kept bobbling the ball. What are you going to work on next week? Obviously you are going to increase the time you spend on holding. That could be in two forms: having your original holder practice holding or replacing him with a new holder.

You would not want to completely drop practice on blocking and snapping because if you do they'll lose the ability to do it correctly. And you have to continue to practice on kicking because you still don't know if that was right because you didn't get the holds.

And let's further say that you scouted your first regular season opponent at their jamboree and you discovered that they overload their right side to try to block the kick.

Given all that I suspect your percentage practice breakdown for the coming week would be something like:

long snap 20%
hold   30%
kick   30%
blocking   20%
    standard blocking   10%
    left overload blocking 10%

Whole team

OK, now consider applying that approach to the whole team. From the head coach's perspective, the original preseason practice schedule should look something like this:

- special teams   40%
- defense   30%
- offense   30%.

The defensive coach's use of his 30% of total practice time would be something like:

- stance   10%
- tackling   50%
- pursuit angles   10%
- job descriptions   10%
- pass coverage   10%
- scrimmage against a variety of offensive formations and plays 10%

Preseason

Our preseason started on July 29, 1991 and ended with our first opponent's jamboree on August 31st. We really couldn't begin the regular season until we had the scouting report on our first opponent. And we didn't have that until August 31st. That's five weeks of preseason. I'll assume your preseason is similar.

Work on both individual skills and team skills in the preseason. Logically, one might say you should just drill on blocking, tackling, and such. But even if that were the logical, it's not much fun. The boys signed up to play football, not to drill. You'd better let them play some football.

No-contact week

The first ten hours of practice must be no-contact in our league. Supposedly, you condition the players during that week to get them ready for contact. I suspect you'd have trouble finding a scientific study that would support that notion. And even if there were such a study, it would probably depend on the first week being spent on a very specific conditioning regimen, not just a general plan that everyone should get sweaty for ten hours before they hit. But like ambulances at games, the one-week-of-conditioning-before-pads ritual lives on because of football's reputation as an injury sport (an undeserved reputation at the youth level).

Because the neck is the area of greatest vulnerability to catastrophic injury in football, you should begin immediately to strengthen the players' necks.

I note that the various football camps whose brochures I have seen are all just one week long and all involve full contact. And camps, being private businesses, are more injury conscious than leagues.

In any event, you can't have the kids hit the first week. But that doesn't mean you can't have extremely useful practices. It may not even mean you can't have the kids in pads.

We always have the kids wear their helmets from day one so their necks get used to the weight and the boys get used to having their mouthpieces in. Logically, you could have the players in full equipment to get them used to the whole ball of wax. You'd just tell them to refrain from hitting. But as a practical matter, it's hard to keep boys wearing full pads to resist the temptation to hit each other. If you've got good supervision and can keep them from hitting, I'd recommend the following if allowed by your league:

No-contact week equipment schedule

Monday	Helmets only
Tuesday	Add girdles with hip and tailbone pads
Wednesday	Add football pants with knee and thigh pads
Thursday	Add shoulder pads but no football shirts over them
Friday	Full equipment

They really need to get used to wearing all the equipment. Furthermore, you need to time them and otherwise test them in pads. The fastest runner in shorts may not be the fastest runner in full equipment. Until you start playing football games in shorts, speed in shorts is irrelevant.

Another reason to add equipment every day of no-contact week is **to teach the rookies how to wear the equipment**. They often don't understand how to put their pads in their girdle and pants. If you wait until Monday of the second week to teach them, you will waste a lot of time that day adjusting equipment. You could even have an injury because players are engaging in full contact with their equipment improperly assembled.

Size is another problem—for both rookies and veterans. If they gradually add equipment each day, improper sizes will be spotted before full contact.

What to evaluate during no-contact week

You can and should evaluate your players on everything listed in the evaluation list above except tackling. Passing, pass catching, punting, place kicking, sprinting, agility, backpedaling, etc. can all be tested without contact.

Player-owned equipment check

Also use no-contact week to check the player-owned equipment like shoes, forearm pads, receivers gloves, etc. Shoes are especially problematic. In our league, they must have at least four cleats on the heel and at least nine on the sole. I bought my son a pair of shoes before the season started and they only had two cleats on the heel and five on the sole.

Fortunately, I had bought them from a store that specialized in football stuff and told them I was leaving it up to them to supply us with legal shoes. The owner took them back and gave me a full refund—but he wasn't happy about it.

Give each parent a copy of your league's shoe rules before the preseason so they can buy legal shoes. It's harder to stay legal with football shoes than Little League shoes because different leagues have different specifications and because illegal baseball shoes usually have some glaring illegal feature like steel spikes. Another disqualifying feature in youth football shoes is detachable spikes. We had a couple junior pee wees show up during no-contact week in detachable spikes and a couple who, like my son, had too few spikes.

Check each players' **shoes** the first week of practice. We did this while they had their feet up in the air during certain calisthenics. Or you can just have them all kneel down.

If you have illegal spikes, you must ban them on any contact practice day. The danger is stepping on another player and that can happen as soon as you start contact. You cannot give a boy a day or a week to get new ones. He must be prohibited from engaging in contact from the moment you discover the shoes until he gets proper shoes. An injury could occur as soon as the **first** contact play he engages in so he must not be permitted to participate in even one play until his shoes are legal.

No-contact-week chalk talks

Just because the first week of preseason is often called "Conditioning Week" doesn't mean you have to spend every minute running your players tails off. You generally need to break it up for variety's sake as well as to give the kids a breather.

I suggest you cover the following topics during no-contact week chalk talks:

* introduce coaching staff
* football rules
* league rules like keeping your grades up and not talking to opposing players
* team rules like those covering player misbehavior
* team history
* team goals for the season
* defense to be used
* football terminology
* introduction of players
* demonstrate skills like

> tackling head on
> tackling from the side
> tackling a passer
> blocking a punt
> wide pursuit angles
> intercepting
> backpedaling technique
> shedding a blocker

Preseason contact period

It took me most of the season to get our players to where they all could tackle a runner going half speed from the side using correct technique. In other words, our players finally all got it when we were preparing for our seventh game—out of eight regular-season games. That's too late. Fortunately, we were in the playoffs by then. But had we played a tougher schedule, not learning to tackle until the seventh game could have kept us out of the playoffs.

Teaching tackling is easier said than done.

So you'd better start right in the first day of contact and work on it every day throughout the season. Furthermore, you need to appoint a coach to be **remedial tackling coach** because the veterans will get it right very quickly, some of the rookies will get it right before too long. But the other rookies will take months to learn—unless you can figure out a faster way to teach them than I did.

Tackling evaluation

You also need to start **evaluating** tacklers immediately. In doing that, keep in mind that there are different kinds of tackles and the fact that a boy can make one kind well does not mean that he can make all kinds well.

There are the close-in tackles like those made by defensive guards when the other team runs a dive play. Those require more wrestling and breaking the holds of the offensive linemen than hitting.

Then there are the open-field tackles. Those require agility and more courage. Many of the guys who are great at close-in tackles can barely succeed at one-hand touch in the open field because they lack speed, or agility, or the courage to hit a fast-moving ball carrier.

Open-field tackles also require judgment. Frequently, the player has all the courage in the world and hurls himself at the runner at top speed. But if the runner sees him coming, he can easily sidestep the tackler. Many times, I suspect the tackler does this knowing full well the ball carrier will sidestep him but taking the attitude, "Hey, what more could I have done? Didn't you see how hard and fast I ran at him?"

The what more he could have done is get himself **under control** as he closed on the ball carrier. That means spreading his feet to about shoulder width and taking shorter steps. This reduces the force of his hit, but it increases the probability that he will be able to cut with the runner and wrap the runner's legs up. Hitting is secondary to wrapping.

Hitting versus wrapping

Hitting is probably overemphasized by youth coaches. Youth coaches explode with delight and praise when a player puts a real hard hit on another player.

I have nothing against hitting. And I'd like my players to hit as hard as they can. But the "as they can" part of that phrase means as hard as they can without taking undue risk of missing or bouncing off the ball carrier.

There was an interesting comment on hitting versus good technique in Tom Landry's autobiography. In the fifties, when Landry played for the New York Giants and New York Yankees football teams, the Cleveland Browns were the dominant team in the league.

> *"It wasn't merely that Paul Brown's teams achieved a string of championships that will probably never be equaled; it was the way they did it.*
> *"...they never beat you with brute strength; they used precision.*
> *"When you played against the Pittsburgh Steelers, guys would stuff extra padding under their hip pads and anywhere else they could get it. Though you expected to win the game against a Pittsburgh club that didn't post a lot of wins in that era, you knew the Steelers would punish you physically. Even with extra padding, Pittsburgh's opponents would be bruised and hurting for the next week. In contrast, teams would go into Cleveland, lose by three or four touchdowns, and wake up Monday morning feeling as if they had taken Sunday afternoon off."*

In baseball, they say, "First the ball, then the play"—meaning make sure you catch the ball before you start worrying about throwing it somewhere or tagging someone out. In football, the rule for tacklers should be,

> *"First make sure of the tackle, then hit as hard as you can."*

Ronnie Lott is famous for hard hits. But he generally can only do that when the player doesn't see him coming or when the player is in a narrow space where he has little room to maneuver.

Start with a snap

To teach and evaluate close-in tackling, set up a two-yard by two-yard lane. Put a ball in the ball carrier's hands in advance. Put the tackler in a four-point or three-point stance depending on which you use. Have a center just outside the lane start the drill by simulating a snap.

You always want defensive drills to start with a ball being snapped. You **never** want defensive drills to start with verbal commands. Even worse is starting a drill with a whistle. You always start with a snap to get the players in the habit of moving when the ball moves in games, **not** when the opposing quarterbacks barks out his cadence. And you want them to go full speed until the whistle blows, at which time they are to stop cold to avoid late-hit injuries and/or penalties. Starting a drill with a verbal cadence or a whistle give the players the **exact opposite** habit from what you want.

Lateral pursuit

To teach and evaluate lateral pursuit, put two tackling dummies about ten yards apart. The ball carrier on one side holds the ball in advance. A center at the end snaps the ball to an imaginary quarterback to start the drill. And the tackler waits on the other side of the line made by the dummies. The ball carrier can cut across the line anywhere between the dummies but he may not run wider than the dummies.

When the ball moves, the ball carrier moves laterally then cuts up across the line made by the dummies. The tackler tries to tackle the ball carrier as soon as possible and for a loss if possible. Reverse the direction of the drill after everybody has done it one way. Here's a diagram to show what I mean.

Lateral pursuit tackling drill

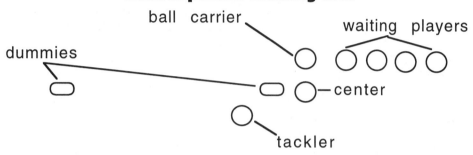

After each snap, the tackler goes to the end of the waiting line, the ball carrier becomes the tackler, the center becomes the ball carrier, and the next person in line becomes the center. You need two balls for this drill: one for the ball carrier and one for the center.

Evaluating tacklers

Carry a clipboard with a roster on it. For evaluations in 1991, I used a special tackle-evaluation roster with excellent, good, fair, and poor columns and common-tackling-mistake columns. That's so I could mark down an evaluation quickly and keep the drill moving. Here's a filled-out example:

Tackling evaluation

Tackle type: _open field_

Name	Excellent	Good	Fair	Poor	Head down	Too high	No wrap	Left feet too soon	Head not in front	Head not on ball
Aaron		III(	I	I				III		
Bob			I	IIII	卌					
Chuck	III	II				I		IIII		
Dennis		II	I	II		卌				
Eddie			III	II		卌			I	
Fred	I	III	I				III			
Gerry	卌									
Hank		I		IIII				IIII		
Irv	II	II		I	I		II	I		
Jim		IIII	I			III		I		
Kyle	III	II				II				
Larry		II	II	I				卌		
Mike	I	II	I	II		卌				
Ned			IIII	I	卌					

Same mistake

Note that the players tend to make the same mistakes every time. Different players have different bad habits. But each player tends to repeat the same bad habit every time he tackles. You can tell him what he's doing wrong—even remind him before each tackle—and he'll **still** do it that way. You really have to bear down to eliminate the problem. Make him do it in slow motion the right way then speed him up and move him farther away from the ball carrier until he's going full speed and still doing it right.

Keep your evaluations in a binder. Show them to the players. Once, I computerized the scores and calculated a composite score to rank every boy on the team according to his tackling ability. An excellent was worth 4 points; a good, 3, and so forth.

I must caution you, however, that the eleven best tacklers in a **drill** are not necessarily the eleven best **game** tacklers. So you have to combine your drill evaluations with observations made during scrimmages.

Also, in 1992, I didn't write down what was wrong with anybody's tackling. I corrected it on the spot. That is I made him do it over immediately the right way—often having him do it at a slower speed to get it right. That instant and universal correction of any tackling error in 1992 paid big dividends. We were a far better tackling team in 1992 than in 1991. In 1991, the game video would often show a player arm tackling or shirt tackling a ball carrier and the ball carrier escaping. In 1992, to get within reach of a Bears defensive starter was to be tackled. We still missed at times when the tackler was not in the right spot and dove at the ball carrier. But you almost never saw an opposing player break one of our tackles in 1992.

Count tackles and assists

Tackling is 90% desire and 10% technique. I have been talking almost entirely about technique in this book. How do you get desire?

I think it's mostly born, not made. It's one of those things you seek rather than create. The way to find it is to count tackles and assists. We told our players to hold their arms out like a ref signalling an unsportsmanlike penalty signal if they made the tackle and to hold one hand above their head if they had an assist.

A tackle is defined as being the first to starting a successful tackle. If the first guy to get to the ball carrier misses the tackle, he gets no credit.

An assist means helping on the tackle before the play's over whistle, that is being the second, third, or fourth guy to join in a successful tackle.

During scrimmage, keep a team evaluation sheet with each player's name on it on a clipboard in your hand. After every play, put a "T" next to the name of the player who made the tackle and an "A" next to the name of each player who made an assist. The players will be holding their arms out or up and asking, "Did you got my tackle, coach?"

As the scrimmage goes on, announce who is leading in tackles and assists. Admonish the guys with few or no tackles or assists to step up their efforts. Remind them that the number of tackles and assists will, more than anything else, determine who starts on defense.

I assume that you are following my advice and giving all your players equal chance to participate in practice. So the total should be the same as the total per play. But in games, you need to switch to counting the number of tackles and assists per play. That is, you must take into account the fact that the bench warmers are not in the game for as many plays as the starters. To put it another way, divide the number of tackles and assists by number of plays the player in question was in the game. Otherwise there is no way the reserve players can match the starters in raw numbers.

In 1992, we had a rookie named Anthony Lomondo. He was smaller than the average player on our team. But he seemed to be pretty good. Nevertheless, his tackle and assist totals were rather low so I did not start him on defense.

Then it occurred to me that I should count game tackles and assists **per play participated in**. When I did that, Lomondo was suddenly the team leader. He made more tackles and assists **per play in which he was in the game** than anyone else on the team. So I immediately made him a starter.

Change every ten to fifteen minutes

You cannot do any drill or other activity like show video tape for more than ten or fifteen minutes. **That may be the most important advice in this book**. You must change activities every fifteen minutes at the latest.

If you don't, the boys will get bored. And when they get bored, they will misbehave. When they misbehave, you will get angry at them and practice time will be wasted. If you repeatedly make this mistake, a permanent rift could develop between you and your team. The team could even fall apart because practice sessions deteriorate into constant misbehavior and punishment.

You **must** change activities every ten or fifteen minutes.

You may think, "Well, this guy coached Jr. Pee Wees. They may have attention spans that short, but my **older** players should get longer drills."

Not true.

All ages get bored with the same activity. Here's what Vince Lombardi had to say about his **pro** players in his book, *Run to Daylight!*:

> *"When a ball club flattens out it is because they go mentally and psychologically, rather than physically, stale. That is why we go to such pains to keep them from becoming bored by this week-after-week routine.*
> *"Everything we do, in these meetings or on the practice field, we do only for short periods, We never stay on one phase of this game for any great length of time, because if I get bored coaching the same thing over and over they are going to get bored learning it, although there are those times when they are not getting something and I must fight that urge to keep them at it until they do."*

Here's what yet another pro book, *Play Football the NFL Way*, says,

> *It is important for a coach to vary the drills daily, constantly challenging his players without subjecting them to endless repetitions. Boredom is one of the greatest enemies of learning, especially in football. Practice time must be interesting and focused, not disorganized. For example, while defensive players should practice tackling every day, the actual tackling drill should vary with each practice. Short, crisp, well-defined drills that concentrate on only one skill keep the players' attention and help eliminate long, tedious practice sessions.*

Different size groups

It is standard in football to work the players in different size groups. You drill one-on-one, two-on-two, three-on-three, etc. One pass defense drill is called seven-on-seven. It is a scrimmage without offensive or defensive linemen. Seven-on-seven assumes there are only four linemen. In my 8-2-1, the no-linemen pass defense drill would be five-on-five.

Different speeds

When I first began coaching, I tended to have the players do everything at full speed. In my second season, I did more walk-throughs and half speed drills. Lately, I've been reading lots of football coaching books and I've been surprised to find that many, if not most, big-time football coaches are rather averse to full-speed contact practice activities.

At the youth level, I'm not sure we can dispense with the full-speed stuff as much as high school, college, and pros can. Many of our kids are still getting religion, that is, overcoming their fear of contact. On the other hand, one coach whose book I read said he believes that full-speed tackling drills are the main cause of kids quitting football prematurely.

My favorite tackling drill

Every coach has favorite drills. The tackling drill I love we call simply side tackling. A ball carrier runs in a straight line and a tackler tackles him from a 90-degree angle off to one side. Each player generally runs half speed although I sometimes have them do it faster or slower.

Somewhere along the line we began laying blocking pads on the ground where the two players land. That was a great idea.

Our team has a bunch of blocking pads which are about four feet high and one foot in diameter. Looked at from above, they are half-circle shaped. We lay four or five of them side by side on the ground—flat side down and half-circle side up. We then take another round dummy and lay it perpendicular to the others on one side.

The ball carrier runs along the round dummy. The tackler must hit him on the thigh pads or lower, wrap tight, and lift the ball carrier over the round dummy and deposit him on the bed of half-circle pads. The pads are very soft so the boys enjoy flopping on them. It's like the jumping on the bed or upholstered furniture that parents won't let kids do at home. The pads also encourage exuberant tackles without fear of injury from hitting the ground. Occasionally when we do this drill without the pads, you can see the kids cut way back on their enthusiasm. They also devote more energy to protecting themselves from the ground instead of concentrating on the tackle technique. Here's a diagram:

My favorite tackling drill

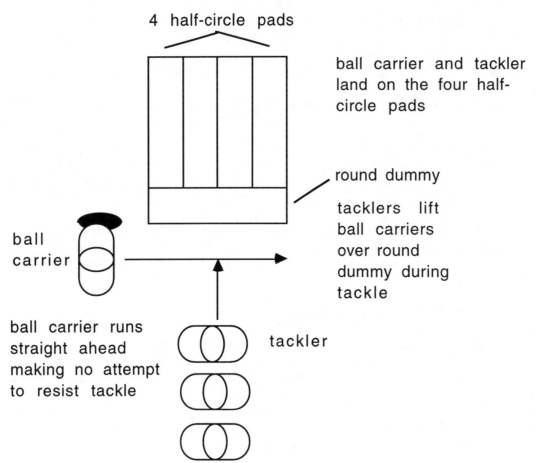

4 half-circle pads

ball carrier and tackler land on the four half-circle pads

round dummy

tacklers lift ball carriers over round dummy during tackle

ball carrier

tackler

ball carrier runs straight ahead making no attempt to resist tackle

If the tackle is done correctly, the ball carrier goes to the back of the tacklers line and the tackler becomes the next ball carrier. During each session, each tackler gets to make one correct tackle of a ball carrier running from left to right and one from right to left.

Importance of lifting

During the 1991 season, we noticed that one of our smaller rookies suddenly started to hurl ball carriers back several feet when he tackled them. Turned out he was lifting them slightly with his wrap. We liked that so we taught it in 1992 as a required part of the tackle.

We then discovered a second reason for requiring lift. Lift forces the tackler to stay on his feet and to get his feet in a proper relationship with the location of the ball carrier. Generally, the tackler should almost be stepping on the feet of the ball carrier when he makes the tackle.

Kids tend not to do that. They prefer to launch themselves through the air from several feet away, attach themselves to the tackler's body, and drag him down with their weight. That's where missed tackles come from.

We had one boy who seemed to be a great tackler. But every now and then he would inexplicably end up on the ground while the ball carrier ran away. We figured out that he was leaving his feet just like the weak tacklers. But his timing was better so it looked like he was driving through the ball carrier. When his timing was off, his feet leaving habit was suddenly revealed.

By insisting on lift, you eliminate the widespread habit of leaving the feet.

Reps

One of the fundamental observations I've made in life is that expertise often consists of knowing how much oomph to apply to a particular problem. I have often tried to fix a car or business machine but stopped short of success because I was afraid I would break it. Then I call a repairman. He does exactly what I was doing but with much more oomph. He knows from experience how much oomph is required and that it will not break the item in question.

It appears to me from observing other teams and from my own experience as a coach that our superior tackling in 1992 stemmed from the fact that we knew how much oomph to apply to the problem of instilling good tackling habits. To be more specific, we knew how many repetitions to require and how much perfection to insist upon. The short answer is lots of each.

When I visited my parents in the Haddon Township, NJ in September of 1992, I visited a local youth football practice. They were doing a tackling drill at what appeared to be the Jr. Pee Wee level. A ball carrier would run at a 45-degree or so angle toward a tackler.

Lousy tackle but 'Good job!'

The boys appeared totally untrained in tackling technique to me. They simply grabbed at the shirt or shoulders of the ball carrier, attached themselves, and dragged the ball carrier down with their weight. As you would expect, this was successful when the ball carrier was a weak player, hit or miss when he was average, and unsuccessful when he was a strong runner.

The coaches would compliment the tackler with, "Good job!" or some such if he was successful or offer a suggestion if he failed. If **we** were coaching those boys, we would do the following:

Boy makes incorrect tackle.
Coach: "You're too high, Johnny. Come here."

We would then have the ball carrier stand still and have Johnny assume a correct tackling position in contact with the ball carrier. We would examine and correct each aspect of his position:

• head up
• shoulder pads against thigh pad
• shoulders parallel to ball carrier's path (assuming side tackle)
• feet spread should-pad width apart
• butt below shoulders
• arms wrapped well around legs.

We would then have Johnny yank his arms up and in dumping the ball carrier to the pads.

Slow it down

Then we would ask them to separate a short distance and do a moving tackle in slow motion—less than half speed. We would gradually speed up the drill insisting on correct technique each time. If the boy was a slow learner, we would have him work separately with another coach so as not to monopolize the drill.

Under no circumstances would we say, "Good job," to a boy who tackled like those New Jersey boys did. We **do** look for things he did **right** and compliment him on those. For example, we might say, "You wrapped good that time, Johnny. But you're still too high." And when the boy gets it completely right, we give him five or hug him or yell, "Yeah! Yeah! That's it! You got it!" But we do not call the incorrect correct.

The basic idea is that you need to make them do it right so many times that it becomes deeply ingrained habit. You need to make them do it so many times correctly that they **forget** how to do it incorrectly.

Our offensive coach made the center and quarterback exchange snaps for ten minutes at the beginning of practice each day. That may seem excessive to others. But we rarely fumbled a snap. Our opponents, on the other hand, fumble a half dozen or so snaps a game even at the end of the season. Their coaches probably teach the same snap technique we do. But they don't teach with enough oomph.

Scrimmage exception

There is one exception to the change-every-10-to-15-minutes rule: scrimmage. You can scrimmage for 30 to 40 minutes without having misbehavior problems from boredom.

Maybe the reason is that scrimmage is varied within itself because the teams run different plays. Whatever, I've found that the players like scrimmage and will play it for extended periods without complaint or boredom-inspired misbehavior.

One exception to the no-misbehavior-in-scrimmage observation is if the scout team coach takes too long explaining plays to the scout offense, the defensive players will get bored waiting and will start to misbehave as they wait. That misbehavior must be avoided because it downgrades what happens when the scout team finally breaks its huddle.

In other words, if you don't keep that scout team moving quickly, you will have a lousy practice. I recommend that the scout team coach draw the upcoming opponent's plays on 8 1/2 x 11 sheets of paper or card stock. Each player's position and blocking assignment should be shown. The play should be called by showing the card to all eleven scout team players.

Don't leave the linemen out of the scout-team huddle. Our scout team coach did that and they started misbehaving. Plus it suggests that linemen are not part of the play. They sure as heck are. And scout team is where bench warmers show their stuff and get promoted. But if they are left out of the huddle, they abandon hope, and cease making the effort to get promoted to first string. Better yet. Don't have a huddle. Show all the play at the LOS.

Scrimmage tackling technique

Almost invariably, players revert to poor tackling technique in scrimmage in spite of your drilling them on correct technique. I adopted a policy of sending defenders who used poor tackling technique to remedial tackling. That is, I would pull them out of the scrimmage immediately, take them to the side, and make them tackle a dummy five times correctly before I would let them rejoin the scrimmage. In virtually all cases, they were tackling high or leaving their feet.

The veterans hated this. Before long, we could see that the veterans were starting to tackle high then would catch themselves and do it right. In one instance, a veteran who had just gotten out of remedial tackling started to tackle high then caught himself and let the ball carrier escape rather than get sent to remedial tackling again. That upset the head coach who wanted to abandon the remedial tackling. But I persuaded him to let me continue and we saw no more instances of a boy deliberately letting a ball carrier escape rather than tackle high.

Tackling against the best players

One of the main reasons rookie coaches are more lenient regarding tackling technique is that the techniques their boys use generally work OK. It doesn't look pretty. But the job gets done.

The problem is the job only gets done against mediocre teams and mediocre ball carriers. When you come up against a good team or a good ball carrier, you'll find your tacklers suddenly look horribly ineffective. And if you make the playoffs, you will certainly come up against runners of that caliber. You must insist on correct tackling technique even though the boys can get by in most games with lousy technique. You must keep your eye on the post-season level of play all season long. If you fail to prepare for post-season play until post-season, it will be too late.

In our league, the standards in recent years have been set by Oakland, Vacaville, and the two Fairfield teams. I'd like to think we became one of the standard setters, too. But you'll have to check with less biased others to find out.

At our practices, you often hear comments like, "Hey, that tackle might work against those guys we beat 28-0 last week. But if you tackle like that against Oakland, the ball carrier's going to go 60 yards. Hit him low and wrap him tight!"

We know that our post-season road to the California Youth Football championship leads through Vacaville (whom we played for the Valley Conference Championship three years running) and the Delta Conference champion (usually Oakland or a Fairfield team). When our kids start getting complacent or sloppy, we remind them that the Dynamites or Falcons or whoever are still out there waiting for us. That usually sobers up the veterans and the rookies sober up when they see the expressions on the veterans' faces.

Find new activities

Not only must you change activities every 10 to 15 minutes, you must change drills and other activities day by day. Drills get stale over the weeks even if they are only run for ten minutes each time they are run. Try to find new ways to teach and evaluate the same technique.

Number of coaches

The number of coaches you have determines what you must do in practice to a large extent. I once was the only coach at a practice with about 25 boys. That was Tuesday which was notorious for bad practices that year. The previous Tuesday had been a disaster.

At the beginning of the practice, I called the boys together and told them that if we had another practice like the previous Tuesday, I was leaving. Our board members could watch over them until their parents came.

After calisthenics, which can be done with one coach because they are done in military formation and in unison, we scrimmaged. We scrimmaged the entire practice. We may have switched to kickoff and punt scrimmages at some point.

We had a very good practice.

For starters, I recommend that you have the full complement of coaches. The more the better.

Drills and other activities need to change every 10 to 15 minutes. But there's another thing about drills: no boy should wait more than about 30 seconds for his turn at the drill. The fewer coaches you have, the fewer stations you have during drills. The fewer stations you have, the longer the line at each station. The longer the line, the longer the wait. And when the wait exceeds 30 seconds, the boys in line will start to misbehave.

Bench warmers in practice

Most coaches I've observed like to put the bench warmers aside and just work with the first string. You can**not** do that.

For one thing, practice scrimmages are about all the bench warmers have to look forward to. They can't look forward much to Saturday games because they don't play much in them. To deprive them of their chance to play football in scrimmage, too, is to recruit for your local soccer league.

Also, bench warmers are entitled to a season-long chance to make the first string. They do that by playing their hearts out in practice scrimmages. You have a duty to both the team and to the bench warmers to pay attention to their efforts. If a kid earns first-string status by his play on the scout team, promote him and demote the first-stringer who failed to maintain his position on the depth chart.

That's very healthy for the team. It sends a message to the first stringers that they cannot be complacent. And it sends a message to the bench warmers that they always have a chance to make the first team if they hustle. If you run your team that way, you will get hustle and avoid complacency.

To a large extent, your bench warmers are your team's future. To ignore them is to ignore your future.

I rotated the bench warmers into practice pretty much the same way I rotated them into games. Only there would be no ten-play limit.

Strong and weak sides

Because we only have about 20 to 25 boys on our team each year, we have to use everyone for scrimmages. I used to put the first-string defense against the other players. Bad idea. The first-string defense would kill such a scout offense. So I started putting first-string defense on only one side of the formation. That would free up a bunch of first-string offense players who I would put facing the first string defenders. And it would give me first-string running backs who could be used on the scout team.

I told the first-string defense to line up in the defensive positions and the rest of the players to line up as the upcoming opponent's offense. Then I would designate one half, left or right, of the first string defense to come over and play offense. And I would send half the second-string guys to the defense. Halfway through the practice, I would select the other half of the first-string defense to play scout offense. And I would ask the second-string guys who did not play defense the first half to go over to the defense.

On the defense right side, the first-string right guard, right tackle, right linebacker, right cornerback, and right end will be in those positions. The first-string middle linebacker may be in his position as well. On the scout offense side, I would have first-string **left** guard, **left** tackle, etc. If not the precise first-string offensive left guard at least I'd have a first-string-caliber offensive lineman and first-string running backs.

The left side of the defense and right side of the scout offense would be second-string players. The result is you have first-string against first-string on the right and second-string against second-string on the left side of the defense. And you have first-string running backs for everyone to tackle.

The coach running the scout team is instructed to run almost all plays to the side where the best players are.

Scout-team center and quarterback

You have to have a good center for the scout team. If not, you'll have a zillion fumbled snaps and you'll accomplish nothing in your defensive scrimmage practice. If the first-string offensive center is not in a strong-side defensive position, use him. If he is in a strong side position, use the second-string offensive center if he's good. Otherwise, you need to have a coach snap the ball to the scout-team quarterback.

We also usually had a coach act as the scout team quarterback because the head coach didn't like the first-string quarterback getting tackled and it takes too long to teach the kid quarterbacks the opponent's offense.

We try to use a kid quarterback when tackling the quarterback is what we expect to do on the play in question like a keeper or pass.

Holding blocking pads

Once or twice, our offensive coach tried having defensive players hold blocking dummies or pads for the offensive blockers to hit.

Forget it.

The defensive players will have continuous pillow fights among themselves with the pads. You can yell at them all night long and you will not stop the pillow fights.

Coaches can hold pads. Or you can use free-standing dummies. And you might be able to have **one** player hold a pad in a closely supervised drill where the pad holder rotates. But if you have more than one player hold pads at the same time in close proximity to each other, you will have pillow fights. And if you have players hold pads for more than one iteration of a drill, you will have pillow fights.

After I saw the unstoppable pillow fights, I argued strenuously against ever using players to do that again.

At the high school level, we **do** have players hold pads. They still get into pillow fights, but less often.

Simulating speed

We did not have speed in 1990 or 1991. In fact, we were slower than every other team in the league except Napa. But we had to **play** against speed.

I believe one of the reasons we lost to Oakland was that our players simply were not **used** to the speed of the Oakland running backs. We would tackle in the usual way—but instead of helmet in front and shoulder into the thighs we would get helmet in back and an ineffective, one-arm tackle.

To put it in skeet-shooting terms, our boys were not leading the target enough because they were used to shooting at slower-moving targets.

We tried a couple things to simulate speed. And I have a couple more ideas which I have not yet tried.

Pre-hand off

One thing we did was give the ball to the scout-team running back **before** the snap. We would use **two** balls: one for the center to snap and one for the running back to carry. Hand offs and pitches slow down the play. By eliminating the hand off, we speeded the play up to the point where our relatively slow scout-team running backs were hitting the hole at about the same elapsed time from the snap as the faster running backs of the upcoming opponent would.

If you are bothered by the defense knowing who has the ball from the start, give **every** back a ball and have all but the designated runner drop to one knee when the snap occurs. Or call out the name of the one you want tackled after the snap

Start early

Another thing you can do is have him start running **before** the snap. This would often be illegal in games because the man before the snap is not allowed to go toward the line of scrimmage. To avoid having your defense know who is getting the ball, you could have **all** the backs, both those faking and the ball carrier to be, start running early.

Coach as running backs

If any of your coaches are as fast as your opponents, you could have them pretend to be opposing ball carriers. Be careful with this though. Only run **wide**, never **at** a boy. Or to simulate a run up the middle, remove your defensive line and just let your defensive backs react to the high-speed coach blowing through the line. And, of course, have them play **touch** rather than tackle. This should be good for practicing wide pursuit against a speedy upcoming opponent.

Older players

You may be able to borrow a player who is as fast as an opponent from a higher level team.

You could also practice against higher level teams in your association. We never did this in 1991, but we always did it before. I understand most associations do this. That is, they allow their Jr. Pee Wees to scrimmage their Pee Wees and so forth.

It seems to me that this may violate the league rules. Obviously, a player can get hurt in a practice as badly as in a game. We had our worst injury, a broken forearm, in practice. We don't let Jr. Pee Wees play **games** against Pee Wees because of the danger of injury. Yet I've often seen the exact same thing allowed in practice. Strikes me as law suit city if there is an injury to a player who was too light to play at the level of the boy who hit him.

In our recruiting, we often assure parents that their son will only be playing against boys his own weight. To put a 60 pounder against a 100 pounder in scrimmage breaks that promise.

One solution may be to limit the participation by the smaller team to those players who are heavy enough and old enough to play on the heavier team. For example, our Jr. Pee Wee team ranged in weight from 50 to 85 pounds. Pee Wees ranged from 65 pounds to 100 pounds. We had many boys who weighed more than 65 pounds and who were old enough to play on the heavier team if, for example, our Jr. Pee Wee team had folded.

Older players may be available to help out if and when their team is eliminated from the playoffs while yours is still playing. Obviously, they cannot play in the actual games. But some may be willing to suit up in practice to help your team. I did not ask for such volunteers this year. But I'll try it in the future if the situation arises.

Suggested practice schedule

Here's a suggested way to organize your practices.

Daily:
6:00 PM	Stretching and warm-up exercises
6:10	Specialty skills
6:20	Special teams
6:50	Emphasis time
7:00	Offensive team practice
7:30	Defensive team practice
8:00	End of practice

You should teach your players a standard way to line up. In the military, each man is assigned to a squad of about 10 men which is one line in a platoon formation. A platoon would typically have four squads. A platoon formation would be a four-by-ten formation. In the military, all formations begin with a report. The platoon sergeant orders "Report!" and the squad leaders report in order, "First squad present or accounted for, "second squad present or accounted for," and so on. Or "Smith absent," if that's the case. I wouldn't allow the "accounted for" line in football. I just want to know who's there.

You may want to use the military format. You need leadership by the players. Squad leader is a role which you could use to develop leadership and to reward it. You could put your most coach-like players in those positions and promote or demote them as their performance and the performance of other players warrants.

Stretching and warm up

I'm rather suspicious of traditional football calisthenics.

For one thing, we only get to exercise the players three days a week after the initial preseason weeks. And in our association the days are Tuesday, Wednesday, and Thursday. As anyone who knows anything about conditioning knows, weightlifting-type activities are supposed to be done every **other** day and at least **three** days per week. So it is impossible to have any kind of weight training with a Tuesday, Wednesday, Thursday schedule.

Weight lifting is not recommended for subteens anyway—although our team medical person says studies have recently found that you **can** do moderate weight training safely and effectively among preteens.

Indirect benefits

I have also never bought the theory that doing X will make you better at Y. For example, a lot of coaches seem to believe that doing leg raises to the point of excruciating pain will make you a better football player. I think it will do nothing more than make you a better leg raiser.

If you want to condition players to play football, you should have them **play** football. To increase the conditioning value of the play, you could insert a special rule like a 10-second clock. That is, your offense has 10 seconds, not 25, in which to snap the ball. If they fail to do so, they do pushups or turn over the ball to the opponent or some such.

Unfortunately, you can only emphasize conditioning at the expense of some other aspect like precision. So be careful you don't end up with a team that is both the best-conditioned and the sloppiest in the league.

High schools today generally do not do calisthenics at all. Rather they just stretch.

Tradition

It appears to me that much of the calisthenics which football coaches make players do are based on **tradition** rather than science. Painful calisthenics are more a masochistic rite of passage into the fraternity of football players than preparation for Saturday's game or the season. "This is what I did when I played football," says the coach. "So now you're going to have to do it, too." It's like hazing college freshmen or new fraternity brothers.

In terms of field strategy and tactics, football coaches have a well-deserved reputation for innovation. Baseball, in contrast, is hidebound. But when it comes to calisthenics, much of the football world is still in the leather-helmet era.

That's especially true of youth football where the least professional coaches are. I recommend that you consult with a '90s sports medicine specialist about what stretching and warm-up exercises your players should do and design your calisthenics accordingly. There is even a question about whether stretching and warm up do any good at all—especially among preteens.

The National Youth Sports Coaches Association football video has a segment on what exercises to use. I'm sure they checked it out with proper pediatric sports medicine authorities.

Are they beneficial?

A study which said neither stretching nor warm-ups have any value was written up on the front page of the *San Francisco Chronicle* a couple years ago. And I read in *Sports Illustrated* 12/23/91 "Sub-Four at 40?" about a New Zealander who hopes to be the first to break the four minute mile over the age of 40. He **never** stretches or warms up.

I have always kept in reasonable shape by jogging or riding an exercise bicycle. But when I began to play baseball at age 42 for the first time in 28 years, I was pulling muscles right and left.

I was still playing in a semipro baseball league year round at age 48 and I rarely pulled a muscle. The reason is I learned to do mild **strengthening** exercises for the muscles most stressed by baseball movements. I **do** stretch both before and after my games (two seven-inning games every Sunday but holiday weekends). I only did it because there's no harm to it and it **might** help.

But my suspicion is that, other than engaging in violent movement immediately after resting motionlessly, there is no danger to exercise without stretching and warm-up. Of course a long ride to the practice field may be enough motionless resting to cool off some players' muscles to the point where they need warm up. Same is true of a player who arrives early and lies down to wait for practice to begin. So you might stretch and warm up to make sure no one is coming off motionless resting. But frequently when you arrive, you will find your youth players running around like maniacs playing with each other. If that's the case, any stretching or warming up you do are clearly closing the barn door after the horse is gone.

I especially suspect that's true of **children**. I am a former child myself. I never stretched or warmed up before playing football or baseball as a kid. I don't remember anyone else ever stretching or warming up. We just played. And I don't remember ever pulling a muscle or seeing a playmate pull a muscle.

I **do** remember wondering why the grown ups made us do calisthenics before football practice when I was a kid. We asked and they always told us it was to prevent muscle pulls. But I figured muscle pulls were a **grown-up** problem and that they were really making us do calisthenics to prevent **their** muscle pulls—sort of like a dieting parent who makes his kids eat the same cottage cheese and unbuttered toast that he's supposed to eat.

Your youth football players can and will pull a muscle if they ask it to do something it is not **strong** enough to do. But I suspect that all of a boy's muscles are warmed up enough and stretched enough to engage in exercise within twenty minutes of his getting up out of bed in the morning. The Kaiser Hospital physical therapist I consult about my sports injuries agrees that children probably need no warm up if they are not coming from a prolonged period of being in a total resting position.

So my exercise suggestion is to simply have the boys play football, gradually building up the intensity of the workouts so that their muscles get a chance to develop the strength needed to perform the movements football requires. Adding more equipment each day of the no-contact week is an example of the gradual buildup which is appropriate.

Chalk talks

I often give chalk talks. We have a white board and felt-tipped marker pens to use on it. I diagram the upcoming opponent's offensive formations and plays and show how we should line up and defend against them. Frequently, these chalk talks take the entire 25-minute defensive time. We often combine the chalk talks with a demonstration in which coaches play the roles of the upcoming opponent's backfield or ends while the players watch from one-knee.

Handouts

I give handouts every week. Usually defensive stats and the diagrams of the upcoming opponent's plays along with comments about how we will line up against each formation and defend against its plays. We give these out at the end of practice and mark the players' name on each one so we can keep track of who did not get one because he was missing that day.

The result

John Madden once asked Vince Lombardi what the difference was between a good coach and a bad one.

Knowing what the end result looks like. The best coaches know what the end result looks like, whether it's an offensive play, a defensive coverage, or just some area of the organization....the bad coaches don't know what the hell they want. The good coaches do.

16

Time outs

You have three time outs per half. So does the other team. When should you call them and what should you do with the ones that you call and the ones that the other team calls?

When to call them

Youth teams ought to have a two-minute offense. But my impression is that they're all oblivious to the clock. That's probably because they have limited passing ability and because their coaches have not given that much thought to two-minute offenses. No thought means no practice and no practice means no two-minute offense.

So time outs may be used less dramatically and less sparingly in youth football.

I recommend that you use them to deal with emergencies like:

- offensive formation which your players don't know how to line up against
- too many defensive players on the field and not enough time to send someone off
- fewer than eleven defensive players on the field
- basketball-style time out to stop momentum and regroup
- to stop the clock when you are behind at the end of a half
- to make a defensive adjustment.

Unknown formation

We never saw an unknown formation that we couldn't easily deal with in 1991. That was because we practiced against everything in the preseason. And because our position job descriptions encompassed almost everything. The halfback always had the widest receiver other than the tight end. It didn't matter if he was a flanker or a split end or one of three split-out guys or whatever. Our boys really did not react in a special way to unusual formations. They simply positioned themselves as their job description said. If some team had come out in a formation we never dreamed of, I suspect our guys would have just picked out their spot and gotten into position as if they had played against it all season.

However, if there had been a formation that our system did not contemplate—like four eligible receivers out wide to one side—and our boys did not line up against it the way I'd like, I'd like to think that I or the field captain would have the presence of mind to call time.

In 1992, Napa scored a point after touchdown against us with a center snapping sideways to a back behind a line that was separated from the center. That is, they had a one-man line where the ball was and a six-man line about five yards away. Our kids incorrectly lined up on the ball ignoring the opposing alignment. Napa scored easily because they had about seven guys against two of ours.

Later in the game, they tried it again. I had told the offensive captain to call time out if he saw that or anything like it. He did. During the time out, I explained that the halfbacks still had the widest receivers on each end of the formation; the linebackers, the second widest; and so forth. I told the middle linebacker or safety to line up half way from each end of the formation. And I told the down linemen to shift over as if the ball were still being centered by the center man in the formation even though it was now the right end who was snapping the ball.

I deliberately explained all this in a calm, no-big-deal tone of voice. After the time out, Napa again came out in that formation, we shifted accordingly, and Napa snapped the ball to the quarterback who was at shotgun depth behind the snapper. We sacked him for a four-yard loss.

Wait until the offense is almost ready to snap the ball so you can get a good look at the formation.

Tell your field captain and back-up field captain that the offense is coming out in a weird formation and that you want them to get a good look at it before they call time. On the other hand, they must call time soon enough to stop the play. Also, once or twice, have a practice referee miss the request for time out to make sure your players understand that they should not just stand there yelling, "I called time out!" if the play starts in spite of their request.

When you talk to the players during the time out, make sure everybody knows where to line up and what to do after the snap for that formation. If you missed it, have the field captain tell you what it was.

Illegal participation

Illegal participation means twelve or more players on the field from one team **during a play**. It is a 15-yard penalty!

If you are about to have illegal participation, your field captain should call time out. To ascertain whether you have 12 players on the field, he should count them before each play.

Too few players

Too few players on the field can be worse. My observation is that the offense's gains of more than two yards are due to a defensive player being **out of position** far more often than a defensive player getting beat while **in** position. Being on the bench when you are supposed to be in the game definitely falls under the category of being out of position.

If your field captain sees too few players, he should call time out if there is not enough time before the snap to fix it without a time out.

Regroup

Our head coach and offensive coaches decided to have us kick off in our first Oakland game even if we won the toss. They knew in would be a tough game and figured our defense would be more likely to demoralize Oakland in the opening minutes than our offense.

To increase the chances of demoralizing Oakland, I called for a four-man blitz for the first time all season on the first play of the game.

Unfortunately, one guy forgot to blitz. And the three who did were not in the same gap as the ball carrier—who ran off tackle for a 60-yard touchdown.

One of our other coaches suggested it would be a good idea to call time and go out and calm the troops down next time we went on defense. Remember, most of our defensive players were playing both ways so they never were available on the sideline to talk to.

So, after clearing it with the head coach, I did just that. Next time we went on defense, I called time before the first play. During the time out, I said something like the following:

> *"Hey guys, about that touchdown on the first play, don't worry about it. It's* **my** *fault. I called for a four-man blitz. A blitz is a gamble.* **I** *gambled.* **I** *lost. Sorry about that. You guys are fine. They tried to run the exact same play for the extra point and you stopped them cold. You guys are just fine. We won't do any more four-man blitzing so we should have no great problem. Just do what you've been doing all season and you'll be fine. What're we gonna do? [players] Attack! What're we gonna get? [players] A sack! Go get 'em!"*

The mighty Oakland team did not score again until the fourth quarter.

When we played Berkeley, we came out on offense with our brand new no-huddle offense. And it worked like a charm. We were chewing up the field in 10-yard chunks. When we got to about the 15-yard line of Berkeley, the Berkeley defensive coach called time to regroup. That was a smart move. His kids were bewildered and lost. He had to call time the way a basketball or volleyball coach does to try to stop the other team's momentum.

Unfortunately for Berkeley, it didn't work. When the time out was over, our offense picked up where they left off and promptly scored. Later, when Berkeley got **more** time to talk and regroup, they were able to stop our offense. We scored 12 points in the first half and that was all the scoring in the game.

If you find the opposing offense has your guys on the run, you'd better call time to regroup. That's especially likely if the opposing offense is using a no-huddle offense. It may even be appropriate if they don't use a no-huddle offense every play but try to use it for just one play.

To make an adjustment

The chapter on tracking plays and making adjustments during the game discusses when you should make personnel or job description adjustments during the game. Time outs are one of the times you make those adjustments.

At what part of the 25-second clock?

OK. You've decided to call time. Now **when** do you call it?

If you're **ahead or tied** against an opponent you think you can beat in overtime, you want to spend as much clock time as possible. That means—if the clock is running—call time **just before the opposing quarterback is about to call signals**. Your field captain might want to tell the referee, "Mr. Referee, sir. I do not want to call it yet, but just before the quarterback is ready to call signals, I'm going to ask you for a time out."

Then your field captain makes sure he has the official's attention and quickly calls time at the appropriate moment. The field captain, however, must be ready to play—that is, in proper position and mentally ready—if the official does **not** call time as he requests.

If you are **behind**—and the amount of time left is short—say, less than three minutes—you will want to call your time outs just **as soon as the play is blown dead**. That way you preserve as much of the game clock as possible for your offense to score the come-from-behind points.

Practice calling time out just before the snap and just after the play is blown dead. In fact, if you can, practice defensive clock management by setting your stadium scoreboard clock at two or three minutes and operate it according to the rules during scrimmage or practice games.

When the clock is not running

Of course, the clock is not always running. You generally do **not** call time out when the clock is not running.

When is the game clock not running?

- during a time out called by the other team
- after an incompleted pass
- after the ball goes out of bounds
- before a kickoff until the kicked ball is touched by a member of the receiving team
- during an injury or other official's time out
- while the chains are being moved
- end of quarter
- try for point after touchdown
- after a fair catch
- after delay-of-game penalty
- a penalty flag is thrown until the penalty is marched off and the chains moved
- after a touchback or safety
- following change of possession
- during a head coach/referee conference regarding the interpretation of a rule.

Causing the other team to draw a delay penalty

You may be able to cause the offense to draw a delay-of-game penalty by shifting during the offense's signal calling to a defense that is likely to inspire an audible—like leaving a wide receiver seemingly uncovered. If the other quarterback has been trained to call an audible, he may stop to see where you end up then take time to call an audible before he resumes his snap count. All that may make him late for his appointment with the 25-second clock. That's a five-yard penalty.

This may be getting too cute for youth football. See if your personnel can handle it in practice before you try it in games.

What to do during time out

OK. Somebody called a time out. Now you're out there. What do you do? Try to look football coachlike?

You need an agenda.

First, there's the **waterboy**. He needs to be filled up and ready to hustle his butt out there as soon as the time out is called by either team. The players need all the water you can get into them. Whenever I saw a time out called, I instinctively yelled, "Water!" in the direction of the bench.

Here is my generic **time-out agenda**. I use this when I did not call the time out for a specific purpose like making an adjustment or regrouping:

- Anybody hurt?
- Anybody tired?
- Are they doing anything we did not expect?
- Are they doing anything we should adjust for?
- Anybody see any keys you should tell your teammates about?
- What technique is their line blocking?
- Review recent plays which warrant either constructive criticism or compliments.

• Show them the opponent's Point-of-Attack Success Chart
• Tell the players about unexpected things which the coaches have noticed.
• Make adjustment in personnel or job description on rare occasion when appropriate.
• Remind them of this opponent's keys.
• Point out game situation:
  time until half or game end
  field position
  down
  yards to go for first down or touchdown
  yards to go for field goal range if appropriate
  likely opponent response to that game situation
  need to manage the clock, if time is short
• Remind to go on the movement of the ball.
• Remind them of the psyche-up theme of the game.
• Get off the field when the time out is over.

I recommend that you put this format or your modified version of it on a piece of paper and put it in a clear plastic sheet cover. You should put your pre-game and half-time formats in there, too. Carry it with you during the game. Then when a time out is called by your team or the opposing offense, you can refer to it as soon as you get with the players.

Where to hold time out

There appear to be **two choices** in where to hold time outs in youth football: you can go out **on the field** or you can have the players come to the **sideline**.

I prefer going out on the field. As do all the coaches in our league except Oakland. The advantage is the offense can't run a quick play without waiting for the defense to return. In 1990, Oakland's defense was frequently still in their defensive huddle or at a time out when our offense was on the line of scrimmage. Unfortunately, our offense patiently and politely waited until the Oakland players were ready before snapping the ball.

I also like to go out on the field to so the players can **rest**. Better I should do the extra running than them.

The only advantage I see to the sideline venue is that more than one coach can talk to the players at once. If you have a pep talk purpose for calling the time out, there is no need for more than one coach to talk to the players. On the other hand, if you have a strong position-coach system, it may be good for your various position coaches to get a chance to give specific reminders, constructive criticism, and compliments to their assigned players.

I have no great preference for either venue. I may try the sideline approach if only because Oakland did it and they are often champions of our league.

17

Half time

The non-football coaching public knows half-time as a time when coaches make fiery Knute Rockne speeches. You can do that if you have the ability and the situation calls for it. The more common use of half time is to make adjustments. Half time is long enough that even if you are going to make a fire-'em-up speech, you can and probably should wait until the last minute or two before second half kickoff.

My half-time format was similar to my time-out format. However, our head coach had no organized format for half time so I just tried to do my thing as best I could.

Team format for half time

I believe the team should have a half-time format or schedule. Assuming half time is ten minutes long, I suggest the following:

0:00	Offensive coach's time
3:00	Defensive coach's time
6:00	Special teams coach's time
9:00	Psyche-up time
10:00	Second-half kick off

If your head coach goes for that format, I suggest you cover the following during your defensive four minutes:

• Anybody hurt?
• Anybody tired?
• Are they doing anything we did not expect?
• Are they doing anything we should adjust for?

• Anybody see any tipoffs you should tell your teammates about?
• Review first-half plays which warrant either constructive criticism or compliments.
• Show opponent's Point-of-Attack Success Chart.
• Tell the players about unexpected things which the coaches have noticed.
• Make adjustment in personnel or job description when appropriate.
• Remind them of this opponent's keys.
• Point out game situation:
    score
    likely opponent offensive adjustments in second half
• Remind them of the psyche-up theme of the game.

Where to hold half time

Half time is traditionally a locker-room activity. But the locker rooms in our league were too far away for us to use them. We mostly went to a private, comfortable, outdoor area away from, but within sight of, the field.

It needs to be **private** because opposing parents and/or players from different level teams are not above **spying**.

One team in our league, Vacaville, held their half-time meeting right on the sideline in the bench area and put up a white board on an easel to diagram adjustments. That strikes me as a very bad idea.

For one thing, the easel faced the Vacaville stands. There could be one or more opponent spies there.

Another problem is the opposing parents who may be on Vacaville's sideline as officials, that is: the mandatory-play monitor, chain gang, and down marker man. If you stay on the sideline, you need to ask them to leave. I don't know why they should. One or more may refuse. Especially if you are the only team in the league that holds your half-time meetings in the bench area.

Another reason to leave the bench area is **comfort**. The bench area is always exposed to the weather. In our league, that usually meant the hot sun. For one game, it meant rain.

In most stadiums, there are shady areas to which the teams can go at half time. On a hot day, you ought to go there.

In some cases, you may be able to get in out of rain or other cold weather. If you can, you should.

The only reason I know to **stay** in the bench area is to avoid wasting time moving to and from the half-time area. But we generally only moved about 60 yards and the walk was a welcome break from the intensity of both the game and the half-time discussions.

18

Tackling technique

My biggest regret of the 1991 season is that I did not **insist** on good tackling technique. I intended to. I resolved that I would. But I didn't.

Not that we didn't work hard on it. We did. And I tried lots of things to get the boys to use proper tackling technique. But I did not do enough.

Saint Bobby and the Barbarians is a book by Ben Brown about Bobby Bowden, the head coach of the Florida State Seminoles. At the beginning of Part III there's a Bowden quote, "You get what you demand."

I didn't demand good tackling technique in 1991. I requested it. I urged it. I pleaded for it. But I didn't demand it.

In 1992, I was better. Early that season I sent players who tackled poorly to remedial tackling if they fouled up. But I got heavy resistance about that from the veterans and one coach.

Still, we had tackling practice almost every night. My demands during tackling practice were strict. And it showed in games. Coaches who had been there the previous season said our tackling technique was clearly better in 1992 than it was in 1991. I told the players that. In the week before the 1992 playoff game against the Fairfield Falcons, I said, "You guys may be the best tackling team in the league. That's great. But it's not good enough. This week we have to stop Fairfield's great running back, #30. He is the best running back I've seen in four years in this league. Your technique is not yet good enough to stop him."

I was right. Number 30 broke loose three times against us in the 1992 Western League playoff game. We lost 19-7. In each case, Bears had opportunities to tackle him and failed. Our tackling had looked pretty darned good throughout the 1992 season. We were 9 and 1 going into the Fairfield game. But an excellent runner reveals tackling weaknesses that remain hidden in games against lesser runners.

On one run, Fairfield's #30 left a string of Bears sprawled on the ground behind him. They had been leaving their feet—all season. That flaw was invisible with other teams because our kids timed it right and hit with enough force to bring the ball carrier down. But #30's speed, balance, and strength were such that tacklers who did not keep their feet on the ground lacked the force to stop him.

How to tackle

First, you have to make sure every player knows **how** to tackle. By knowing how, I mean he has to be able to make a correct tackle on request in a tackling drill. The speed at which your players will arrive at that stage will follow a bell-curve pattern. That is, a few players will be able to do the first week you are in pads, most will be able to do it during the first month of the season, and the few who still cannot do it at that point will be able to do it by the sixth or seventh game.

Teaching good tackling technique is fairly straightforward.

1. Explain and demonstrate step-by-step what a good straight-ahead tackle, side tackle, and pass-rush tackle look like.
2. Have each player assume a correct straight-ahead, side, and pass-rush tackling position on an opponent.
3. Have the tackler lift the ball carrier off the ground, carry him two yards, and dump him. The ball carrier is to give only token resistance.
4. Have the two players do it over in slow motion this time starting with them a yard apart.
5. Gradually spread them out farther and increase the speed until you are at half speed. Texas Tech coach Mike Bobo says you should **never** have youth players tackle full speed in drills. Rather they should only tackle full speed in scrimmages and games. I evolved into that approach before I read his book because I found that the boys learned better when we tackled at half speed. At full speed, the ones who could not do it seemed to make no progress. But at half speed, everyone made progress. I don't know that I agree with **never** having the players do a full speed tackling drill. Drills are still the best way to isolate one thing like tackling technique. And there is a distinct difference between half-speed and full-speed tackling. So I suspect you need to do **some** full-speed drills as the final stage before scrimmage or games. Even in *Play Football the NFL Way*, author Tom Bass says, "Most drills should begin at a relatively slow pace. This is especially true where contact is involved. The coach must make sure that all players are using correct technique and have overcome their natural fear of contact before increasing the speed of a drill. If players are afraid of being injured, they will learn very little."
6. Whenever a player does it incorrectly, drop him back to a closer distance and slower speed. Keep decreasing the distance and speed until he gets it right. Then increase the distance apart and speed gradually making sure he does it right every time. Do **not** allow a player to repeatedly make incorrect tackles. Always drop him back in distance and speed to the level at which he can make a correct tackle.

Motivating them to use correct technique

The problem is not **teaching** the players to tackle correctly. I did that with each and every one of my players—even players who were extremely weak at first. You don't have to be a rocket scientist to learn to put your helmet in front, hit in the legs, and so forth.

The problem is **persuading** players who **know** the correct way to tackle to **tackle** the correct way in game situations. In my experience, most simply **refuse** to do it the right way, even when they **know** the right way.

If you promised any of my players $100 for a correct tackle toward the end of our 1991 season, they'd all get their $100 the first try. But if you watched our last game, you'd have often wondered, "Didn't the Bears coaches ever teach these boys how to tackle?"

Why the difference? No $100—or other adequate motivating factor.

Common player preferences

Most players do not want to tackle below the crotch. They prefer tackling **above the waist.** Ours knew they were **supposed** to tackle below the crotch. They always did it that way in drills toward the end of the 1991 season. But as soon as they got in a scrimmage or game, most went for the chest or shoulders or arms of the ball carrier.

The players also do not like wrapping their arms around the ball carrier. They prefer to **grab his shirt or arm** with their hands. Some like to swing the ball carrier around in circles after they get hold of him—letting loose after they've reached a speed at which they believe he will fall down.

Some fancy themselves Ronnie Lott-style hard hitters and run **full speed** at the ball carrier regardless of the fact that this often causes them to miss or bounce off. To them, tackling is all hitting and if they run at the ball carrier full speed, they have done all they could. Their attitude is that it's not their fault the ball carrier escaped for a touchdown.

Common mistakes

The following are **mistakes** the players often make. I call them mistakes rather than preferences because I believe the players did not **want** to do these things. They are simply bad habits left over from their pre-football days. These mistakes are relatively easily corrected by repetitive drills and verbal corrections.

- head behind ball carrier in side tackle
- head on wrong side in straight-ahead tackle
- leaving feet before the ball carrier is lifted off his feet
- no wrap, just shoulder hit
- head down
- no shoulder hit, all arms or hands
- hit with side instead of top of shoulder (rank-beginner mistake)
- out of control (too fast—sometimes mistake; sometimes deliberate).

Our lost championship

We won the division and conference championships in 1991 and 1992. But we lost the Western League championship both years. Had we won the Western League Championship, there is a very good chance we would have won the whole California Youth Football Championship. Oakland beat us 25-0 for the Western League in 1991. (19-0 actually. We sort of gave them the last touchdown by letting our players blitz just for fun at the end. The last touchdown came on an end sweep when our end blitzed inside the wingback instead of going to his normal sweep-stopping spot.)

Oakland went on to win the CYF Championship in a rout. The Falcons did the same in 1992. We would have been favored against all Eastern League opponents both years according to how each of us did against common opponents or opponents of common opponents.

How did we lose the two championships? If you look at the video of the Oakland Western League Championship game, two things jump out at you: Oakland's superior **speed** and their superior tackling **technique.** And actually tackling is the whole problem because the antidote to their superior speed is to tackle them before they get going. We failed to do that.

Oakland tackling technique

How did Oakland tackle in the Western League Championship game? The same as we did—in our practice drills. How did **we** tackle in that game? We too often tackled **high.** We too often grabbed shirts and arms. We too often came in too fast and missed. Our helmets were too often behind on side tackles. Mainly, we tackled high—above the waist.

Oakland outcoached us—**not** in terms of **teaching** technique better. Our kids knew the same techniques. Rather Oakland outcoached us in terms of **motivating** their players to **use** the correct technique.

If I had the pre-Oakland **week** over again, I doubt I could win the ball game. Tackling high was too ingrained a habit. But if I had the **whole season** to do over, I'd have a shot at beating them. What I would do differently is **insist** on correct tackling technique throughout the preseason and regular season. (In 1992, the Fairfield Falcons eliminated Oakland from the playoffs before Fairfield beat us in the semi-final game. We did not play Oakland in 1992 but we **did** beat Vallejo 13-6 and Vallejo beat Oakland 21-7.)

'Unless there's no other way'

At the beginning of the 1991 season, I told the players that you tackle low unless high is the only way you can get him.

Big mistake. In fact, speaking those words was probably the biggest mistake I made as a coach.

Why? Because most of the players took it to mean they could tackle high **all the time**. Whenever you would try to criticize them for tackling high, they'd answer,

> *"But it was the only way I could get him. You said..."*

If you tell your players it's OK to tackle high whenever it's the only way, they will tackle high 98% of the time and swear it was the only way they could do it in that particular situation.

Here's what I **should** have said:

> *"Never tackle above the crotch unless the ball carrier is cocking his arm to throw a pass or one of your teammates already has him below the crotch."*

Leaders

In any organization, there are leaders. They may hold formal leadership positions like team captain. Or they may be informal leaders who exert their control in subtle ways.

Veterans tend to be leaders. The rookies look up to them—especially at the beginning of the season.

If some or all of your veterans refuse to tackle low and wrap with their arms, some of the rookies will get the idea that that particular teaching can be ignored. You must stamp out that kind of harmful leadership.

One way might be to appoint team leaders. You have the defensive **field captain** who is required for games. You also need **coin-toss captain(s)** who may or may not be the same as the field captain(s). You can appoint squad leaders or line leaders for calisthenics. You need demonstrators for drills.

I suggest you give out these positions strictly on merit and merit includes correct tackling technique. Veterans who insist on using **in**correct tackling technique do not get any leadership positions at all. And if you appoint a veteran to a leadership position at the beginning of the preseason, then find that he is refusing to use correct tackling technique, counsel him to clean up his act. If he doesn't, demote him and tell him why.

I've noticed a tendency among coaches to **never** demote players from either playing positions or leadership positions. The reason is the coach does not want to hurt the player's feelings—or he may not want to admit he made a mistake.

To heck with that. If you entrust a boy with a leadership position, and he leads the team down the path to poor tackling technique, he must be straightened out or moved out of that position. He deserves a second chance and maybe a third chance. But no more.

If you leave him **in** the leadership position, you send a very **bad** message to the team. That message is we tolerate poor technique. If you send that message, you will **get** poor tackling technique. And if you get poor tackling technique, you will have a poor record. And from a citizenship standpoint, you will have taught a team of boys that sloppiness and slacking off is OK.

On the other hand, if you replace a leader who refuses to exhibit correct tackling technique with one who **does** use correct tackling technique, you send the exact opposite message: Poor tackling technique is not tolerated on this team. No matter who you are or how many years experience you have, if you use poor tackling technique, you will hold no leadership position.

In *Play Football the NFL Way*, Tom Bass says,

> *...do not allow your players to develop bad habits or incorrect techniques. Point out bad technique immediately. Then change it and practice it correctly.*

Awards

You could award a Best Tackling Technique trophy or certificate each week. The winner could be announced in the team newsletter and/or over the PA system at the game during half time or before the game. You might let the winner of the Best Tackling Technique award be the defensive coin-toss captain and have the PA announcer so state when the captains go out for the coin toss.

Motivation in general

I note that there is a movement afoot in youth sports to eliminate individual recognition. The reason seems to be it hurts the feelings of the non-awardees. The natural progression of that theory would lead us to not keeping score—the way they do in Little League Tee Ball. After all, losing hurts the feelings of the defeated team.

I am less interested than most in the various child-raising theories which go in and out of fashion—because of my West Point background. Here's what I got out of my leadership education there and my experience in various leadership positions.

Leadership means getting people to do that which they ought to do, but would not do if you were not their leader. Coaching is leadership.

You motivate people to do that which they ought to do but are not inclined to do on their own by, among other things, **carrots and sticks**.

X and Y theories

People who have little leadership training or experience tend to adopt what I call the nice-guy, carrots-only approach. In the seventies, this was called the Y theory of leadership. The X theory was the hard-ass, sticks-only approach. Theory X was generally regarded as bad and wrong and ineffective.

In the nineties, the same theory is still around. But now the Y approach is called "positive reinforcement." And in our current, shrill, politically-correct, psychologically-correct era, deviations from the positive-reinforcement approach are now called child abuse.

The proponents of these various warm-and-fuzzy approaches to motivation have names like Dr. Benjamin Spock, Leo Buscaglia, T. Berry Brazelton, and Mister Rogers. And the nice-guy, carrots-only approach has been reinforced by such television families as Father Knows Best, My Three Sons, The Donna Reed Show, The Andy Griffith Show, and so forth. One of the great things about the Cosby Show and Roseann is that the children are realistically somewhat unresponsive and the parents are somewhat more realistically impatient than the usual TV family. That's closer to what we encounter in the real world of football coaching.

At West Point, we cadets tended to fall into either the X or Y theories in our barracks debates—at least during our first two years. During your first two years at West Point, you are generally a **subordinate** to junior and senior cadets. We reacted to the various leadership styles as they affected us personally. And we made the very common mistake of assuming that everyone else responded the same way we did.

But then we became juniors and seniors. And we were in leadership positions. And we learned a lesson. **Neither** the X approach nor the Y approach works all the time. You have to have **both** in your repertoire.

Some of the people respond to some **carrots** some of the time. And some of the people respond to some of the **sticks** some of the time. If you use the nice-guy, positive reinforcement, Y theory, let-'em-eat-carrots approach all the time, you will get a response from your players which is **partially** satisfactory. The same thing will happen if you use a hard-ass, you-never-do-anything-right, X theory, spare-the-rod approach all the time. And in today's world, you will also be cashiered as a youth coach for lack of modern enlightenment if you use strictly the X theory.

Motivation is difficult

The first thing the touchy-feely types need to understand is that motivation in the real world is **difficult**. The children on TV shows respond so well to the nice-guy approach because the script writer told them to. And the child actors who play those TV children are not about to give up their video fame and fortune by misbehaving the way they do at home. TV shows are produced in Hollywood.

But the motivational techniques which TV-show parents and teachers use are just that—Hollywood. If your players are getting $50,000 a year to play on your team—and appearing on nationwide TV weekly—there is no doubt in my mind that they will respond to any positive leadership technique you want to use. But if you have **real** boys in the **real** world, trying to mimic an old-time TV father will most definitely produce disappointing results.

True, there's good in everyone which can be tapped. But there's also bad in everyone which can get in the way. We are all lazy at times. Most of us have a panoply of other faults and weaknesses. We are all also former kids. And we were not angels when we were kids. Neither are our current football players.

The goal: win the championship

In order to motivate people, you need a well-equipped tool box of carrots **and** sticks. And the higher your goal, the greater the need for the maximum possible number of carrots and sticks. In a youth football league, each team has as its goal, by definition, winning the league championship. To adopt any other goal would be to plan to throw a game. Because if you play to win each game—and succeed in winning—you will be the league champions.

My question to any team which said the championship was **not** their goal would be to ask, "Exactly which game were you planning on **losing**? And if you plan on losing, why practice the week before and show up at all? And isn't that a little unfair to the opponent who wanted to test themselves against a worthy competitor?"

So by starting a football team, you implicitly adopt a goal of winning the league championship. And you know that the league is full of other teams with the same goal. They and their coaches are striving mightily to beat you. As a result, you must strive mightily to beat them.

The Y theory of leadership abandons the sticks of leadership. The X theory abandons the carrots. Using either approach exclusively ties one leadership hand behind your back. If your goal is easy, like getting each player to put his helmet on, you can succeed with one hand behind your back. But if your goal is hard—like winning the championship or getting your players to use the tackling technique which is necessary to win the championship—you can**not** succeed with one hand tied behind your back.

The greatest problem with the carrots-only approach to leadership is its naive assumption that everybody responds satisfactorily to that approach all the time. They don't.

Recognition

One carrot you can use is individual recognition. This can be in the form of awards like trophies, plaques, or certificates. Or in the form of publishing the individual's achievement in the team newsletter, over the PA system at games, or just verbally to the players at practice.

The military and boy scouts award uniform decorations like medals, badges, patches, shoulder cords, and special hats. Oriental martial arts instructors award different colored belts.

In football, you have helmet decals, team jackets, badges, patches. Some teams have different color practice jersey for different levels of players. For example, the Permian High School football team has often won the Texas State High School football championship in spite of having less raw talent than many of their opponents. In practice, by "long-standing tradition," their starters wear black football shirts and their substitutes wear white ones. In the book, *Friday Night Lights*, which is an in-depth account of Permian's 1988 season, the following appears on page 195,

> *"In the life of a player few single moments were more stirring than to open a locker one day and find a black practice jersey...Conversely, few single moments were more humbling than to have that black shirt taken away and given to someone else"*

Now I know that the author of *Friday Night Lights* regards the Permian High School football program as a classic example of competitiveness run amok. And having read it, I agree that it is just that in many respects. However, I also believe that the Permian High coaches were excellent coaches in many respects. And recognizing the starters not only on Friday nights at games, but also during the week with black practice jerseys, is an excellent example of the kind of motivation that coaches can use.

Coaches strive for, among other things, justice, in their decisions about who plays how much and where. And the best justice is **swift** justice. When a player behaves so as to warrant his demotion, he should be demoted **promptly**. Prompt demotion will best impress upon him and his teammates the consequence of slacking off and the need to do your best at all times. And that is a lesson which must be impressed on all who would succeed in football—or in life for that matter. Frequently, demoting a player with first-string ability serves as a wake-up call. It shocks him out of his complacency and inspires him to redouble his efforts. It tells him you do not succeed in football or in life by resting on your past laurels.

Depth chart

Sports teams whose rosters are large enough to have substitutes have depth charts. The depth chart may exist only in the mind of the coach—and he may not use the phrase depth chart—but all coaches have depth charts nevertheless.

Publicizing your depth chart can serve as a carrot and stick motivator.

When a player is promoted, or demoted, he ought to know it.

Furthermore, in practice, you can promote and demote repeatedly and from moment to moment. For example, if your starting right linebacker tackles high in a scrimmage play, send him to remedial tackling and put the second-string right linebacker in his place.

Tell the former first-string right linebacker that he has just lost his job but that he can get it back by tackling properly. And tell the second-string player who was just promoted to first string that he can keep the position if he plays well. But that if he uses poor tackling technique or otherwise screws up, the former first-string player, or a third player, will be brought in to replace him.

Remedial tackling

Defensive practice ought to be a two-ring circus. One ring is main-stream practice like scrimmage. The other is remedial tackling.

If a player uses poor tackling technique, you send him to remedial tackling where a coach who is assigned to that duty works with just him and any other players needing remedial tackling. If there's only one player there and you need a second in order to do the drill the coach wants to do, take the worst tackler on the team to make a twosome even though he may not have used poor technique lately.

Being sent to remedial tackling makes sense from an education standpoint. Either the player doesn't **know** proper tackling technique—or the **habit** of using proper tackling technique is not yet deeply ingrained enough. Either way, he needs to do some tackling drills.

Sending a boy to remedial tackling also makes sense from a carrot and stick standpoint. It is the equivalent of Permian High School's taking away your black practice jersey. It sends a message to the player in question and to all the other players that he just behaved in an unacceptable manner And that when you do that, you at least momentarily lose your job.

While the player is at remedial tackling, another player takes his place in scrimmage. As anybody who has ever played sports knows, a coach's decision to let someone else play your position—even if intended to be temporary—can result in a **permanent** loss of your job if the sub does well.

Wally Pipp

The classic case of that was New York Yankee first baseman Wally Pipp. He was well established as the Yankees first baseman in 1915, a member of the Yankees' "Murderers' Row" hitting line up, and twice led the American League in home runs. But in 1925, he sat out a game and let a new guy play. The new guy was Lou Gehrig who proceeded to stay there for the next 2,130 games, a consecutive-games-played record which still stands. You ought to tell your football players—especially your veterans—the story of Wally Pipp.

By sending the first-string guy to remedial tackling, you create an opening for a second-string guy to became first-string. That should be a great motivator and morale sustainer for the second-stringers. They know that they will get many opportunities to show what they can do.

Remedial format

Remedial tackling ought to be productive time. It will inevitably have a connotation equivalent to sitting in the corner wearing a dunce cap. But it ought to be more than a punishment or embarrassment. One format would be to have the player who just made a tackle incorrectly do that same type of tackle correctly twenty times in remedial tackling before he is returned to the scrimmage.

The coach who refers the player to remedial tackling should tell the remedial tackling coach what the player did wrong. Like, "Hey Bob. Remedial tackling for Joey. He put his head down." Then the coach works with Joey on keeping his head up when he tackles. When Joey makes twenty head-up tackles, he is returned to the scrimmage.

Zero tolerance

The main idea behind sending players who use poor tackling technique to remedial tackling is that you must not tolerate even one instance of incorrect technique. That's not to say you should yell at the boy or treat him harshly. Just tell him what part of his technique was incorrect and tell him to go see coach So-and-So to work on it. And tell the next player on the depth chart to take the place of the remedial player. In time, the whole team will figure out what's going on and a referral to remedial tackling will have all the effect you need.

Eventually, the players will wince at their own error when they do it wrong—knowing they're about to be sent to remedial tackling. And hopefully, between remedial tackling drills and the desire to avoid being sent to remedial tackling, the players will lose their poor habits and replace them with good ones. The goal is to make them incapable of using poor tackling technique because they are so used to doing it right and they instinctively fear what will happen to them (remedial tackling and possibly losing job) if they do it wrong.

Under-the-pads tackling drills

One drill we found effective at teaching to tackle low I'll call our under-the-pad drill. Our team owned a bunch of four-foot long blocking pads. We would put a ball carrier on one side running in slow motion along the pad which was held about three feet off the ground by a coach at each end of the pad. The tacklers were lined up on the other side of the pad and had to go under the pad and make a correct tackle. The tackler starting in a "good football position," that is, knees bent, hands and arms dangling loosely in front of the thighs, bent at the waist. You do **not** want the tackler to start from a three- or four-point stance. Although, like all defensive drills, it should be started by a snap. You need two balls: one for the ball carrier and one for the snapper.

Here's a diagram:

Under-the-pad tackling drill

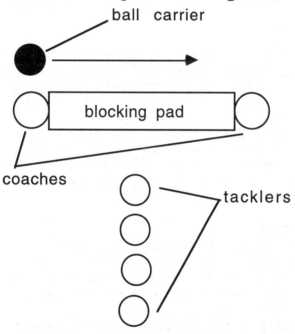

The players rotate after each tackle. When everyone has tackled a ball carrier running to the tackler's right, the ball carrier moves to the other side and runs to the ball carrier's left.

We found this drill to be amazingly successful. The same players who would ignore repeated admonitions to hit below the crotch in the same drill with**out** the coaches holding the pad, would almost invariably hit low when they had to go under the pad.

I often wished we could practice in a chute—a sort of four-foot-high table with no top. Because the low man usually wins in football. And the players' natural tendency is to stand up. Most high schools have chutes. Ours did not. In 1992, one of our coaches made several chutes out of PVC. They worked pretty well. Chutes may also be a problem in that the players may bump into them as they shift sideways to meet the ball carrier.

Practice games with special rules

Another idea is to have intrasquad game with special rules. For example, tackling above the crotch when the ball carrier is not in the act of throwing a pass or already being tackled below the crotch by someone else will draw a 15-yard penalty. Reward the winners of the practice game or punish the losers. The typical way this is done is by excusing the winners from post-practice equipment clean-up on the grounds that they must have gotten enough exercise in the game when they out-hustled the other team.

Here are some other technique-oriented penalties you could adopt to discourage poor tackling technique:

- leaving feet in an unsuccessful tackle attempt
- head behind the ball carrier in a side tackle
- head not on ball side in straight-ahead tackle attempt.

Lift

The tackler ought to lift the ball carrier off the ground. You don't have to lift him high.

Youth football cleats are no more than one half inch long by rules. All you have to do as a tackler is get those cleats out of the ground. Once the ball carrier's connection to the ground is broken, knocking him down is easy. I sometimes demonstrated that to players by having one jump up an inch or so off the ground next to a bunch of blocking pads. When he cleared the ground, I would, with a flick of one wrist, lightly flip his heel sideways. That would send him sprawling to the pads.

On the other hand, as long as the ball carrier has cleats in the ground, strenuously pushing him horizontally or, worse, downward, accomplishes little or nothing. This is especially true if your angle of attack is from the front and the ball carrier's knees are bent. With his cleats in the ground, it's the tackler's leg strength and desire versus the ball carrier's strength and desire. That's a wrestling match, not a tackle.

Paradoxical as it may seem to the players, the best way to get a ball carrier **down** is to first lift him slightly **up**.

Subtle technique

Lift is an extremely important, but extremely subtle, part of good tackling technique.

We had one player really master this toward the end of the 1991 season. We taught trying to get slight lift. But this boy was more self-taught than coach-taught. He just figured out how to do it at some point and was able to do it most of the time thereafter. And he was one of our smaller, lighter, rookies.

His tackles looked pretty much the same as everybody else's—except that other players would drop the ball carrier where they hit him—and this one player would deposit the ball carriers three or four feet **back** from where he hit them—even when the ball carrier was significantly heavier than he was.

The lift comes from four things:

- a tight wrap with both arms and
- the shoulder attacking the ball carrier at a slightly up angle—maybe just five or ten degrees above the horizontal and
- the tackler firing out at the ball carrier from the proper distance—that is, the tackler's foot or feet were on the ground within inches from the ball carrier's nearest foot when the tackler exploded into the ball carrier and
- jerking the ball carrier's legs backward and upward between the tackler's legs.

If the tackler has no tight wrap, his upward thrust will generally just slide up the uniform of the ball carrier.

If the tackler does not thrust upward, obviously there will be no lift.

And if the tackler fires out from **too far away** from the ball carrier—a common mistake—his explosion will be mostly spent when his shoulder hits the ball carrier.

Coaches should **insist** on the deposit-the-ball-carrier-six-feet-back tackle.

Stopping contest

I recommend you run a tackling contest in which the object is to stop the ball carrier as close to his starting point as possible—or drive him back as far as possible. One coach would act as an official. He would closely observe where the ball was when the ball carrier was officially tackled and mark the spot accordingly. The distance from the starting line would then be measured and recorded. As always, there would be an extra ball and a center whose snap would start the players moving. No verbal start command should be used.

The players would start facing each other and three to five yards apart. You should limit lateral movement to five yards or so unless you are specifically interested in wide pursuit. The field ought to be small enough so that there are no total misses.

On the first iteration, match the players at random. When you've gone through the whole team once, you will have distances for everyone as a tackler and everyone as a ball carrier.

For the second iteration, match the best ball carrier (got the farthest distance in the first iteration) against the best tackler (held his ball carrier to the shortest distance in the first iteration) and the second best against the second best and so forth. Keep repeating the contest until you have a good fix on the ranking of every player on the team as both a ball carrier and as a tackler.

This is a good drill for teaching the players to hit as close to the ball carrier's center of gravity as possible. Of course, you don't want to hit right on the center of gravity—which is probably above the belly button—unless it's a straight-ahead tackle—because you have to immobilize the legs. In any event, this contest should encourage optimum technique because anything less will allow the ball carrier to gain extra feet or yards after the hit.

Since football is a game of inches and first downs and touchdowns, making the tacklers forward-progress conscious as opposed to just get-him-down conscious should pay dividends in games.

The contest results will also serve as yet another evaluation upon which to base your position and playing time decisions.

Two-man teams

Two two-man teams play each other inside a five-yard by five-yard box. One offensive player centers the ball to the other from one yard line who tries to score by advancing the ball to the next yard line five yards away. The two defensive players line up on the other side of the neutral zone in a similar formation nose to nose with the center and try to stop them. That is, one defensive player would be directly behind the other. If you have trouble with the snap, have the ball carrier start out with the ball in his hands and have the center snap an invisible ball. Here's a diagram:

Two-man team competition

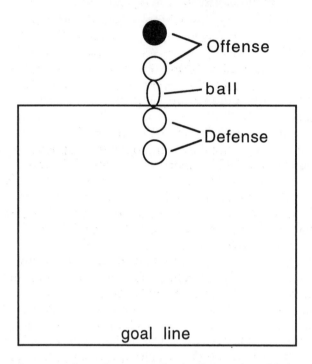

Each team gets two downs unless they turn the ball over in which case the team which recovers the turnover then gets two down from the spot of the recovery. Each team gets to have the ball for four series. The team with the most scores wins.

In a 30-player team, you'd have 15 teams. Run the contest as a single elimination tournament with consolation games so that you end up with an overall ranking of each team. Retain the results as further evaluation material for making position and playing time decisions.

I have found competitions to be great fun and great motivators. The kids generally love them and play with full intensity. If the game is designed to be close to game conditions, valuable learning takes place.

Pass-rush tackle

When making a pass-rush tackle, your defense should charge with hands held high overhead. That obstructs the vision of the passer and may deflect a pass. Pass rushers must be taught **not** to jump up in the air until they see daylight between the ball and the passer's hand. If they jump up in the air in response to the passer's arm going forward, they are susceptible to being pump faked out of the play.

The passer pump fakes a pass. Then he simply trots to one side or the other and throws a real pass while the rushers are descending to earth and changing direction.

When the pass rusher gets to the passer, he should drop his raised hands down onto the shoulders or passing arm of the passer. That way he will interfere with any last second pass attempts. If he tackles low as we normally require, the passer will get an extra second or so to get the pass off.

You have to practice pass rush tackles. Don't use your real quarterbacks. Have the passers try to fake the rushers off the ground.

Video examples

You should show your players video examples of excellent technique tackles. There are some great ones on NFL Films tapes. Unfortunately, the vast majority of the tackles on

NFL Films tapes employ terrible technique from the standpoint of what we are trying to teach our kids. Most NFL football players are like the major league baseball outfielders who catch fly balls one-handed. It's wrong. It's bad technique. But when you're a pro making a couple million a year, you do what you want.

That's not to say the NFL players don't know what they're doing. NFL Films concentrates on the very best players and they know exactly what they are doing most of the time. It's just that the high hits they employ work for them because they are so skilled. Our kids can do that when they become pros. But if they try to use those techniques as kids, they'll just miss tackles.

NFL Films are also replete with garbage behavior like taunting opponents and bleeped-out foul language and guys saying they want to put their opponent in the hospital. The NFL Films narrator sounds like a 1920's sportswriter with all his ponderous, overblown "Four Horsemen of the Apocalypse" rhetoric.

I recommend that you cue up an NFL Films video to one of the tackles which demonstrates the kind of technique we want and run it over and over—with the sound off.

Bo Schembechler's "Teaching Kids Football" tape illustrates good tackling technique. Unfortunately, it does so in a very unexciting way.

Most colleges sell video tape highlights of their seasons. I haven't seen any of them. They probably vary from school to school. Get one from your alma mater or some team you especially admire and see if it has examples of good technique.

Finally, you can probably make a video highlight tape of your own team's best tackles from a technique standpoint—or of the best tackles from your team and your opponents.

NFL Films are probably the best because of the super high quality of the camera work. Just make sure you only show the good-technique examples and then only the video, not the audio.

Video on the bench

It has been established by studies that showing an athlete a video of excellent play just before he engages in his sport can significantly improve performance. I'd like have a video showing excellent tackles running (and maybe some sacks and interceptions) in the locker room before a game and on the bench during a game. I'd have the players watch it just before they went into the game the way pros sometimes take oxygen (although scientists say oxygen's a waste of time in such situations). High school rules, which are used by most youth leagues, prohibit "mechanical devices" being used during the game.

I've seen the effect on myself when I watched a game on TV before going out to play with friends. I also saw it once at a baseball batting cage where I watched an excellent hitter just before I got in the cage to hit myself. To my amazement, I was doing things that he did—like flicking the bat at near strikes to foul them off—things that I had never done before.

I **did** have a flip-card thing of Don Mattingly hitting a home run. You bent the stack and let the cards flip past quickly. Each was a photograph of part of Mattingly's swing in sequence. The effect was as if you were seeing a movie. I showed it to some of my Little Leaguers just before they went up to bat. It did not seem to have any effect. One problem may have been that Mattingly bats left and all my players batted right. Maybe they couldn't relate to it.

Gang tackling

Gang tackling is extremely important. It can make up for poor individual tackling technique. We did not do enough of it in the 1991 season. We talked about it in practice. But we never practiced it *per se*. We should have. Here are some drills to try.

Last man out

One is a scrimmage policy that the last man to get in on a tackle gets replaced. Players would be taught to get in on every tackle if they could do so before the whistle. If the whistle blows, they are to run to the scene of the tackle as fast as possible and put their hand on the body of one of the tacklers. Last one who gets there is out like a musical chairs players who doesn't get a seat when the music stops.

You could also put a stop watch on the time which elapses from the first hit to the last touch of the tackler by a defender. Over time, you would develop an understanding of what a good time is.

Do your job drill

Another gang tackling drill we used worked like this. We would line the defense up against air. We would place several free-standing heavy tackling dummies around the field. The players would get set and the coach would yell, "Do your job!" Each player would move forward and freeze in a cup shape around the offensive backfield. The coaches would check their positioning then the defensive coordinator would point at one of the dummies and yell, "Gang!" Then plyers would then all run and tackle the dummy en masse at full speed. The players loved this drill and we felt it did an excellent job of teaching the habit of gang tackling.

Leave him standing

The *1985 Coach of the Year Clinics Manual* contains the following from Claremont, California High School coach, Bob Biaz,

> *In practice we come in on the ball carrier or receivers with the same force as we would in a game, except we do not bring them down. We hit and lift, and wrap the arms. This leaves the back standing. We picked this up from UCLA a few years ago. Everyone on their team gets to the ball on every play. All defensive backs will run to the ball carrier regardless where he is, and get their hand on him. Even if the man is going back to the huddle they will go after the man. By doing this we encourage gang tackling. We get 5 or 6 men on each tackle.*

Point system

A point system occurs to me. A tackle is worth eleven points. If a player single-handedly makes a tackle, he gets all eleven. But if others assist before the whistle—regardless of whether the first tackler needed the help or not—he shares the points with the assisters. The point system would go like this:

	1	2	3	4	5	6	7	8	9	10	11
1st	11	6	4	3	3	2	2	2	2	2	1
2nd		5	4	3	2	2	2	2	2	1	1
3rd			3	3	2	2	2	2	1	1	1
4th				2	2	2	2	1	1	1	1
5th					2	2	1	1	1	1	1
6th						1	1	1	1	1	1
7th							1	1	1	1	1
8th								1	1	1	1
9th									1	1	1
10th										1	1
11th											1

(Number of tacklers)

Playing time and positions would be awarded according to point scores. Plus just publishing the point scores would encourage competition between players. To avoid late hit penalties, you'd better subtract points for late hits. A point a yard sounds appropriate. Fifteen points for a fifteen-yard penalty infraction.

Another point system

Biaz uses the following point system which sounds good to me also:

Behind line of scrimmage tackles	4 points
Unassisted tackles	3 points
First hit	2 points
Assist on tackle	1 point
Cause fumble	5 points
Recover fumble	5 points
Interception	5 points
Deflect pass	3 points
Big hit (not defined by Biaz)	3 points
Blocked kick	6 points

Actually, the technically-correct thing to do would probably be to assign points according to the system on page 71 of *The Hidden Game of Football* by Bob Carroll, Peter Palmer, and John Thorn. They advocate the following point system for rating offenses. Of course, rating the offense is nothing more than an upside-down rating of the defense.

Points	1st down	2nd down	3rd or 4th down
-4	Turnover	Turnover	Turnover#
-1	-3 yards or more	-3 yards or more	-3 yards or more
0	Less than 40%	Less than 60%	Less than 100%
1	40 to 79%	60 to 79%	100%
2	80%	80%	—
3*	11+ yards	11+ yards	11+ yards
4*	21+ yards	21+ yards	21+ yards
5*	41+ yards	41+ yards	41+ yards

* Subtract one point if not first down
# 0 if on 4th down inside opponent's 35-yard line on play that would not have otherwise registered a first down. Biaz's system—and mine—give credit for tackles and assists no matter when or where they occur. In fact, when and where they occur make all the difference in the world. A turnover on 4th down inside the defense's 35-yard line when the ball carrier or intended receiver would not have made a fourth down anyway gets five points from Biaz but none from Carroll, Palmer, and Thorn. That's because such a turnover is meaningless. The team which was on defense was going to get the ball anyway. In fact, if the field position changed in favor of the offense—as is typical on an interception—the team on defense is actually **hurt** by the turnover. For example, the offense has fourth and 16 on your 25. They pass and your safety intercepts at your 27 and is immediately tackled. You'd have been better off if the defender batted the ball down instead of intercepting it. But in Biaz's point system, deflecting a pass is only worth three points and intercepting is worth five.

Perhaps the best system would be to reverse the signs on the *Hidden Game* system. That is, make a turnover worth positive four points and a 41+ yard gain by the offense worth minus five. Then multiply the points by ten to make them easier to distribute among eleven players. Then the question is how do you allocate responsibility on each play for what happened. That would require a sort of cost-accounting analysis of each play in accordance with the team's job descriptions.

Gang tackling against Fairfield in 1992

When we scouted the Fairfield Falcons in preparation for the 1992 Western League championship, we concluded we could only stop their # 30 with gang tackling.

We tried some drills the week before the game. But the thing that seemed to work best was simply to **talk** a lot about the need to gang tackle. That included explaining the importance then yelling "Gang! Gang! Gang!" during scrimmage and the game itself.

It may be that the Falcons' #30 will grow up to break O.J. Simpson's records. In which case our holding him to three touchdowns will seem like an accomplishment. We succeeded against him when we gang tackled him. On some plays, our boys gave textbook examples of gang tackles with several players looking like the Marines raising the flag on Iwo Jima and others flying onto the pile before the whistle.

Our first guy could usually make #30 at least change direction. That slowed him up. When more Bears flew in from all directions, #30 generally went down on the spot. He could break tackles all day. But even he could not break **gang** tackles. Unfortunately, we had three too few of them.

19

Stance

Down linemen

The down linemen should be in a four-point stance. I know that a three-point stance with your up hand sticking out in front of you is in. But low man usually wins and it's tough to get football players to stay low. The purpose of the four-point stance is to get the players low. Our charge-through-the-gaps defense in particular needs the four-point stance.

Here are the check points for the four-point stance:

• head up
• toes under butt
• back parallel to the ground
• feet shoulder-pad width apart
• shoulders parallel to the ground
• 25% of weight on hands
• hands on ground about three inches in front of helmet
• knees behind elbows.

If the back is horizontal and the toes are under the butt, the other points will generally all fall into place.

Here are the things the players tend to do if you don't keep after them:

• head down
• toes way behind butt as if to do a pushup
• butt way below shoulders as if squatting to defecate in the woods
• feet together

- one shoulder down; the other, up
- no weight on hands, they just dangle directly below the shoulders as if there were a rule requiring the player to touch the ground with his fingertips until the snap
- knees turned outside body.

Remedial four-point stance

We emphasized the stance at the beginning of the 1991 season and got great results. But as the season wore on we paid far less attention to stance and the players stances deteriorated as a result. You have to stay on this all season long. In 1992 we pushed it longer and got better results. It's really something you have to check everyday. What you don't check and correct daily will deteriorate. Our offensive coach said after the season that one of our great early strengths—good faking—virtually disappeared later in the 1991 season when he was too busy teaching new plays to focus on it.

As with tackling, zero tolerance of poor stance is the only way. When you see a player in a poor stance, correct him immediately. If he does it again that practice, send him to the remedial coach. Have the remedial coach put him in a proper stance and charge on movement of the ball twenty times.

Fingertips, knuckles, or palms

You're supposed to put your weight on either your fingertips or knuckles. Our players seemed physically incapable of putting weight on their fingertips. Their hands would immediately collapse when they tried. I was a bit skeptical. It seems pretty easy for me to do it. I've never heard that children's finger muscles were weak.

So we told them to make a fist and put the weight on their knuckles. That, they could do and did.

Some tended to put their palm on the ground. That makes their shoulders a bit **too** low. It makes it harder for them to get up. My high school coaches always said our hands would get stepped on if we put our palm on the ground.

Other stances

In general, the other players should be in a two-point stance—that is, they should stand up on their two feet. I suppose there's some great "right" way to take a two-point stance. I must confess, however, that I can't get excited about it. Basically, I just want the player to be comfortable and ready. That is, he ought to be on the balls of his feet.

I have considered a sprinter's stance for my defensive ends at times. For reasons unknown to me, defensive ends frequently do not penetrate to the depth of the ball as they're supposed to in my 8-2-1. Sometimes they are blocked enroute even though they were supposed to line up far enough outside the opponent that they could get to their sweep-stopping spot untouched. Other times they inexplicably stop even though there is no block.

A sprinter's stance is basically a three-point stance with the strongest leg foot staggered behind the other foot as in a track sprinter's starting blocks. I figured the sprinter's stance would shoot the end across the line of scrimmage so fast he would neither be blocked nor be able to stop his momentum before he got to the right depth. I never really gave it a good try. Rather I offered it as a suggestion to the players and they are generally opposed to all stances other than standing straight up.

Hallmark of a well-coached team

It seems to me that stance in youth football tells you immediately whether the team is well coached. On the first scrimmage play, you see the other team's stance. If their butts are down, feet close together, etc., you're generally not facing a well-coached team. They may have overwhelming talent in spite of their poor stances. And you don't know about the whole team until you also see the unit that operates on the other side of the football, that is, until you see both their offense and defense. It may be their offensive coach allows the defecate-in-the-woods stance, but the defense coach does not. But I always breathe a bit easier when I see an opponent come out in bad stances.

Sometimes, the stance varies from player to player. If I were an offensive coach, I'd try running plays at defensive linemen with poor stances. They ought to be easier to run over. And the rest of their technique, like tackling, probably is not so hot either.

20

Coaches meetings

Some people are anti meeting. I'm one of them. When I worked briefly for a bank I noticed that there were meetings going on from morning until night—so many meetings that I could attend meetings all day and claim a reasonable reason for being in each one. Those meetings were poorly organized and virtually always a waste of time. That bank has since gone out of business.

But when it comes to coaching football, I believe well-organized, weekly coaches meetings are essential. I've read many books about famous college and pro coaches and coaches meetings were almost a **daily** occurrence if I understood the books correctly. Watching film was also a daily activity for them and served as an additional coaches meeting of sorts.

Why meetings? Two heads are better than one. A football team requires teamwork between the coaches as well as the players. Practice and game chores must be assigned. Players must be discussed, evaluated, and assigned to position coaches. Practice schedules must be coordinated. The psyche-up theme of the week must be chosen. Coaches' objectivity must be checked. Coach and player absences must be accommodated. And more.

Topics

Here's a list of topics which should be covered at coaches meetings. That's not to say that you should cover **all** these at **every** meeting. Rather each individual coach should use this list as a check list when he is preparing for what he wants to say or ask at the next meeting.

- Player evaluations
- Discipline problems

• Hand out and discuss scout report on upcoming opponent
• Scouting assignments for upcoming weekend, if any
• Psyche-up theme of the week
• Video of last game or practice
• How can we keep practice fun and interesting this week?
     e.g., new drills, competitions
• Any coaches going to miss any practice time or the game this week?
• Do we need to change our system (formations or job descriptions) on
     offense
     defense
     kickoff team
     kick receive team
     punt team
     punt receive team
     place-kicking team
• Do we need to change personnel (what position and how much playing time) on
     offense
     defense
     kickoff team
     kick receive team
     punt team
     punt receive team
     place-kicking team
• Practice schedule for the week
• Coach evaluations
• Nepotism check—Ask the group if any coach's son is getting too much or too little playing time, too few or too many carries or passes, or is playing in the wrong position.
• Hand out videos of last game if not already distributed
• Goals for the week
• Do we have any equipment problems?

WHERE to hold meetings

You really ought to have a blackboard or white board or overhead projector. And it would be nice to have a TV and VCR.

What you should **not** have is players present. The coaches should be able to discuss the team and players with complete candor. It's not a good idea to do that in front of or within earshot of one or more of the players. So the meetings ought **not** be held at the home of a coach who is also a parent of a player if the player will be in the house during the meeting.

We held one team meeting in a community center. It had both a TV/VCR and a white board. That would have been a good place to hold our coaches meetings. The meeting room of a local pizza place or other restaurant might work. You need to be sure no spies from another team can eavesdrop or see what you're doing. Some banks will let the public use their conference room. The school whose field you play on may have a room you could use.

Attendance

Coaches very quickly get mad at players who are late for or miss practices. But many coaches do not hold themselves to the same standards. The attitude seems to be, "Hey, I'm a volunteer. I don't get paid to do this. I'm doing the league and the players a favor to be here at all."

It seems to me that the time a coach spends attending and preparing for team activities should be one of the main criteria for selecting and retaining coaches. Ned McIntosh coached Little League baseball for 15 years before he wrote the book, *Managing Little League Baseball*, a book which was "fully approved by Little League Baseball." On page 136 he says,

> *If there is one single factor above all, that will affect the success of your team it will be the amount of time you are willing and able to spend with your boys...*

Coaches can debate how much time a youth coach should devote to the team. I know **spouses** of coaches debate it.

But I don't think there's any debate that the **more** time a coach spends on his team, the more success they will have on the field and the more success he will have at providing the players with the best experience possible regardless of the team's record. Accordingly, I think youth football boards ought to ask the candidates for head coach how much time they can and will devote to the team. And they should heavily weight that factor in choosing the head coach.

A guy who was all-state in high school, all-American in college, and all-pro in the NFL will do very little to help your team if he's rarely there. Indeed, a coach who is consistently absent from team activities can **hurt** his team to the extent that the responsibilities assigned to him are neglected as a result of his absences. An absent coach is not pulling his oar and he forces his fellow coaches have to pull their own oar and his as well.

Resumes and good intentions don't win ball games—or even help the players have an enjoyable experience. Work wins ball games and enables the players to get the most out of the experience. Ohio State's Woody Hayes used to say that the opposing coaches may be smarter than he was but that they would never outwork him. (Hayes teams' record was 205-61-10. They went to the Rose Bowl seven times and won 13 Big Ten Championships. He was revered by virtually all of his many players and erstwhile assistant coaches.)

Once the head coach is chosen, he, in turn, should choose his assistants in large part on how much time they will be able to devote to the team. All coach candidates should be asked how explicitly how many hours per week they are willing to spend on the team before they are assigned specific responsibilities. Better yet, the head coach should create a schedule for the preseason and show it to the coach candidates. He should ask them if they have a problem with any of it.

The head coach ought to confirm with each coach candidate approximately how many coaches' meetings they will be able to attend. Once it has been established that the coaching staff has committed to attending the meetings, the head coach should poll the coaches to find the most convenient day and time for the meetings. Once the coaches have committed to attend in general and approved the specific day and time, they should be held to their commitment.

Coach discipline

Any coach who subsequently makes a habit of missing all or part of numerous coaches meetings ought to be spoken to about the matter. His availability in general ought to be reconfirmed and his availability on the particular day and time should be reconfirmed. Once he has reaffirmed his intention to be there and still fails to make it, his coaching responsibilities should be reduced or eliminated to reflect the amount of time he has actually been spending rather than the amount he promised to spend. In other words, if a coach frequently misses meetings, arrives late, or leaves early, demote or fire him, replacing him with a coach who is devoting more time.

This applies regardless of whether the absences are the result of bad faith or just unexpected changed circumstances which prevent the coach from meeting his original good-faith commitment. Absence is absence. There is no place on the scoreboard for excuses, good or otherwise. Nor does the fact that an absent coach had a good excuse for his absence make up for the fact that players had to spend twice as much time standing in line at practice.

Coaches who complain that they don't like meetings in general or that your meetings in particular are a waste of time, should be asked for **constructive criticism**. If the criticism raises valid points, corrective action should be taken to improve the meetings. But general aversion to meetings or vague protestations that your meetings are a waste of time should not be accepted as valid excuses for absence form all or part of coaches meetings.

Ideally, all coaches will spend the same amount of time and that time will be an adequate amount. But lack of volunteers may mean that you have to accept some coaches who can only spend limited amounts of time. If the amount of time spent by the coaches is not equal, the head coach ought to be the guy who spends the most time, the offensive and defensive coordinators the second most, and the position coaches, the least.

Duration of meetings

Meetings can drag on. In the real estate property management business, condominium management agreements generally require the property manager to attend monthly condominium association meetings. But they also limit the number of hours the manager has to stay at the meetings. That's because condo association meetings typically last until the wee hours of the morning.

I tend to be one of the guys who made our coaches meetings run on. On December 14th, 1991, I attended a real estate conference at which one of my fellow real estate gurus told me his wife told him, "If Jack Reed is there, remember you have to be home by 4:00." That's because he and I often talk for hours on the phone. That same evening, I went to our San Ramon Bears coaches post-season cocktail party and one of the coaches told me his wife warned him not to "spend the entire evening talking to Jack Reed."

Hey, I'm a writer. What do you expect?

To protect the coaches who have a life outside football from guys like me, the coaches ought to agree to not only a starting time but also a **stopping** time for the coaches meetings. The head coach then needs to keep things on schedule and his assistants need to help him by trimming their contributions accordingly.

I don't know what the "right" amount of time is for coaches meetings. If all the coaches were like me, the meetings would probably last three hours. The coach's biographies I've read almost all talk about coach's meetings routinely lasting into the wee hours, like condo meetings.

The head coach ought to decide how long the coaches meetings will last before he makes his preseason "Is-this-schedule-OK" schedule. Then, the duration of the meetings should only be changed by consensus of the coaching staff.

Partial attendance by non-coaches

Certain non-coaches might be asked to attend your coaches meetings at least briefly. **Board members** probably ought to attend from time to time to make sure the coaches are keeping league purposes and rules in mind—and to answer coaches' questions.

Your **equipment manager** ought to be invited but not expected to stay the whole time. Ours generally did attend meetings and stayed the whole time because he wanted to. But it's not necessary that he stay the whole time.

You may want to invite your team's **cheerleader coach** to coordinate the theme of the week with their efforts. Ditto your team mother to coordinate parental support efforts.

Your **video taper** ought to be invited at least once so he or she can see how their tapes are used and how important they are.

Your **team doctor or medical technician** may want to make a presentation at one or more meetings.

Your **scout(s)**, if they are different from your coaches, should attend for the purpose of reporting on the upcoming opponent.

The attendance of those who only come for part of the meeting should be scheduled at a particular time. It need not be the first thing on the agenda. But the meeting should be run so that the part-timer's part of the agenda starts at its scheduled time. That way the part-timer can do his or her business then leave in a minimum amount of time.

21
Pursuit angles

When the offense sweeps, players need to pursue at particular angles depending on their position. If you do not train them to do this, and drill them on it repeatedly, some, if not all, will pursue at the wrong angle.

Ends

Backside ends must pursue through the offense's backfield at the depth of the deepest offensive player in case the play is a reverse. We stopped Vacaville in the 1990 Conference Championship game until one of our ends failed to do this on two plays, both of which resulted in touchdowns. We had trained our ends to pursue through the backfield. And although the end in question had also been so trained, this was his first game at end.

In 1991, our ends never made this mistake that I recall. Every time the opposing team tried a reverse or bootleg, our end was there. He didn't always make the tackle. But he was always there. In 1992, one started to stray so I replaced him.

Of course the playside end must get to the sweep spot and refuse to let any blockers or ball carrier run through there. He must force the ball carrier to cut up inside or go deeper to get around him. He must **not** give ground toward the sideline.

Other players

All other players except those in the immediate vicinity of the ball carrier must take a head-'em-off-at-the-pass angle. That is, they must run to the spot the ball carrier will pass through after he turns up field. Players must **not** pursue a ball carrier from **behind** when he is running toward the sideline. As long as he's running in that direction, he is not helping his team. He only helps them when he turns upfield.

In addition, unless the pursuer is faster than the ball carrier, he cannot catch him from behind. Ball carriers are generally the fastest guys on the field. So the defender must use the knowledge that the player has to turn upfield eventually to take a short cut to the tackle. Here's a diagram.

Wide pursuit angles

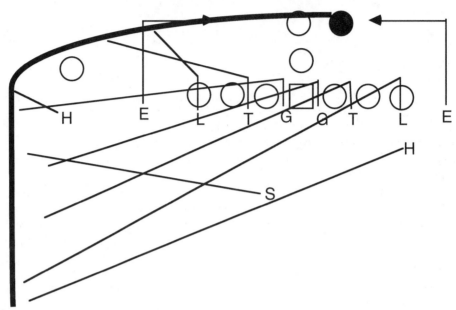

The basic idea is that everyone except the end on the side **away** from the flow of the play must head for a spot he can get to before the ball carrier.

We taught this during our first pre-pads week. Walk through it at first. To do that I gave the command, "Ready—step" for each step. We would check each player's position then order the next step. And we came back to it from time to time during the season.

Loafing

One of the problems is that they take the right angle but they **loaf** on the assumption that someone else will make the tackle. To counteract that we showed videotape of how loafing hurt us during one game. And we did some of our wind sprints in wide pursuit angle format. We would start the players from a normal formation on a snap. Then I would point to one side and yell, "Sweep!" They would then take their wide-pursuit angles.

During those wide-pursuit wind sprints, I would yell, "Full speed! Full speed!" to remind them to keep moving at full speed until the whistle. Stragglers would be singled out for correction.

Sometimes, after I had them going, I'd yell "Reverse!" at which time they would have to cut back at a wide pursuit angle toward the **other** side of the field.

We had the second slowest team we saw. So we pointed out to our players that taking proper pursuit angles at full speed was the only way they were going to catch the faster players we faced.

Overdoing it

In 1992, I think we overdid the pursuit angle drill. Or at least we allowed the angles to get out of whack. Our head coach liked doing the pursuit angles drill as an end-of-practice wind sprint. I got in the habit of telling everybody except the ends to go at a 45-degree angle. That's really incorrect if you look at the above diagram. But it makes for an easier-to-monitor wind sprint.

As the season progressed, our angles of pursuit were great—best in the league probably. Our game videos looked like training films with the offside players blowing back at full speed to form a gauntlet along the sideline the sweeping ball carrier was heading for.

But I also noticed we seemed to be playing the sweeps too **softly**. The ends generally did their job of forcing the ball carrier off his intended track. That should have given the other ten defenders time to make the tackle. They did make the tackle—but not until the ball carrier had picked up five or ten yards some times. We may have lost the Western League Championship and, thereby, our first California Youth Football Championship in 1992 because of this little flaw in our drill.

The problem was the defenders closest to the ball carrier were running away from him just when he was most vulnerable. They were not afraid of him. Rather they were highly disciplined to blow backward at a 45-degree angle when they heard the coach yell, "Sweep!" If the closest linebacker and cornerback had gone straight to the ball carrier at the time the end was fouling up his route, we probably could have stopped him for a loss. But by our playside cornerback and linebacker taking pursuit angles, we turned a sweep into a play that was more like a punt return. Their best back had the ball and was loose with our players scattered over a wide area.

We only lost two games in 1992. So we were not **too** weak against the sweep. But we were weak enough to lose it all against the Fairfield Falcons. Their star running back, Gregory Reed, got around us four times. We tackled him close to our end zone on two of those sweeps—once because a kid took a correct pursuit angle. And we held them out one of those two times. But another time, he swept left, our kids all took 45-degree angles toward that sideline, and he cut back against the grain and ran about 60 yards for his third touchdown of the day. Our pursuit angles had been so disciplined and fast that we had absolutely no one to stop him inside the hash marks.

You need to have some of your players covering the sweeper from the outside in—like the ends and cornerbacks—and others pursuing inside-out—like the safety and inside linebackers. The inside-out pursuers prevent the cutback. Inside-out pursuers must stay one step behind the ball carrier as they run sideways.

I must add the Farifield Falcons running back was about the best running back I've seen in four years in the California Youth Football League. It would not surprise me to see him playing on national TV in a decade or so. His great ability notwithstanding, I think we could have won the game if the linebacker or cornerback had made a bee line for him at about the time our defensive end was forcing him to change course. We lost 19-7.

A better drill

The lesson I learned is the pursuit angle drill must look like the above diagram. Everybody other than the ends can**not** take a 45-degree angle. Rather everyone must take a **unique** angle designed to deliver him to the ball carrier's probable path at the earliest possible moment. And full speed may be a little too fast. It can cause you to overrun the play allowing the runner to cut back behind everyone.

I suspect the best way to run the drill is to have coaches who are in shape or fast players try to get around the end, cutting back against the grain at times. You should also station players who run reverses to help the ends maintain their anti-reverse discipline. Run the drill as a two-hand touch game with each player stopping at the spot where he touched the ball carrier. Coaches could then check each player's position against the diagram.

We also trained our players to go to the ball when a pass was in the air. When the opposing quarterback cocked his arm to pass, I'd yell, "Pass! Pass!" When it left his hand, I'd yell, "Air! Air!" During the "Pass!" phase, the backs were supposed to get behind and stay with their man—the middlelinebacker was supposed to stay behind **everybody's** man. The linemen and linebackers who did not have a wide receiver to cover, were supposed to rush the passer. The ends were also to rush the passer—only on a square-in route. (If the offense lined up in a **shotgun** formation, we would have the ends blitz straight at the passer and have the tackles get up in a two-point stance and loop out behind and around the ends for containment duty.)

But when I yelled, "Air!", all eleven were to turn and hightail it to the ball.

22

Awards banquet

Whenever amateur speakers take the microphone at organizational dinners, they bore the audience silly with endless thank yous. Heck, even the Academy Awards winners, most of whom are professional performers, bore their worldwide audience with their endless thank yous.

Then there's the "lovely wife" syndrome. At one annual dinner of a civic organization, another husband and I amused ourselves by keeping track of the number of times the phrase "and his lovely wife" was used by the speakers.

Thank but no thanks

All organizations have many members who have contributed to the success of the organization.. The members of all-volunteer organizations, like youth football associations, are even more praiseworthy. But the fact that an organization has many members who are praiseworthy does not make the delivery of that praise any less boring. So if you want your end-of-season banquet to be a success, I strongly urge you to abolish oral thank yous. I suggest **written** thank yous instead—in the team year book or banquet program—or on certificates of appreciation handed out diploma style.

A few words about each player

It is a standard and expected ritual at the end of youth football seasons for the coach to say a few nice words about each player at the year-end banquet. In youth football, that includes the cheerleaders.

It is also standard to say a few nice words about each coach—both football and cheerleader—and the team moms and the president of the league and the equipment manager.

At our 1991 end-of-season banquet, we said a few nice words about 24 players, seven coaches, one equipment manager, four videotapers, a trainer, about a dozen cheerleaders, and several cheerleader coaches. That's around 50 people.

In addition, boys who played both ways were commented upon by both their offensive and defensive coaches.

If you have an hour and a half—and that's about all the audience can take—you can only devote 108 seconds to each person. Applause takes up about ten of those seconds. Actually handing the player his trophy adds another five or ten seconds to the post-remarks celebration. That leaves 108 - 20 = 88 seconds to sum up the player's season. If you read the words off a cue card or TelePrompTer and avoid searching for words or ums and ahs, you can say about 200 words in 88 seconds. An amateur speaker who did not rehearse or create cue cards can probably only get out about 100 words.

If you run a highly disciplined, rehearsed, cue-card-directed program, you can make nice comments about each player. I doubt that most youth football programs will go to that much trouble. If you won't go to that much trouble, I urge you to forget about the nice-remarks-about-each-player routine.

Public speaking

Another thing to keep in mind is that not all coaches are public speakers. For some reason in 1992—probably to prevent us from preparing overly long speeches—our head coach refused to tell us which kids each coach was to talk about until the middle of the awards. You found out you were supposed to tell about little Johnny when the head coach said to the audience, "Now Coach Reed will give Johnny his trophy."

That was not a problem for me. I am a trained and experienced professional speaker. I've spoken to audiences of thousands in convention centers like the New Orleans Superdome and to millions on live TV shows like *Good Morning America* and *Larry King Live*. But it was aparently a shock to one of our rookie assistant coaches who was suddenly asked to present a trophy to one of our weaker players. Between the coach's discomfort with public speaking, the boy's limited playing time, and the coach's relative unfamiliarity with the boy in question, it was a disaster.

Lesson learned: Don't assume anybody is a public speaker. Some people, even otherwise tough football coaches, are terrified of speaking in public. Ask each coach if he would like to be excused from speaking to the awards banquet.

Others are not afraid to speak in public, but they are still terrible speakers—for example, they read every word of their speech. If you really want to make sure the public speaking is good, have each speaker put on a dress rehearsal in front of you. At West Point, they taught us you **NEVER** make a speech without first rehearsing it in front of an audience. I'll bet General Norman Schwarzkopf rehearsed that Desert Storm briefing that was so well received. Schwarzkopf graduated from West Point in 1956 and was a professor there when I was a cadet.

Weaker players

Another lesson learned: The weaker the player was, the more time it takes to come up with remarks that emphasize his strengths. Give the coaches who have to speak about the weakest players lots of warning. It's best to assign such players to the coach they worked most closely with.

Fathers and sons

Don't have the boy's father/coach make the remarks about his son. Fathers tend to shortchange their sons because they dont want to seem immodest. They are also hardest on their own sons and tend to see more to criticize than other coaches would see in the same boy.

What to say

Here's another reason to not have a nice-remarks-about-each-player segment in your season-end program. What are you going to say?

Inevitably, your player profile will follow a normal distribution. That is, you will have 25% excellent players, 50% average players, and 25% below-average players. If you have less than the league minimum number of players on your team, then you were not allowed to cut. That probably means you have several players who never had any success in a game or who had minimal success like an assist on a tackle.

These days, trophies are invariably uniform. Uniforms are uniform (they don't allow helmet stickers showing the number of tackles or whatever). So the nice-remarks-about-each-player is a significant departure from the current don't-acknowledge-any-differences-between-players fashion.

I'm a great believer in keeping and publishing detailed statistics during the season. But at the awards banquet, I tend to agree that uniformity is appropriate. Your audience consists entirely of parents and relatives. They are ultra sensitive to any slight of their son. If he gets fewer nice words, they are hurt. If he is described less glowingly than others, they are disappointed. And they are embarrassed by their son's lack of accomplishments if he is one of the below-average players.

Graduation format

You have to do something to mark the end of the season. A football season is an epic struggle. Attention must be paid to it's end.

But so is graduation from high school or college the end of an epic struggle whose end is invariably marked by ceremony. And I think the academic folks have a better format than the nice-remarks-about-each-player routine you see at sports banquets.

The typical graduation format is a few introductory remarks by an official of the institution, calling out the name of each graduate and giving him a diploma, a commencement speaker who generally gives the graduates advice on how to live the rest of their lives, a valedictorian, and a final-moment ritual like the famous one at the service academies where the superintedent says, "Class dismissed!" and the entire class throws their hats high in the air.

That is a program which generally leaves each and every proud parent and graduate happy. Now, how can that format be modified for a youth football program.

The differences

Here are my suggestions for your awards banquet based in part on the differences between graduation from an educational institution and completion of a youth football team's season.

• **Team result.** Graduation is an individual effort. The result is a diploma. A football season is a team effort and the result is a team record. That record must be acknowledged. I think a **highlight video** of the season is the best way to summarize a season. Indeed, that's how college and pro football teams do it. During the season, the cameraperson ought to make an effert to capture a characteristic portrait of each person associated with the team and to capture a characteristic shot of the various ambient rituals of the season: practice, pregame preparation, pep rally, weigh-in, pre-game announcement, half-time, time outs, and post-game "nice-game" receiving lines.

To show the highlight video to an audience of 100, you'll probably need to hold the affair in a place which already has an elevated big-screen TV—like a pizza restaurant—or make arrangements to get an elevated big screen TV or projection TV and screen in your not-so-equipped meeting room. If you are bringing equipment to a non-equipped meeting room, you'd better check it out there in advance of the actual banquet to avoid unforeseen glitches.

- **Remarks by coach**. I believe having the head coach and/or offensive and defensive and special-teams coordinators say a few general remarks about the program, the season, and the next season is appropriate. A five-minute limit per coach is probably best.

- **Remarks by league president.** You can't stop them—especially from the lowly position of defensive coach—so plan on this and try to limit it to five minutes as well. The speakers should coordinate their remarks so as not to duplicate or steal thunder from subsequent speakers. I suggest the following division of topics:

League president:	Purpose and history of the local association
	Introduction of next speaker
Offensive coach:	Summary of offensive results
	Introduction of next speaker:
Defensive coach:	Summary of defensive results
	Introduction of next speaker
Special-teams coach	Summary of special-teams results
	Introduction of next speaker
Head coach:	Summary of season
	Preparation for next season

- **Awarding of trophies and gifts**. Each player will get a trophy and each coach generally gets a plaque or other token of appreciation. That ought to be done the way diplomas are handed out. The players and coaches line up, the person's name is announced, they stride toward the official who is handing out the trophies, receive their trophy, and depart along a receiving line of coaches and other officials. Applause takes place between the annoncement of each name. No nice-remarks-about-each-person are made by anyone at any time.

- **Commencement speaker**. Not appropriate. The players will be back together in eight months. Even when they leave the program at age fourteen, they reunite on the high-school team eight months later, if not in a winter football weight program. It's not such a momentous occasion to require or warrant a commencement speaker.

- **Valedictory speech**. Also not appropriate. In educational institutions, the educators who choose the valedictorian have observed that person in an academic setting which is similar to making a valedictory speech. Football coaches have not. The most valuable player, for example, may be petrified of speaking to 100 people. Besides, even college valedictorians are boring. That's a tradition which no one but the valedictorians and their parents would miss.

- **Final moment ritual**. Most teams have favorite cheers. Some may have a song. We San Ramon Bears adopted the University of California (Berkeley) Bears fight song. We clapped exuberantly to the tune and shouted, "Go Bears!" on certain note pairs. I suggest you **end** your banquet and your season with a rousing rendition of your favorite cheers or team song. It should be led by your best cheerleader—which may be a cheerleader *per se* or a coach or player.

   I was a delegate to Boys State in my youth. I've always been impressed by a next-to-last-moment-ritual we did there as part of our graduation program. Picture it, Rutgers University, 1963. A thousand boys are assembled on the ground floor of an auditorium in Boys State uniform (T-shirt and khaki pants). In the balcony are the parents. At the end of the program, we serenaded the parents with several songs the counselors had taught us: *God Bless America, This is My Country*, etc. The sound of 1,000 boys singing patriotic songs is pretty powerful stuff. But I thought one of the songs was out of place—until we performed it for the parents. It turned out to be our show stopper. We sang *"I want a girl just like the girl that married dear old dad."* In keeping with current football tradition, you could top it off with a rousing, "Hi, mom!"

Your team may not have any good singers. But I guarantee that if you have your team perform a football song (fight song or "You've got to be a football hero") and "I want a girl…," no parent will ask for a refund.

- **Program**. Put your thanks here. The league president can call the audience's attention to the thanks section of the program at the beginning of his or her remarks. People will look themselves up and be satisfied. Colossal boredom will be avoided. Do your best to acknowledge everyone who put forth an extraordinary effort. In our association, that would include acting as a volunteer mandatory play monitor, chain gang, videotaper, sign-painting party host, announcer, team mom, or clock operator. Service as a ticket seller or snack bar worker was required of everyone. Such universal service should not be acknowledged except as part of general thanks for parent support.

   The program should also contain a schedule of the night's events so the parents can see that the end is in sight.

- **Noteworthy player contributions**. I believe in giving credit where credit is due— namely MVP recognition and such. But I seem to be out of step with the times on that subject. Suggesting any player is better than another now seems to be considered a form of child abuse. That being the case, don't mention anything about a player except his name and possibly number during the banquet. Even mentioning positions played can be non-egalitarian because the weaker players will have fewer positions.

- **Music**. Other than the team chorus described above, you ought to have a little musical football ambience. You can buy cassettes of college football fight songs in music stores. Get a couple and play them as background music during pre-speech and post-speech portions of your banquet.

You probably ran a good football program. But you can undo a lot of the good you did during the season if your banquet is not up to the same standard. It will **not** be up to the same standard if you allow it to degenerate into everybody thanking everybody and coaches struggling to make even-handed speeches about stars and players who never made any tackles but are really nice boys to work with.

23

Parents meeting

You should have a pre-soason parents meeting. I coached one football team and one baseball team where I was unable to hold such a meeting and it caused trouble in each case.

Here's a suggested list of things you may want to cover in your parents meeting. You and your league will almost certainly have your own additional items.

- Purpose of the league
- Practice schedule including:
    - time
    - dates
    - days of the week
- Practice location
- Practice uniform (Pre-pads and regular)
- Legal football shoes
- Legal face masks
- Jock requirement
- Optional protective gear
    - forearm pads
    - down linemen gloves
    - neck rolls
    - rib pads
    - protective chin strap
    - teeth protector with lip shield
- Sporting goods stores which sell football accessories
- Game schedule including:
    - time
    - dates

- days of the week
- Game locations
- Game uniforms
- When and where equipment will be handed out
- How playing time is allocated
- How positions are assigned
- Need to recruit more players
- Age and weight rules
- Weight watchers
- Introduction of coaches including their relevant background
- Differences between youth and higher level football
  - special rules
  - less complexity
- Need for support staff including:
  - videotaper
  - scouts
  - weighmaster
  - chain gang
  - down marker holder
  - team mother
  - sponsors
  - two mandatory play monitors
  - snack bar workers
  - ticket window workers
  - scoreboard operator
  - public address announcer
  - newspaper liaison
- Officiating
- Scholar-athlete awards and scholarships
- Pep rallies and sign painting parties
- Fund-raising activities
- Homecoming
- Awards banquet
- Rules for parents observing practice
- Offensive system, if known
- Defensive system, if known
- Need to memorize defensive job description
- Need to study scouting reports
- Roster corrections (Hand out rosters and ask for corrections)
- Describe team newsletter
- Picture day
- Birth certificates and payments
- Parent behavior during games including where permitted
- Team logo clothing and other items which can be purchased
- Mouthpiece fitting and replacement
- League organization and playoff schedule
- Post-game pizza parties
- Yearbook
- Policy on lates, absences from practices or games
- Recommended videotape: ESPN's *Teaching Kids Football*
- Recommended book: Joe Namath's *Football for Young Players and Parents*
- **Not** recommended: NFL Films videotapes. They are full of lousy technique and unsportsmanlike conduct.
- Team play

- Unofficial coaching by player relatives
- Question period

Team play

Parents need to help stamp out children's normal tendencies to put down weaker players and to act on their dislike for some of their teammates. Team play requires that weaker players be helped and that dislikes be suppressed. The rule is, "Thou shalt not speak ill of a teammate." And this is not some boilerplate loyalty oath to niceness. It is a policy that you not only have to explain but also **enforce** for the good of the team.

Unofficial coaching by player relatives

Unofficial coaching by player relatives is **dangerous** at worst and disruptive at best. You must tell fathers, grandfathers, etc., that the official coaches are in charge of both the techniques used and the defensive system. If a father has a suggestion, he must clear it with the coach before urging his son to follow it.

Here are some specific reasons why. As I said earlier, I generally did not allow stunts by the defense. I can imagine some father looking at our defensive papers that we sent home with the players and thinking, "This is too unimaginative." Whereupon, he tells his boy how to loop or do some other stunt. "It'll help you get through the line untouched. Try it. You'll see."

If a boy did that on my team, I'd ask him, "What the heck was that?" If he told me his dad suggested it, I'd talk to him and his dad and tell them I need to know who's going to be where and doing what on every play. I cannot have players doing their own thing and thereby leaving a hole uncovered or getting on the way of another player.

If, on the other hand, the boy just shrugged his shoulders, as they often do, I'd tell him not to ever do that again. If he **did** do it again, I'd probably replace him with the next player down the depth chart.

Getting diametrically **conflicting** advice from two different adults can demoralize a boy. And, like an orchestra with two conductors conducting different songs, a football team whose players are disregarding their coach's instructions and following their father's or other relative's will play terribly.

I would tell parents that I am not necessarily more knowledgeable about football coaching than they are—but that I am in charge and we can't have more than one person in charge. I would tell them I welcomed constructive criticism and suggestions—but that it could hurt the team and hurt their son if they did not clear any unofficial coaching they did with me in advance.

Parents who coach their son tend to make **rookie coach mistakes**—like being too complex or thinking youth football is like pro football. One of our parents told his son to try to steal the ball from an opponent in 1991. The player tried to do that the next game and the ball carrier he could have tackled ran for a 40-yard touchdown. Fortunately, the refs called it back on a tripping penalty.

Parents also often do not know the **rules** that are unique to youth football—like no blocking below the waist outside the free-blocking zone. Parents also often base their coaching on vague memories of their own football careers and on out-of-date information they got back then. For example, coaches used to tell players to drive their helmet into the ball carrier. That is now strictly forbidden because it risks injury to all concerned—most especially it risks breaking the neck of the player who does it.

Some parents believe it is smart to teach their sons how to **cheat** (holding usually) and not get caught. That's unethical. It also rarely works. I had a player once who had been taught to cheat by coaches in another area. He led the team in penalties for a stretch.

Other fathers may feel their son should be taught to play **dirty** and teach them to pinch or punch opponents when they think no one can see. Tri-Cities players pinched our running backs at the bottom of piles in the 1990 season. Some fathers teach their son to try to intimidate opponents NFL style with verbal taunts, threats, and abusive language.

In short, youth football is much more tightly regulated than the football most fathers are used to. As a result, they may inadvertently teach their son something that will hurt the son or his team or both.

Hand out

You should present your parents meeting information both verbally and in writing in the form of a handout. Parents rarely take extensive notes. They may miss something. Some parents will not attend the meeting.

24

Other defenses

In this book, I advocate the 8-2-1- and 10-1 defenses. But you may not be able to use one of those two for some reason. Maybe your head coach is chicken. Maybe you have to use your local high school's defense. Or maybe you aren't convinced that the 8-2-1 or 10-1 are the best. So let's discuss the other defenses and considerations on which defense you might to use and how to teach and staff it.

Strength against strength

Remember that the basic principle of defense is **strength against strength**. That means you must design your defense primarily to stop your **toughest opponent's best play**. If there is no dominant opponent, you need to design your defense to stop the play that is most successful for teams **in general** in your league. In my experience, and in the experience of many youth coaches who have called me from around the country, the most difficult play to stop is the **sweep**.

The sweep

If you have two very fast, sure tacklers, it probably does not matter what defensive alignment you use. They can simply run from wherever they line up to the ball carrier and tackle him before he gains any yards. I know because that's what our fast opponents did to our ball carriers when **we** tried to sweep.

If you are like most teams, you don't have the talent to line up anywhere and still stop the sweep. In that case, you have to preposition a player in or near the sweep path. In general, that means you have to put a player outside the offense's tight end either on the line of scrimmage or close behind it. This diagram shows what I mean.

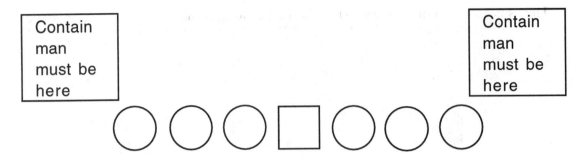

You must have a contain man on each side of the offensive formation. He can be a lineman or a linebacker. In general, he should probably be in a two-point stance so he can see what's going on better and so he has maximum maneuverability.

Wide offensive players and stopping the sweep

What if the offense places one or more players out wide? If your contain man is flanked, that is, there is an opposing player to his outside, he probably will not be able to stop the sweep. The wide offensive player has an ideal blocking angle and will be able to block the contain man in, which is fatal to your sweep defense. The general solution is to have the man who has pass responsibility for the wide player to **take over contain responsibility** when he sees the wide man block down on the normal contain man. Here's a diagram.

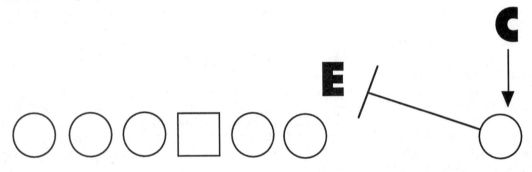

In this sweep to the right, the split end is blocking down on the defensive end (E). So the cornerback (C) comes up to take over the end's contain responsibility. You have to practice this to make sure the cornerback does, in fact, take over containment.

You must also have your scout team run plays in which the split end **fakes** a block on the defensive end, then goes out on a pass. Someone must cover a block-faking wide offensive player when he goes out for a pass. There is no set rule.

The cornerback could yell "Switch," in which case the defensive end would take over covering the split end on a pass and the cornerback would take over containment. Or, if you had a deep pass coverage man, like a safety, behind the cornerback, he could take over the pass coverage of the wide offensive player.

The basic principle is that somebody who is not being blocked from the outside must take care of containment and somebody who is not worrying about containment must cover the wide player if he goes out for a pass.

The blast play

The second-most dangerous offensive play in youth football, in my experience, is the blast or isolation play. That is a play in which the ball carrier dives through the A (center-guard) or B (guard-tackle) gap with one or two blockers leading the way.

This is not a problem for the 8-2-1 or the 10-1 as long as the defensive players lined up in the A and B gaps **stay low**. But it is very difficult for a more common defense, like a 5-3 or a 4-4 to stop the blast.

Unlike the 8-2-1 or 10-1, the defenses with three, four, five, or six linemen have what are called "bubbles." Bubbles are empty spaces in the defensive line. Here's a diagram.

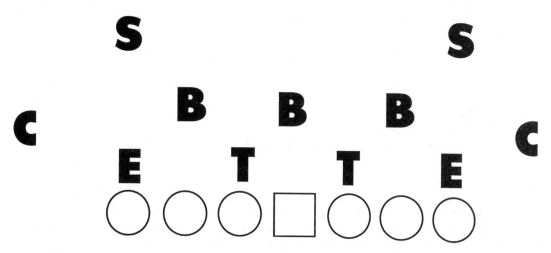

In the above diagram, you see a 4-3 defense. It has three bubbles: one in front of the center and one in front of each tackle. In a well-designed defense, all bubbles are the responsibility of a linebacker. But he is usually **several yards back**. And he typically has **other responsibilities**, like covering the hook zones if the play is a pass.

Linebacker keys

Linebackers have **keys**. That is, one to three offensive players that they must concentrate their eyes on. When the ball is snapped and those keys start moving, the linebacker must react. He cannot react too rapidly to some movements, because they are fakes. But he must react instantly to a blast play by attacking the lead blocker head on. That makes for a fierce collision. It takes a special player to play that position and execute his many varied responsibilities well. Many teams have no such player at all.

In my experience, linebackers must be **veterans**. I have never seen a rookie succeed at linebacker. The need for extremely well-suited, strong players to play linebacker is one of the reasons I use defenses that do **not** require linebackers.

Off-tackle play

In high school, the off-tackle play is the most dangerous one. But the off-tackle play is no slouch in youth football. Especially when run as a power play, that is, with one or more lead blockers.

The **good** news is that the off-tackle play takes a little while to develop. Blasts and quarterback sneaks hit fast so your best chance of stopping them is to have a player in the A and B gaps. With the off-tackle play, if you have a bubble at the off-tackle hole, you can probably get a linebacker to fill it as he sees the off-tackle play develop. In other words, if you insist on having less than eight men on the line, which, in turn, creates bubbles, the best place to have bubbles may be at the C (tackle-end) gaps.

Dual responsibility

Another ramification of having less than eight men on the defensive line is that your **contain** man has to take on **dual responsibility**. He has to cover both the off-tackle play **and** the sweep. You may have one of your down linemen in the C gap, which is the off-tackle gap. But that man will be flanked by the offensive end. Just as I described above, when a man is flanked, he needs help if the offensive player blocks down on him.

In this case, the offensive end blocking down on a defender in the C gap is usually a **double-team** block involving the offensive end and offensive tackle. Double-team blocks are generally highly effective. Two against one—what would you expect? The only way the defender can even hold his position is to drop to the ground. He will almost never make the tackle on a ball carrier coming through his hole if he is double-teamed. That's why the defensive end (sometimes called an outside linebacker) must help out on stopping the off-tackle play. Here's a diagram showing the off-tackle play using a double-team block against the defensive tackle with the defensive end helping.

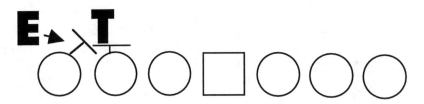

Such dual responsibility makes the defensive end's job much harder. Whenever a defender has a dual responsibility, the smart offensive coordinator will use **play pairs** that start to attack one of his areas of responsibility, then abruptly attack the other. For example, it is common to design the off-tackle play so the ball carrier starts out as if he were running a sweep. If the defensive contain man falls for that, he tends to step outward. The ball carrier then cuts up through the off-tackle hole and whoever is assigned to block the defensive end out has his job made easier because of the defensive end's initial outward movement.

The solution is that the defensive end must be trained to **key on the helmet** of the offensive end. He must react a different way for each helmet movement. He must be drilled until his reaction becomes instinctive. He has no time to rely on anything **but** instinct.

Fewer than eight men on the line

These are all ramifications of using the popular defenses which have fewer than eight men on the line. The **offense**, by rule, **must** have **seven** men on the line. When you have seven men on the line, you create **eight gaps**. If you use a fewer-than-eight-men defensive line, you create bubbles in the line and you require at least four of your defenders to discharge dual responsibilities. Linebackers have to "commute" to their gap responsibilities, as well as to their pass zone responsibilities.

Various defenses

Here are various defenses aligned against a double-tight-end offense. I list my source on each so you can research it further if you wish.

```
                    S
      C                        C
        B        B        B
        E   T    G   T    E
        O   O   O   ⊠   O   O   O
```

5-3 In
Directory of Football Defenses

```
            S           S
      C            B    B            C
        E   T      G    T   E
        ◑   O   O   ⊠   O   O   ◑
```

5-4 Oklahoma
Directory of Football Defenses

```
      C          S
            B            B          C
        E   T    G        G   T   E
        O   O   O   ⊠   O   O   O
```

Wide-Tackle 6
Directory of Football Defenses

```
      C              S
                  B   B
        E   T   G          G   T   E
        ◑   O   ◑   ⊠   ◑   O   ◑
```

Split 6
Directory of Football Defenses

```
             S
      C                        C

      E  B  T  G     G  T  B  E
        O  O  O  ⊠  O  O  O
```

Gap 8
Directory of Football Defenses

```
                  S
      C                        C
        B     B     B     B
        E        T     T        E
        O   O   O   ⊠   O   O   O
```

4 - 4
Football: The Violent Chess Match

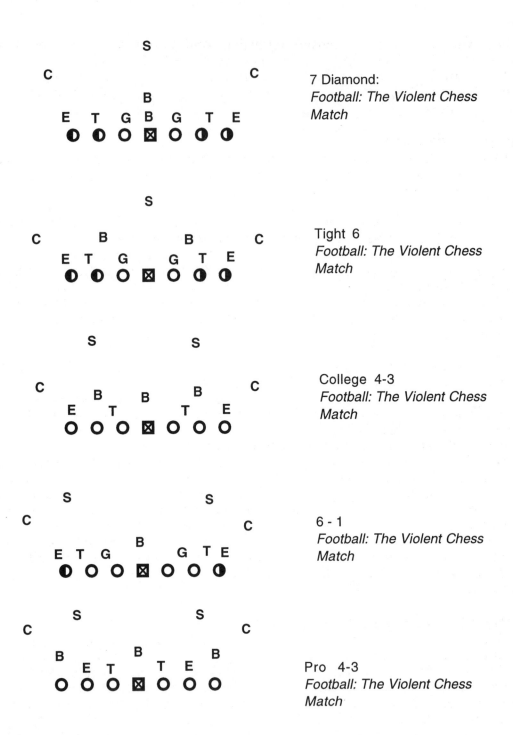

7 Diamond:
Football: The Violent Chess Match

Tight 6
Football: The Violent Chess Match

College 4-3
Football: The Violent Chess Match

6 - 1
Football: The Violent Chess Match

Pro 4-3
Football: The Violent Chess Match

That may not be every defense known to man. But it's most of them. You can be a lot more creative on offense than on defense, where you have to react to the offense's formation, motion, and flow.

Alignment varies according to offensive formation

Note that I have diagrammed these defenses against a double-tight-end offense with no wide receivers. Whichever defense you pick, you must tell your players where they line up against **every** conceivable offensive formation. And players whose job descriptions change if the offense lines up certain ways must memorize those changes.

You must also teach **who** adjusts to **motion**, if any, and **how** they adjust. My defenses always used **man** pass coverage so the adjustment to motion was simple: if your man goes in motion, go with him.

Large-split rule

Defensive players who are supposed to line up in the **gap** between offensive linemen need no large split rule. But any player who lines up **on** an offensive player **does** need a large split rule. The rule I used at the high school levels was,

> *If the guy you are supposed to line up on is split more than three feet from his inside neighbor, forget lining up on him and line up **in** that wide gap.*

My youth defensive ends were told to line up one yard outside the offensive end. But if the end lined up especially far from the tackle, the defensive end was to make a judgment call. He was to keep moving out until the offensive end was so far out that the defensive end was sure he could get to the sweep spot, untouched, from an **inside** alignment. As a practical matter, that meant

> *If the end splits out more than two yards, line up in the gap between the split end and the offensive tackle.*

If you do **not** use a gap defense, you must have a large split rule for your defensive linemen and practice it. At the lowest levels, that is up to about 12 years old, I would consider a split larger than eight inches to be extraordinarily large.

What happens if you do not have a large split rule? The varsity coach where I coach high school football told me he once faced an opponent who apparently had no large split rules. Every time he sent a play in, he told the offensive linemen to line up a foot wider than the previous play. They got to eight-foot splits and the defense still kept moving out with them. They never lined up in those huge gaps. Dumb players. Dumb coaches.

Players who are supposed to line up in the gap anyway don't need large split rules. But any player who is to line up on or near an offensive lineman must be taught **and tested** on a large split rule to prevent him from being taken out of the play merely by the offensive alignment.

Gap defense against the rules

One coach who read the first edition of this book called and told me lining up in the gap was **illegal** in his league. I'll bet I know exactly why. Some coach in years past used a gap defense and tore up the league. The losing coaches, in a fit of sour grapes, claimed that children have an innate inability to stop gap charges and they outlawed the gap defenses. I have seen that outlaw-the-successful-coach's-tactic response many times in baseball. The coaches who do that are contemptible.

But if I were in the league that outlawed lining up in the gap, I would tell my offensive linemen to take eight-foot splits. Then I'd put my offensive backs around the quarterback and have them charge *en masse* through one of the A gaps. The defensive linemen, who would be forced to go way out and line up with my eight-foot-split linemen, would thereby take themselves out of the play. They would not have to be blocked.

Not lining up in the gaps when the offensive line takes extraordinarily large splits is nothing less than unsound defense. A rule that prohibits gap defenses is a rule that requires unsound play if the offense splits wide.

Blitzing

There is nothing more macho in football than blitzing. It's a way for coaches to prove their manhood. I wish I had a nickel for every youth defensive coordinator who told me he blitzes a lot.

I blitzed a lot when I coached defense in high school. One reason was the head coach would not let me use my 8- or 10-man fronts. Blitzing was the closest I could come.

But in **youth** football, blitzing is generally a waste of time. The reason is the line splits are too narrow. In 1993, when I coached offense. We used zero line splits. One upcoming opponent blitzed a lot. So I had a scout team player imitate him. He disappeared into the mass of players at the line of scrimmage on every play he blitzed. In the game, the same thing happened. The guy just took himself out of the play when he blitzed.

The idea behind blitzing is that it complicates the blocking assignments of the offensive players. That, in turn, means one or more offensive players is likely to block the wrong guy, thereby allowing one or more defenders to get to the ball carrier scot free.

Blitzing the run

If you blitz when the offense is doing a **running** play, you are likely to blitz yourself out of the play. The purpose of blitzing is to sack a quarterback who is dropping back to **pass**. A running back, on the other hand, is most likely crossing the line of scrimmage going the other way when the blitzer arrives in the offensive backfield.

Since the blitz is primarily an anti-pass tactic, and there are few passes in youth football, blitzing is usually a bad idea in youth football. That's especially true where the line splits are so narrow that a blitzer cannot get through even when the play **is** a pass.

Passing situations

Although there is relatively little passing in youth football, a passing situation is a passing situation, even there. So if there is a wide enough lane to blitz through, it may make sense to blitz when you are pretty sure the offense plans to throw a pass.

The general principle of blitzing the passer is that **if he's good**, you gamble and **blitz**. If he is **not a very good passer**, the blitz gamble is **not worth it**. So the indicators for a blitz are

- it is a passing situation
- the passing game of the opponent is good
- there are wide enough gaps to blitz through

If you do not have all three of those factors present, blitzing does not make sense.

As I have said elsewhere in this book, I only blitzed when I knew that the ball carrier was **going to a particular spot outside the tackles**. One year, every time Elk Grove lined up in a slot formation, it meant that they were going to sprint out to a spot just behind where the slot lined up and throw a pass. I told my middle linebacker to line up in front of the slotback and blitz to that spot on those plays. We practiced it and I yelled "Slot!" during the game. He lined up correctly but inexplicably failed to blitz. But I am darned sure it would have worked if he had blitzed.

It's hard to blitz a passer who is between his tackles when there are narrow splits because you cannot get through the offensive line and a guy coming around the end has farther to go.

Cover one

At Miramonte High School, when I was J.V. defensive coordinator in 1994, a blitz automatically meant cover one. That is, if any member of the linebacking corps was departing to go on a blitz, the pass defense had to switch to cover one, which meant one free safety who covered the entire field and all other defensive backs and linebackers in **man** coverage.

If you use **zone** pass coverage, a blitz generally forces you into man coverage for that play at least. The reason is that you do not have enough guys left to cover all the zones.

Zone blitz

In 1995 in the NFL, you may have seen the **zone blitz**. That's a new wrinkle, at least to me. What they mean by zone blitz is that although blitzing usually requires man pass coverage, in a zone blitz they are able to stay in zone pass coverage. They do that by having a **defensive lineman drop back into pass coverage**. Essentially, the blitzing linebacker and the dropping lineman trade jobs. This had an element of surprise—especially in 1995 because I do not recall it being used in previous years. But it also represents a new gamble. It could result in some guy like William "The Refrigerator" Perry trying to cover Jerry Rice.

The zone blitz actually makes more sense at the youth level if you have weight limits. (A coach that called me recently said his youth football program has no weight limits.)

The main thing you must remember is that blitzing is generally **not** consistent with **zone** pass coverage. So if you call a blitz, you probably have to switch to man pass coverage for that play.

Red dog

Suppose you're already in man coverage? Does that mean a blitz does not change your pass coverage? No. You probably still have to change your coverage, although much less. Man coverage means each eligible receiver is assigned to a linebacker or a defensive back. When you blitz a linebacker, he can no longer cover his man. Somebody else has to.

At Miramonte, whenever an inside linebacker blitzed and we were already in man coverage, the outside linebacker (defensive end) on that side had to take over the man coverage responsibilities of the inside linebacker in question.

As a general rule, the inside linebacker has man coverage of the first back out of the backfield on his side. So when the outside linebacker took over those responsibilities, he would recognize that the play was a pass and begin his contain rush of the passer. Frequently, the running back would be his blocker. But if the running back swung out on a pass route, the defensive end would break off his pass rush and go with the running back. Our J.V. head coach called this "red dogging." I have not seen that terminology used in that way elsewhere.

This shows one of the dangers of blitzing. When the outside linebacker goes with the running back, there is no longer a contain rusher on that side. The quarterback could scramble out that way for a big gain. Furthermore, the outside linebacker is probably not accustomed to covering receivers. Finally, it is very difficult for a pass rusher to suddenly change gears and directions when a running back, whom he is trying to get past, swings out.

Confuse the offense

It is standard in the college and pro ranks to disguise your pass coverage and what defense you are in. This is done by last-second shifts on the part of defenders, Linemen stem (jump sideways to a new alignment). Linebackers act like they're not blitzing then blitz, or vice versa. Defensive backs may line up in cover two (two safeties each covering half the field) then suddenly switch to cover three or cover one.

The purpose of all this is to mislead the quarterback when he makes his pre-snap read of the defense. As a general rule, I doubt that youth quarterbacks make a pre-snap read. I further doubt that many of them can read defenses. And finally, even if a youth quarterback was trying to make a pre-snap read and could call an appropriate audible, I doubt he and his teammates could execute the new play well enough to be a threat.

So I recommend that you not try to confuse the offense in that manner. You are just as likely to confuse your own players if you try. And it is crucial that your own players not be confused. Keep It Simple Stupid.

Delayed blitz

The blitz that I used most successfully in high school was called Okie Lightning. Here's a diagram.

I think the reason this worked so well is that the right offensive guard made his own pre-snap read and decided he was going to block the nose guard or the left inside linebacker. On the snap, he pursued one of those two. Meantime, the right inside linebacker looped around through the offense's right A gap. This is a delayed blitz in that the blitzer's path is not evident before or even immediately after the snap.

This could work even when the offense has zero line splits. That's because once the play gets underway, offensive linemen generally move around. They go off to block someone thereby leaving a hole. If the blitzer does not reveal himself before or immediately after the snap, he may be able to sprint through that hole.

Linebacker play

In my 8-2-1 and 10-1, I had one linebacker. My instructions to him were, "Do whatever you want." My middle linebacker was generally my best defensive player. His instincts were great. He was a veteran. I gave him no training other than tackling technique. Furthermore, all gaps were filled with linemen so he had no gap responsibility. He was essentially a **spare** whose job was to back up his teammates.

But that's only true of the 8-2-1 and 10-1. When you start running a 4-, 5-, or 6-man front—the most common defenses in youth football—you force yourself to teach traditional linebacker play. That is very complicated and schizophrenic.

Mirroring

One technique is mirroring. The linebacker lines up facing an uncovered lineman. An uncovered offensive lineman is one who does not have a defensive lineman in front of him. The linebacker focuses his eyes on that lineman and mirrors his movements.

If the lineman attacks **straight at** the linebacker, the linebacker must attack straight at the lineman. When the offensive lineman attacks the backer, the play is generally a dive. The backer needs to attack the dive to stop it.

If the uncovered lineman pulls in an **outward** direction, the inside linebacker move sideways mirroring the pull. That will lead him to the play which is off-tackle or a sweep.

If the uncovered lineman stands up and **drops back** into a pass-blocking stance, the inside linebacker drops back into his hook zone pass coverage.

There is one **exception** to the mirror rule. If the uncovered lineman pulls in an **inward** direction, the linebacker must **stay** where he is. That's because an inward pull often signals a **counter** play. That is a play where the flow goes one way initially then a running back cuts back diagonally the other way. A typical play looks like this.

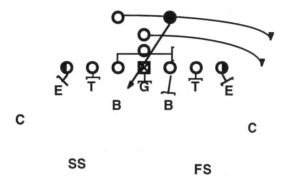

As you can see, if the left inside linebacker mirrored the inside pull of the uncovered guard in front of him, he would take himself **out of** the path of the counter play. The way we taught this was to tell the linebackers that if they see the offensive backfield flow to the side **away** from them, they should stay put and switch their focus from the **near back** (the one lined up on their side before the snap) to the **far back** (the one lined up on the other side before the snap).

Drill, drill, drill

To get your inside linebackers to do this, you must drill them over and over against a skeleton offense. They need an uncovered lineman to mirror as well as a couple of backs. The skeleton offense must run all the various run and pass plays so the linebacker can practice his reactions. The most common mistake linebackers make is reacting too quickly. That causes them to take false steps in response to fakes, which, in turn, cause them to take themselves out of position to make the tackle.

This is extremely complex. It is so complex that I do not even attempt to teach it to youth players. But most youth defensive coordinators **are** running a defense with a 4-, 5- or 6-man front defense, which, in turn, requires that they teach all this stuff—or some other system of keys. Of course, you also have to teach the linebacker whatever blitzes you want him to run. And you have to teach him how to do both man and zone pass coverage.

Books

In my other football book, *Coaching Youth Football*, I strongly urged readers to get a book on their favorite offense. That way, they would get a proven, tested playbook with much detail on the kind of kids needed for each position, the drills to do, and the play diagrams. To a large extent, you can do the same with defense—and you should.

Here are all the books I've read on defense:

Football's Super Split by Bill Siler	Split-4 defense
Football Winning Defense by Bud Wilkinson	General discussion
Football: The Violent Chess Match by Flores & O'Connor	General discussion
Coaching Football Successfully by Bob Reade	5-2 Rover defense
Coaching Team Defense by Fritz Shurmur	General discussion
Football's Modular Defense by John Durham	Variation of split-6
Coaching Football by Flores & O'Connor	General discussion
Directory of Football Defenses by Drew Tallman	Various
Missouri Power Football by Devine & Onofrio	Wide-Tackle 6
Ara Parseghian and Notre Dame Football	Split-6
Multiple Monster Football by Warren Washburn	6-2
Modern Football by Fritz Crisler	Wide-Tackle 6

Vince Lombardi on Football by Vince Lombardi	4-3
Coaching Football's Split 4-4 Multiple Defense Pete Dyer	Split 4-4
Building a Championship Football Team by Bear Bryant	Multiple
Hot Line to Victory by Woody Hayes	5-2
Functional Football by John DaGrosa	Various old-time
Championship Football by D.X. Bible	Various old-time
The Slanting Monster Defense by Dale Foster	Wide-tackle 6
Football's Fabulous Forty Defense by Jack Olcott	4-3
The Modern Short Punt by Lou Howard	Wide-tackle 6
Simplified Single Wing Football by Ken Keuffel	5-4 Oklahoma
Option Football by Scarborough & Warren	5-4 Oklahoma
Secrets of the Split-T by Don Faurot	Various old-time
Complete Handbook of Winning Football Drills Don Fuoss	Drills
Principles of Coaching Football by Mike Bobo	Various
Fundamentals of Coaching Football by George Kraft	Various
Game Plan to Winning Football by Gordon Wood	4-3, 65 Tandem
AFCA Guide Book to Championship Football Drills by Jerry R. Tolley	Drills
Football Drill Book by Doug Mallory	Drills

Here are some more which I have not yet read:

Football's 4-4 Stack Defense by Tom Simonton	4-4
Defensive Secondary	
Coaching the Defensive Backfield by Greg McMackin	
Defensing the Delaware Wing-T by Bob Kenig	3-4 slant
The Eagle Five-Linebacker Defense by Fritz Shurmur	Eagle 5
The 5-2 Defense by J. Campbell (also books on each position)	5-2
Pressure Defense Made Easier by Scott Pelleur	4-4, 4-3
Complete Book of Linebacker Play by J. Giampalmi	
Pro 3-4 by M. McDaniels	Pro 3-4
Coaching the Defensive Secondary by M. Schuster	

I strongly urge you to refrain from inventing your own defense. The vast majority of youth coaches simply do not understand the principles of football and defense well enough to create their own schemes. I have made an enormous effort to study football over a number of years and I still do not trust myself to create a defense or an offense. Rather I find a proven system that makes sense to me and adopt it. That gives me an integrated, comprehensive guidebook which is based on years of someone else's experience.

Videos

There are also many video tapes available to train defensive players and coaches. I have generally been disappointed with football coaching videos. Most are poorly organized and very amateurish. But they are probably also worth their price, albeit barely. Several companies offer many videos on various defensive positions and situations as well as on team defense.

The publishers of these books and videos are listed in the back of the book.

Order of selection

In my offense book, I made a big deal about the order of selection. That is, which position do you choose a player for first, which second, and so forth. I pointed to A. Allen

Black's book *Modern Belly T Football* as the best example of a thoughtful discussion of the subject.

In other books, I have seen it said that you should pick your quarterback first, then your defense, then the rest of your offense. That assumes that no one is going both ways. At the youth level, with its unsophisticated passing game, I wouldn't even pick the quarterback first. Heck, in my only year as offensive coordinator, I did not **have** a quarterback. We snapped the ball to a tailback.

Best eleven on the field

I oppose platooning, that is specializing players as to offense or defense. Platooning is the rule at the pro and college levels. Also, many high schools platoon.

I think you will have your best success when you strive to have the best eleven players on the field at all times. That will lead to some natural platooning. There are some kids who will be among the best eleven defensive players, but not the best eleven offensive players, and vice versa.

There is also the fatigue factor. Your best player will not remain your best player during the game. At some point, he will get tired and a fresh second-stringer will be able to outplay him because he is fresh. You need to monitor each player's fatigue level and substitute accordingly.

Defense first

Having said all that, I will now discuss platooning because you may have it crammed down your throat by your head coach or by your league rules. I gave this some thought lately because I heard one of our local football leagues had 22 players on a team and insisted that each player play the whole game on one platoon or the other. Players may only go both ways when a player is hurt or absent.

Defense is **reaction** football. Offense is **assignment** football. Reaction is harder than assignment. So you need the best players on defense if you have to put them on one unit or the other. NFL coaches and players says you can tell whether a player is on defense or offense by the neatness of his locker. Offensive players are neat; defense, slobs.

In assigning your players to platoons, you should put the athletic, messy room types on the defense and the rest on offense. Actually, I would run a lot of scrimmages in practice and see who played defense the best rather than relying on the condition of their rooms. But you need your best on defense.

With the offense, the coordinator can be creative and finesse a lot of weaknesses. But the defensive coordinator has little ability to be creative. His alignment is largely dictated by the offensive alignment. And his players' post-snap movements are also dictated by the offensive play.

Here's what Hall of Fame Coach Bud Wilkinson of Oklahoma had to say on the subject in his book, *Football Winning Defense*.

> *Each of the three phases of football requires athletic ability, but most coaches agree that playing effective defense takes far more physical and mental ability than the other two phases. Primarily, this is because playing defense calls for immediate response to an unknown situation.*
>
> *Given average ability, a boy can be taught, through proper practice and repetitive drills, to be an effective offensive player. Because of the difficult physical and mental reactions that are necessary to play defense, however, it is very difficult for a boy who does not possess outstanding athletic ability to become an effective defensive player.*

Here are the comments of Gordon Wood, the winningest football coach in Texas High School history.

Every coach should realize that any competent athlete can, through practice become a good offensive football player. It takes a great athlete and a real man to play defense.

Here's Penn State head coach Joe Paterno:

...the first source of football success is defense, the second is kicking, the third is offense. The strongest team is the strongest defensive team.

Northwestern and Notre Dame head coach Ara Parseghian:

...we believe that our defensive unit should be given first choice of the personnel to make sure we will have the fastest defensive team.

NFL legend Vince Lombardi:

...it is defense more than anything else that wins championships.

Ohio State great Woody Hayes:

The first selection on the football team is the quarterback, the second and third are the two linebackers. Interior defensive linemen usually are selected ahead of interior offensive linemen.

The advice I'm giving, give the defensive coordinator first dibs if you are playing two platoon football, is really head coach advice. If you are a mere defensive coordinator, you have to try to persuade the head coach to let you have the best players. Unfortunately, the typical head coach also takes the offensive coordinator's job.

Offensive coordinators are usually more interested in their unit's success than they are in the **team's** success. They will fight fiercely to keep you from getting their favorite players. I never won a single one of those fights. Good luck to you if you are in one.

'Iron men' are best

As stated above, the correct approach is to put the best eleven on the field. In 1993, the high school team where I coached got knocked out of the playoffs by Foothill High School, which went on to win the North Coast Section Championship—the highest we can go on the field. Foothill's star scat back, Fontaine, played both ways. In 1994, my high school was defeated by Northgate in the league championship game. Their quarterback, Matt Harden, was also strong safety, punter, punt returner, and holder. In 1995, we were eliminated from the playoffs by Bishop O'Dowd, another team with many starters going both ways.

As long as you keep an eye on the fatigue, both offensive and defensive coordinators should have equal access to your team's talent.

Not equal practice time for two-way players

In terms of practice time, two-way players may spend more time on one side of the ball than the other. For example, linebackers need mucho practice. The offensive position of fullback, generally requires less practice. If one linebacker is also starting fullback, you should make sure that he spends the majority of his practice time at linebacker. Conversely, a quarterback/free safety should spend most of his time practicing his quarterback skills. Whether a two-way player should spend more practice time on one side of the ball or the other varies from position to position.

The 'right' defense for various offenses

As I said earlier, you should adopt the defense that is best suited to stop the dominant opponent in your league. If there is no dominant opponent, you should adopt the defense that is best suited to stop the most common offense used by your opponents.

Homer Smith's book, *Football Coach's Complete Offensive Playbook* has an interesting section where he traces the history of football's arms race between offense and defense. In most cases, someone came up with a new offense which the defenses of the day could not stop. Then, eventually, a defensive coordinator figured out a new defense to stop the new offense. Smith shows the various offenses and the defenses that he says stopped them. Here's my version of what he says. It should help you pick a defense for the season as well as deal with a particular challenge that you are facing in a given week.

Single wing

One of the earliest offenses that had some thought behind it is the single wing. I used that offense in 1993 and had an extremely successful offense—second best in the league as far as I could tell. Here is the defense that Smith says was best for stopping it.

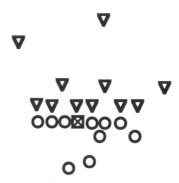

Nobody ever tried that defense against me. But looking at it, I'm glad they didn't. We did have a little trouble running **extra points** in that season—when we tried to go through the A, B, or C gaps. But we were successful **sweeping** for extra points. We probably had trouble because the defense went to their **goal line** defense, which bore some resemblance to the defense depicted above.

T formation

The T formation is completely balanced—equal number of backs and linemen on both sides of the ball and all at the same distance from the ball and depth as their counterpart. So you would expect an equally balanced defense. Here's what Smith said the defenses switched to when the T became dominant.

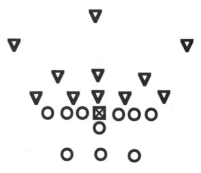

And here's the goal-line defense to stop the T.

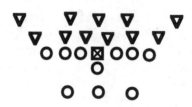

As you can see, both these defenses are as balanced as the T formation itself.

The Split T

I have long wondered what happened to the split T. Oklahoma coach Bud Wilkinson made it famous. Oklahoma's split-T-powered consecutive-win streak from 1953-1957 (47 games) still stands.

The split T was the first incarnation of the triple-option offense. The triple option is still going strong in other forms, namely the veer and the flex bone. Nebraska won national championships in 1994 and 1995, in part, with the triple option.

But Homer Smith says the split T "disappeared overnight." Why? Coach Wilkinson started the demise by inventing the Oklahoma defense. Somebody else figured out that you could start the play with four defensive backs then rotate toward the flow of the play so that you end up with two defensive backs and you outnumber the offense on the side the play is going to. Here's the Oklahoma 5-4 versus a split-T formation.

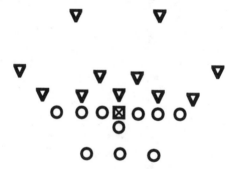

Smith says a 6-2-3 can do much the same thing also by rotating the backside (away from the flow of the play) cornerback back into a two-men deep coverage while the playside (the side to which the play is going) cornerback comes up to stop the run. Here's that defense.

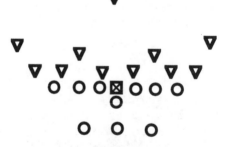

Wide receivers

Offenses then discovered the wide receiver. All these defensive backs rotating toward flow are great at stopping the run. But who's gonna stop that wide receiver from catching a pass if everybody's rotating toward the run? Defenses then put a guy in a **walk-away** position. That is, about halfway between the wide receiver and the widest tight offensive player on that side. The walk-away defender is in addition to the cornerback who lines up on the wide out.

If flow comes **toward** the walk-away guy, the **cornerback** on that side **drops** back to cover the wide receiver in the deep third of the field and the **walk-away guy** comes **up** to stop the run. If flow goes **away** from the walk-away guy, he rotates **back** to cover the deep middle third and the **cornerback** on the playside comes **up** to stop the run.

This is called inverted or "Sky" (strong safety) coverage as opposed to "Cloud" (cornerback) coverage. Here's a diagram.

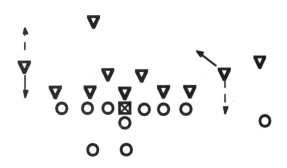

The Wing T

The wing T is a combination of the old single wing and the T formation. It was started by Forest Evashevski and David Nelson. Evashevski won the Big Ten and Rose Bowl championships in 1957 at Iowa. Nelson had so much success at Delaware with the wing T that the offense has come to be known as the Delaware Wing T and they still run it there.

According to Smith, and others, the solution to the wing T is the **slanting monster** defense. In the slanting monster, the defense lines up in a sort of Oklahoma 5-4 then, on the snap, the interior linemen slant in a predetermined direction and the inside linebackers slide with the offensive flow. The effect is that in an instant after the snap, the defense has transformed itself from an Oklahoma 5-4 to a wide-tackle 6 with a middle linebacker on the play side. The normal wide-tackle 6 does not have a middle linebacker.

The wide-tackle 6 is strong for stopping runs to the play side and the middle linebacker and slanting linemen are in a good position to stop the many counters run by Wing T teams. There's a whole book called the *Slanting Monster Defense* by Dale Foster. Here's a slant right against a wing T.

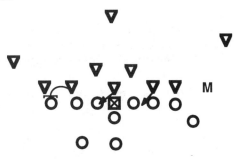

The same University of Oklahoma team that set consecutive win record in the mid fifties sent a bunch more records in the early seventies. As in the '50s, they did it with the triple option. But two things had changed. The coach was Barry Switzer, not Bud Wilkinson and the offense was the wishbone triple option, not the split-T.

Using the relatively new wishbone, Oklahoma set the still-standing records for the most yards gained per game (472.4 in 1971), highest average rush gain per game (6.8 yards in 1971), most rushing first downs per game (21.4 in 1974), and most rushes per game (73.9 in 1974). As is usually the case with such success, other teams adopted the wishbone and

defensive coordinators figured out how to stop it. According to Homer Smith, they did it
with this defense:

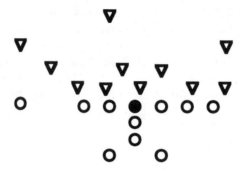

Here's the version to stop the veer triple option.

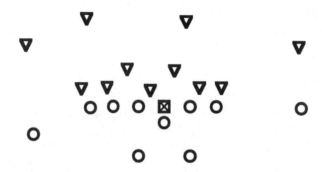

The 4-4

The 4-4 never stopped any famous offense as far as I know. But it is a common **high
school** defense and because of that, I should devote some space to it here.

The 4-4 is more or less a defense for teams that have **weak defensive personnel**. It
substitutes **trickery** for ability. It uses the element of surprise by constantly varying the
charges of the linemen and linebackers. There's nothing wrong with that. And it works
reasonably well at the high school level. I would be inclined to run the 4-4 if I were a high
school defensive coordinator and could not get the job done with another defense.

'It saved our team'

One high school varsity coach I know had a championship season in which he had
great players and used the 5-2 defense. The following season, the great players had
graduated. The new players were far less talented. He started the season again using the 5-
2. He got killed, switched to the 4-4, and was able to have a successful season. Upon
hearing the comment that the 4-4 was an interesting defense, he laughed and said, "It saved
our team in '84."

Lots of stunts

The 4-4 is a **stunting** defense. In fact, it's probably the best stunting defense there is.
In his book, *Football's 44 Stack Defense*, Tom Simonton says you should **not** use the
defense at all if you do not plan to stunt frequently. The high school coach who used it to
save his season says, "You'd get killed if you just sat in the 4-4 without stunting."

The 4-4 in youth football?

Will it work in youth football? I do not recall ever seeing it during my youth football
coaching. I just checked a year's worth of scouting reports from and every youth team we
faced ran either a five- or a six-man front. I never tried to run the 4-4 in youth football.

I suspect it would **not** work well because it relies on stunting and virtually all youth football teams have extremely tight line splits. Extremely tight line splits make it hard to stunt between the tight ends. And passing is so rare in youth football that having four linebackers back in the medium passing zones is not a smart deployment of defensive strength.

A friend who coached a 8-10-year old team tried the 4-4 one season. He said it was lousy. Contain responsibilities were shared by four players. They often got confused and no one contained at all. The many stunts were too confusing. And trying to teach four guys to contain—the most important defense responsibility in youth football—resulted in unsatisfactory execution.

You may be coaching youth football in a feeder program for a high school that runs the 4-4 and therefore wants you to run it. It might work at the highest levels of youth football, that is, the midget (13 and 14-year olds). You should probably resist using it at the lower levels.

The 10-1 as run by others

I have described my version of the 10-1 in this book. There are other versions. Coach G.A. Moore of Celina, Texas High School has run a form of the 10-1 for sixteen years—with great success. I believe he has won four state championships at various levels. He was the winningest active coach in Texas High School football two years ago. His version of the 10-1 is described in his Bob Rexrode video: "The 10-1 Even Pressure Defense."

Coach Moore does a number of things differently from the way I ran it. For one thing, he has his down linemen line up in the gap but angle outward on the snap. They are in a four-point stance with their inside foot up and take their first step with their outside foot. The reason is he says everyone blocks down against his defense. By angling outward, his guys cancel out the inward block and end up in the gap where they started and where they want to be.

In high school, it is generally not possible to use **one** defense. The opposing coaches are too aware of the weaknesses of each defense and they will run plays that exploit those weaknesses. My limited experience in high school is that the defensive coordinator has to **vary** what he does—by using stunts from one defense or mixing different defense. When I was a junior varsity defensive coordinator, we used 17 defenses if you count stunts and variations in alignment. We won the league championship and lost only one game. Each stunt is really a different defense. For example, when a 4-4 coach stunts one linebacker, he will actually be in a 5-3 for that play.

Moore has a down lineman in each of the A, B, and C gaps like this.

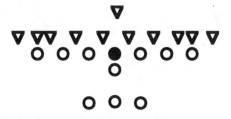

Like me, he plugs the tight ends so they cannot get out on a pass route quickly. He does not box his contain men the way I did. Rather, he has them play the near back man-to-man. They play man-to-man on the **run** as well as the pass. If the near back attacks them, they attack the near back. Pass coverage is necessarily man-to-man whenever you rush this many guys. The pluggers have the tight ends. The contain men have the near back. And the middle linebacker has the fullback. The middle linebacker has any back who goes in motion outward leaving the contain men to take the remaining near back.

If the tight end blocks down on the C-gap defender, Moore has his plugger crash hard.

When the offense only has six men tight on the line, that is, they have a split end, Moore runs a 9-2 rather than a 10-1. The contain man on the split end side drops back to free safety. The C gap lineman gets up from his 4-point stance into a 2-point stance and becomes the contain man.

Against the veer triple option, Moore likes to run a stunt he calls 10-1 loop. The C gap defender crashes down hard the way the plugger does above. The B gap defender pops up out of his 4-point stance and loops out to where the C-gap defender started.

The form of the 10-1 that Moore says he runs the most is really a sort of 8-2-1. A nose tackle covers both A gaps. Two inside backers watch the backs and there is a free safety.

Moore's other variation has the A gap defenders and a nose tackle in **two-point** stances. One, two, or three of them can charge through the A gaps and/or the center into the offensive backfield while the remaining ones drop back into linebacker positions.

The Kent State 10-1

Coach Trevor Rees ran the 10-1 at Kent State University in the late sixties and early seventies. His defense was similar to Moore's. But he did not have his tight end plugger crash when the tight end blocked down on the C-gap defender. He did not want his plugger to cross the line of scrimmage. Rather he wanted them to stay parallel and look for the ball.

Here's how Rees' team lined up against various offensive formations:

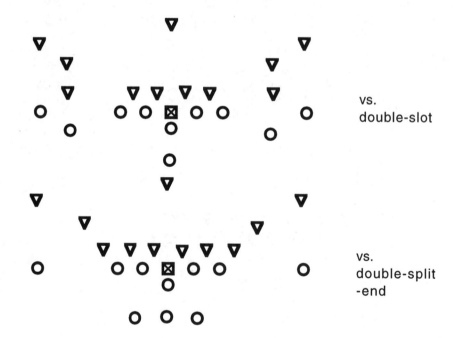

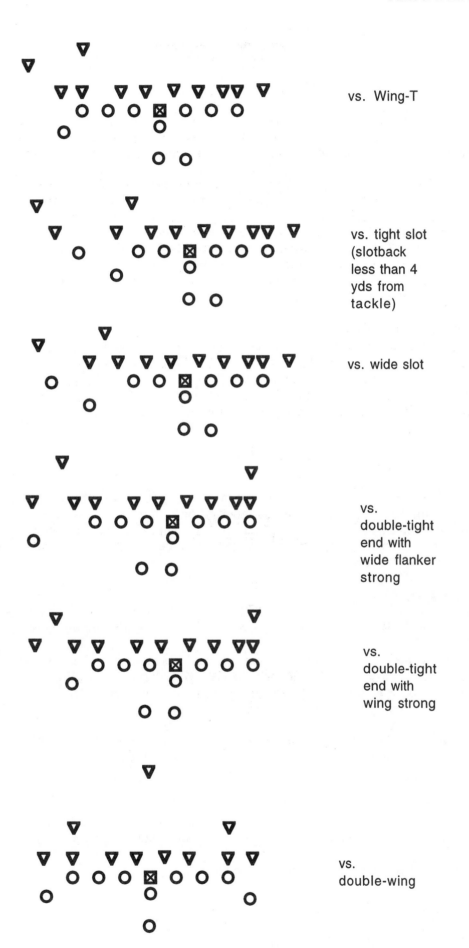

vs. Wing-T

vs. tight slot
(slotback
less than 4
yds from
tackle)

vs. wide slot

vs.
double-tight
end with
wide flanker
strong

vs.
double-tight
end with
wing strong

vs.
double-wing

25

Teamwork

Helen Keller said, "There is plenty of courage among us for the abstract but not for the concrete." A similar thing could be said about everyone's love of teamwork.

Everyone is in favor of teamwork, the abstract concept. But when it comes to being on a real team with real people, most players cannot resist the temptation to engage in behavior which is **destructive** to teamwork.

We are family

The Pittsburgh Pirates team led by Willie "Pops" Stargell was fond of the song, "We are family" a number of years ago. They meant the word "family" in the sense of "one big happy."

I think the word "family" applies to **all** teams. But I mean it in the sense of "You can pick your friends, but you can't pick your relatives—or your teammates."

Family are people you **have** to get along with. With non-family members, if you don't get along with them, you can avoid them. But since you can**not** avoid family members, you **must** get along with them.

Once you join a team, you cannot avoid the other people associated with the team—players, coaches, parents, board members, etc. So to join a team is to join a family of sorts.

No criticism, no put downs

Every team you have ever been on or ever will be on has **weak players** and **jerks**. That applies not only to athletic teams but also to all groups of people who are working together.

So what do you do about weak players and jerks?

Very simple. You **help** the weak players and you keep the fact that you think someone is a jerk **secret**.

Notice I did **not** say you should pretend to like someone whom you think is a jerk. That would be phony. The Stargell Pirates were criticized for that sort of phoniness. Phoniness doesn't do a team any good. And it's not the kind of value we should be teaching to kids. But asking a player to keep his dislike of a teammate **secret** is not the same as asking him to pretend he likes the player in question. Everybody ought to be able to keep a secret. And everybody ought to be able to resist the urge to indulge their darker side in destructive comments or nonverbal communication.

That is teamwork. Or at least that's the **hard** part of teamwork. Working with teammates you like is necessary, too. But most people do that almost automatically. Restating it so no one will miss my point:

The hard part of teamwork consists of two elements:

- **help** weaker players
- keep **secret** any personality clashes.

"But I have evidence"

The typical teamwork pattern on real, concrete teams is that everyone is in favor of teamwork when they first join—Helen Keller's abstract teamwork. But as they get to know their teammates as individuals, they start to see weaknesses in some and jerkiness in others. And many kids have the habit of putting down the weak and verbally or even physically attacking kids who they think are jerks.

That must not be permitted on a team.

If you confront someone who is putting down a weaker player, they will typically say, "But you don't understand. He's really bad. He did this and he did that." In other words, yes, they promised to work like a team but this kid is **really** a lousy player. Listen to all the **proof** I have.

I am not interested in the proof that someone is a weak player. We coaches have little else to do but figure out who the weak players are. We generally don't need help from players in that department. Furthermore, the real reason why one person puts down another is to elevate himself by comparison. That's destructive to the team. It can cost the team victories and advancement in the playoffs. The team must work as a team and it will not if any of its members are putting down others of its members.

Suppose you confront someone who is feuding with a player whom he considers to be a jerk. You will get the same, "Yes, I'm in favor of teamwork but wait until you hear about the jerky things this guy did."

I'm not interested. He is your teammate. If you don't like him, you must keep it a secret.

Everybody gets to be the weak guy or the jerk

Young players need to be told that one of the reasons they must help the weak and keep secret their feelings about the jerks is because if they play enough years, **they** will be one of the weaker players on some teams and, inevitably, someone will think **they** are a jerk. Knowing that, helping the weak when you are not one of them is nothing less than the golden rule. And so is keeping secret your dislikes.

Teamwork drills

There are some drills which could teach teamwork to those who fall off the wagon. One is the three-legged race.

Three-legged race

Let's say you catch Sean and Ben bickering. Take them aside and explain that bickering is destructive to teamwork and will not be allowed. Then assign them to **remedial teamwork**. A coach will then take them to a separate area where they cannot be seen by the other players and have them run three-legged races against a stop watch. You can strap them together with three football belts. To graduate from remedial teamwork and rejoin the "general population," they must run 50 yards strapped together at least 50% as fast as the slowest of the two's solo 50-yard time.

There is no way you can run a three-legged race successfully without cooperating.

This is a legitimate cooperation-teaching drill. But it's also a **punishment** in the sense that the last thing you want to do with the teammate you most hate is be tied to him and have to cooperate with him in a strenuous three-legged race. I suspect that most feud-prone players would not want to do the three-legged race routine **twice**. So they will, in the future, keep their dislike secret—which is precisely the standard I want met.

A player who can**not** refrain from verbally or physically attacking a teammate he doesn't like may quit the team if you make him run three-legged races with the teammate in question. So be it. In any organization, the leader **must** establish reasonable standards. If anyone does not meet the standards, he must either **straighten out or move out**.

Another staple of church picnics might serve this purpose well—human wheelbarrow races with the two bickering players paired as a team.

The army has a **log drill** for building team cooperation. They have a group of six or eight men pick up a heavy log which they could not pick up if they were a smaller group. They then execute various maneuvers with it. That might be too dangerous for youth football players. Except for one log drill: joint sit-ups. Have a group of six players do sit ups while all are holding a log which is big enough to pin any one or two of them down. There is little danger of dropping the log in sit-ups. Another example: a group of tires might be tied together making a mass which the players could only lift if each member of the group does his share.

Blocking **sleds** are an excellent way to teach teamwork. The two-man sled could be used to teach cooperation to two feuding players. Make them push it in a straight line at a respectable speed. The speed should be high enough that only true cooperation will work. Larger sleds can teach cooperation to larger groups.

Another army device for building teamwork assigns groups of men tasks which can only be performed by a team which works together. These tasks involve moving objects too heavy to be lifted by one or two men from point A to point B. Or climbing over an obstacle so high that no one man can do it alone. Or maneuvering around or over an obstacle which is structured so that one man must use his eyes and voice to give directions to other men who are performing a task which requires the information provided by the man with the visual vantage point. All of these tasks are performed against a stop watch and group times are compared. The key is to design drills which require cooperation then assign any bickering or feuding players to perform those drills until they cooperate adequately. Hopefully, that will make the point that cooperation is necessary between members of the football team.

Player coach

If a Sean puts down Ben as not playing well, try appointing Sean to be Ben's player-coach buddy. Sean will stand next to Ben in all practice drills in which they are in the same group. Sean will help Ben learn to do better at whatever it was that Sean felt the need to criticize. Whenever Ben is sent to remedial whatever, Sean will accompany him and help the adult coach teach Ben to do better.

When Ben screws up, both he and his player coach Sean will do whatever punishment is assigned. Whenever Ben needs a demonstration of the correct technique, Sean will provide it.

If Ben plays a different position than Sean, Sean will move to Ben's position and show Ben how it **should** be played. This would be common between running backs who say the line isn't blocking and linemen who say the backs aren't hitting the holes quick enough. Each can **show** the other how it should be done.

When to stop this routine is up to the coach's judgment. The basic criterion should be when the critic has learned to either help the weaker player or to refrain from putting him down.

MUST be corrected

The main point I want to make is that the coach can**not** tolerate players who put down or otherwise mistreat their teammates. This is not behavior you can excuse as unavoidable boys-will-be-boys conduct. Antagonistic behavior adversely affects both the football experience of the boys on the receiving end and the team's ability to compete in games. The offending boys **must** be straightened out either by one of the methods I've suggested or by your own approach. If during-practice teamwork drills won't work, the offending player should be suspended or thrown off the team.

I am familiar with a couple elementary schools where child cliques have taken over classes. In one affluent suburban school, girls who are not in the in-crowd refuse to go to the playground or other outdoor areas at recess or lunch. Rather they stay in the classroom reading a book so as to have teacher nearby to prevent the incessant, vicious harassment which is inflicted upon them in the school yard. Most youth sports teams probably have one or two members who would, if unchecked, make life miserable for other players for their own sadistic amusement. You cannot prevent that from happening in school or elsewhere in children's life. But you can and must prevent it from happening on your football team.

26

Flip Flopping

One of the issues you must address as a defensive coordinator is whether to flip flop your players and, if so, which ones and how. Flip flopping means assigning players to a side other than left or right. If you do not flip flop, everyone's position name starts with the word "left," "right," or "middle." For example, you have a left cornerback, a right tackle, and so forth.

When you flip flop, the position names start with words like "strong" or "wide."

Keep It Simple Stupid

The Keep It Simple Stupid principle applies here. Not flip flopping is the simplest method. I recommend that method if you can get away with it. That is, your left cornerback always lines up on the left side of the defense (with the possible exception of when the offense has three or four receivers on the other side).

I did not flip flop in 1991 or 1992 and I had one of the top two or three defenses in our 28-team league.

In 1993, I made a video of every sweep ever run against us to figure out how we could improve at stopping the sweep. I noticed that we had the most trouble when the offense ran to the wide side of the field.

Left is wide when the ball's in the middle of the hashes

When the ball is smack dab in the middle of the field, there is no wide side. In that case, we designate the defensive left as the "wide" side. The reason for that is that most offensive players are right-handed and prefer to run to the right. So when the ball is in the middle (half-way from each sideline), we figure it is more likely they will run to their right which is our left. Our middle linebacker is in charge of yelling out "Wide left!" It is important that one player and only one player be in charge of designating the wide side. There is not time to debate the matter.

Wide side when ball is not in the middle

When the ball is not smack in the middle of the hashes, the wide side is the wide side. That is, the side with the farthest sideline is the wide side.

I designated three players as wide. I had a wide cornerback, a wide defensive end, and a wide linebacker. Those three operated as a team and always lined up on the wide side of the offensive formation.

I also had three short-side players: a short-side cornerback, a short-side defensive end, and a short-side linebacker.

This is flip flopping. But it is a rather simple form of flip flopping. The main benefit of using hash position to guide your flip flopping is that you get plenty of time to flip. Once the previous play is blown dead, you know the hash position for the next snap. No one should even need to have anyone designate the wide side most of the time. It's obvious— or at least it's obvious once you have taught your players what you mean by wide side.

How did it work?

We never had a confusion problem with our wide side-short side flip flopping in 1993. Did it work better? I believe so. We had a lousy defense in 1993. But that was due to the fact that we had only one boy who had ever played defense before and only two who had ever played football before. You need at least five veterans to have a decent defense. The veterans play the non-line positions. You can put rookies on the defensive line including at defensive end. But you can almost never get away with rookies in the defensive backfield (cornerback or linebacker).

There is no doubt that the sweep is far more dangerous on the wide side. It is also true that I have never had personnel who were equal in ability. If the wide side is more dangerous, and your personnel are not equal, you should assign your best players to the wide side and your second best to the short side.

Strong and weak

When most coaches speak of flip flopping, they mean strong and weak. Most common offenses of the '90s have a strong side. The strong side is the side with the tight end if there is only one tight end. I've heard at least one youth coach refer to the strong side as being the one with the most players. You can use whatever terminology you want. And there are a few teams at the high school and higher levels that use the word strong to mean most player side. But it is almost standard throughout football that strong side means the side with the tight end in a one-tight end set.

The weak side is the side with a split end rather than a tight end.

Double tight

What if the offensive formation has two tight ends? That's called "double tight." If the formation is totally balanced, that is, there are the five and a half players on each side of the ball and they are all the exact same distance from the ball, you need to make an arbitrary designation of which side is strong. Most teams designate the wide side of the field as strong if the offense is totally balanced. And if the ball is smack in the middle of the field, they do like I described above. They designate the defensive left as the strong side on the grounds that the offense is probably right-handed and likes to run to its right.

If the seven offensive lineman are all tight, the backs may be unbalanced. For example, a double-tight formation with a wing back would be strong to the wing side. Any imbalance in the offensive backfield renders the side with the most backs the strong side.

If there are no tight ends, the strong side is the one with the most players. If the formation is totally balanced, for example a double slot or double split-end, double-flanker, and the one back is directly behind the quarterback, the strong side is the wide side or the defensive left if there is no wide side.

Yell it out

If you flip flop strong and weak, you must have a player who designates which side is strong before each play. And he must be quick. He will not know which side is strong until the offensive team lines up. Furthermore, the offense may shift or put a man in motion, thereby changing the strength of the formation at the last second.

A no-huddle offense that flip flops its strong and weak sides can drive you nuts. So can substitute tight ends when you get used to looking for a certain jersey number to figure out which side is strong.

The linebacker in charge must yell "Strong right!" or "Strong left!" as soon as he can tell which side is strong. If you attend a high school football game, you will probably hear a linebacker making such a strength call.

Who changes?

Some defenses that flip flop only flip one guy, typically the strong safety. Others flip their whole outside unit like I did. That is, a cornerback, defensive end, and linebacker.

I've even seen some that flip flop their entire eleven-man defensive unit.

Pre-call alignment

Any players who flip flop must line up on the ball until their linebacker in charge designates the strong side. If they assume they know which side is wrong, and they are wrong, they have farther to run to get to the actual strong side.

Last-second flip flops

As I said above, defenses that try to flip flop according to the strong side of the offense often have to contend with confusing last-second offensive flip flops. The offense only has to be set for one second after they shift. And they can have one guy in motion at the snap. So you could get less than one second notice as to which side is strong.

The more guys you flip flop, the harder it is to adjust to last-second flips. Accordingly, you must ignore some offensive flips because you do not have time to adjust.

Flip wide, not strong

I hope I am convincing you to **forget** flip flopping strong and weak. It is very **confusing** if the offense varies its strong side. I recently attended a football clinic where a **junior college** coach said his players could not figure out which side was strong and he had to quit flip flopping. If a junior college has trouble with flip flopping, what do you think your **youth** players will do?

Confusion is fatal to a successful defense. Your players **must** be **certain** of their alignment and assignment. You do not want a weak-side defender to suddenly find himself dealing with a tight end when he has not practiced against a tight end. But that is sure to happen if the offense flips at the last second or your linebacker in charge makes a mistake about which side is strong.

Flip wide and short, not strong and weak.

27

Our worst game

Our worst game of the 1991 season was against Oakland in the Western League Championship game. We lost 25-0. Here is a play-by-play account which I made to figure out what I did wrong. I was also interested in what Oakland did right. Because they were clearly the best defense in the league.

Play	Poss.	Down	To go	Ball on	Result	Comment
1	Bears			O40	0	Kickoff to Bears, grounder down middle to our best returner
						He touched knee to ground when picking up ball.
2	Bears	1	10	B32	0	Oakland defense in 7-3-1. The 3 are no wider than our tackles.
						Noseguard shoved center into QB causing fumble to Oak.
3	Oak.	1	10	B32	26	I formation. Off tackle left. Untouched at line of scrimmage
						(LOS). Tackle by safety who was hurt on the play.
						Extremely fast execution by Oakland.
4	Oak.	1	6	B6	2	Dive right guard-tackle gap. Hit at LOS by our left tackle
5	Oak.	2	4	B4	4 TD	Same play. Hit by 2 defensive linemen at LOS. Tacklers fell
						down. Ball carrier bounced left. Other defenders appeared to
						assume ball carrier was tackled and stopped before the whistle
6	Oak.	PAT	3	B3	-3	Fumble by Oakland QB recovered by our right tackle.
7	Bears			50	15	Kick off to Bears, grounder down middle to our best receiver.
						Caught on second hop at 28 and returned to our 43.
8	Bears	1	10	B43	0	Off tackle right. Oakland's left end penetrated past ball carrier.
						Stopped at LOS by line and LB.
9	Bears	2	10	B43	4	Same play to left. Two good blocks.
10	Bears	3	6	B47	13	Pass to wing who faded out to right on LOS. No defender
						around. Fullback faked dive into line then came over and
						lead blocked a would-be tackler down.
11	Bears	1	10	O40	-3	Sweep right. LE penetrated. RTE could not get
						angle to block in because LE lined up outside RTE. ·
12	Bears	2	13	O43	2	Fullback dive right. Tripped over someone's leg.
13	Bears	3	11	O41	1	Off tackle right. Line blocked well but LB came
						up fast to make sure tackle.
14	Bears	4	10	O40	5	Offsides Oakland.
			5	O35	-15	Fake punt pass to right wing who was wide open. He caught
						ball and was not tackled until the 21. But OLE called for
						illegal block downfield. 15-yard penalty and loss of down.
14	Oak.	1	10	O40	9	Dive right. Six defenders missed tackles.
						Generally because of leaving feet. Tackle by LE.
15	Oak.	2	1	B41	-1	Sweep right. Our LE was hit by two successive blockers but
						seemed not to notice. He got hand on ball carrier then 3 guys
						gang tackled.
16	Oak.	3	2	B42	14	Off tackle left. Hit at LOS by RLB. But bounced to ball carrier's
						left. RHB fell down. Good pursuit angles caused ball carrier to
						stutter step allowing LLB to catch.
17	Oak.	1	10	B28	17	Sweep left. RE did not penetrate to depth of ball, got blocked
						in. RHB gave ground then tackled assisted by LLB.
18	Oak.	1	10	B11	11 TD	Roll-out pass left. RE did not cross LOS. RLB, RHB, and RE
						at left hash at 5-yard line. Wide open back caught in end zone.
19	Oak.	PAT	3	B3	2	Dive right. Hit at LOS by LT. No point.
20	Bears			O40	7	Kick off down middle to second-best returner.
						Picked up at 30 and tackled at 37.
21	Bears	1	10	B37	4	Fullback dive right. Hit at 39 but fought to 41.
22	Bears	2	6	B41	0	Incomplete pass to right wing same as play #10.
23	Bears	3	6	B41	-2	Sweep right. NO LE but linebackers came up
						fast and ball carrier slipped when he tried to cut.
End of first quarter						

Play	Poss.	Down	To go	Ball on	Result	Comment
24	Bears	4	8	B43	19	Punt to O38
25	Oak.	1	10	O38	20	Sweep right. LE stopped but face masked.
						Gain of 5 and 15-yard penalty
26	.Oak.	1	10	B42	1	Sweep right. LE held but got arm on ball carrier.
						LT hit at LOS and staggered. Finished by S.
27	Oak.	2	9	B41	11	Sweep left. RE grabbed arm 3 yards behind LOS, swung ball
						carrier 360 degrees and let go. Ball carrier did not go down.
						Ran up sideline. Hit high by several defenders. Fought to 30.
28	Oak.	1	10	B30	3	Dive right. High tackle after hitting ball carrier in backfield.
29	Oak.	2	7	B27	-15	Sweep right. LE was held but made tackle at 25
						15-yard penalty against Oak.
30	Oak.	2	22	B42	-5	Sack. Great pressure from RE, RLB, RT, RG.
31	Oak.	3	27	B47	-15	QB fumbled then recovered. LE lunged inside. QB escaped
						outside for 15 gain. Clipping. 15-yard penalty
32	Oak.	3	42	O38	2	Shotgun pass attempt. Pressure by LE.
						QB escaped and was driven out by tackle.
33	Oak.	4	40	O40	30	Punt to B47 rolled to B30 untouched.
34	Bears	1	10	B30	-1	Sweep right. Much penetration.
35	Bears	2	11	B29	1	Oakland now in 5-5-1. Fullback dive right.
36	Bears	3	10	B30	22	Pass to linebacker. Tackled by center. Oakland clipped.
37	Oak.	1	10	O48	3	Dive right. Tackled by LT.
38	Oak.	2	7	B49	2	No huddle. Same play. Same result less 1 yard.
39	Oak.	3	5	B47	-1	QB keep sweep left. Played perfectly by RE who solo tackled.
40	Oak.	4	6	B48	34	Punt to 24 rolled to 14 untouched.
41	Bears	1	10	B14	2	Sweep right
42	Bears	2	8	B16		Half-time
End of first half						
43	Oak.			B40	0	On-sides kick. We almost recovered.
44	Oak.	1	10	O46	11	Off tackle left. RE overpenetrated. RLB blocked in. LLB tackled
45	Oak.	1	10	B43	3	Dive right. Stopped by defensive line.
46	Oak.	2	7	B40	6	Pass to right flat. Intercepted by LHB. Offensive interference
						declined.
47	Bears	1	10	B34	-1	Fumble to Oakland.
48	Oak.	1	10	B33	2	Deep penetration by 2 defensive linemen but missed tackle.
						Penetration forced ball carrier to stutter step. LLB tackled.
49	Oak.	2	8	B31	0	Sweep right. Our tall LE tossed lead blocker aside. Closely
						following ball carrier suddenly found himself nose to chest with
						our LE who wrapped and took down.
50	Oak.	3	8	B31	0	Pass to left flat. Same play as #18 TD. Our RHB got piece of
						ball. Incomplete by milimeters.
51	Oak.	4	8	B31	12	Punt to 19. No attempt to catch but Bears bounce.
52	Bears	1	10	B19	2	Off tackle right. Oakland's line was handled but no one blocked
						linebackers who came up fast.
53	Bears	2	8	B21	-6	Roll-out pass right. Sacked by linebacker and noseguard.
54	Bears	3	14	B15	1	Fullback dive fumbled to Bears.
55	Bears	4	13	B16	5	Oakland offsides
			8	B21	-6	High lob snap. Punter sacked by apparently untouched
						noseguard.
56	Oak.	1	10	B15	-1	Shotgun roll-out right. Great pressure by LE who fell down.
						Tackle by line. Almost face mask penalty.

Play	Poss.	Down	To go	Ball on	Result	Comment
57	Oak.	2	11	B16	-5	Shotgun. High snap. Illegal procedure before snap.
			16	B21	-6	QB under center. Roll-out left. Sacked by RE and RG.
58	Oak.	3	22	B27	15	Quick kick. Almost blocked. Had to pull down & take approach steps a 2nd time to kick. LE leaped into air to block 1st attempt.
59	Bears	1	10	B12	1	Fullback dive. Hit at LOS, Spun to 13.
End of third quarter						
60	Bears	2	9	B13	8	Sweep right.
61	Bears	3	1	B21	2	Off tackle left. One LB penetrated but missed. Other LB tackled
62	Bears	1	10	B23	2	Fullback dive stopped by Oakland line and linebackers.
63	Bears	2	8	B25	-3	Sweep right. RTE missed block on LE who made tackle.
64	Bears	3	11	B22	-4	QB sacked attempting to pass.
65	Bears	4	15	B18	-5	Illegal procedure.
			20	B13	12	punt out of bounds at 25-yard line.
66	Oak.	1	10	B25	14	Dive right. Hit at LOS. Most players stopped assuming play over. Breaks loose. Tackled high by LHB after being dragged several yards.
67	Oak.	2	4	B11	11TD	Off tackle left. 2 tacklers hit high, left their feet, and put their helmets behind the runner. Safety tackled ball carrier, but two yards in end zone.
68	Oak.	PAT	3	B3	3	Same play. RLB arm tackled with head behind ball carrier. RLB may have been held on the play.
69	Bears			O40	-2	Kickoff grounder down the middle to our second-best receiver. Ran East-West (sideways). Picked up ball at 22, tackled at 20. Unsportsmanlike conduct against Oakland.
70	Bears	1	10	B35	3	Fullback dive right. Hit at LOS high and battled for three yards.
71	Bears	2	7	B38	3	Fullback dive right. Hit at LOS high by lineman, dragged him 3 yards until hit low by linebacker.
72	Bears	3	4	B41	2	Fullback dive right. Hit at LOS and battled for two yards.
73	Bears	4	2	B43	1	Fullback dive right. Defensive lineman submarined and tripped up fullback.
74	Oak.	1	10	B44	1	Off tackle right. Hit at LOS and swarmed under.
75	Oak.	2	9	B43	-3	Sweep right turned upfield by LE. Tackle by LLB.
						Time out Bears. Told players to have fun. They asked, "Can we blitz?" I said, "Yeah, what the heck."
76	Oak.	3	12	B46	10	Off tackle left. RE lunged around back side of blocker. RLB apparently held. RHB retreated as if pass defending and was blocked easily while going backwards. Safety was blocked. Decent pursuit angles by other players. Ball carrier got to the end zone but touchdown was called back by clipping. Dead ball unsportsmanlike conduct by Bears, i.e., talking to other team, canceled out clipping penalty yardage.
77	Oak.	1	10	B36	36TD	QB keep sweep right. Both the LLB and the LE blitzed inside. The LLB just missed the QB and fell down. The LE was easily blocked in by the TE because the LE went straight for the QB instead of taking his usual square-in route to stop the sweep. All pursuing defenders took great angles but the QB was just too fast to catch.
78	Oak.	PAT	3	B3	-3	PAT fumbled and recovered by Oakland.
79	Bears			O40	?	Video camera did not pick up point at which ball was picked up. Returner was tackled at the B28.

80	Bears	1	10	B28	-3	Oakland now in 5-5-1 defense. Reverse tackled by LB and line.
81	Bears	2	13	B25	5	Off tackle right. Good blocking.
82	Bears	3	8	B30	6	Pass thrown to linebacker. Tackled by intended receiver after one-yard return.
End of game						

Here is a statistical analysis of our 1991 loss to Oakland:

Category	Oakland	Bears
Non-PAT scrimmage plays	38	41
Non-PAT yards gained	159	39
Non-PAT yards per play	4.18	.95
Penalties	90	50
Kickoff returns	1	5
Kickoff return yardage	0	20
Yards per kickoff return	0	4
Average field position after kickoff return	Own 46	Own 32
First downs	6	2
Non-PAT successes on defense (less than 4 yd.gain)	25	20
Non-PAT failures on defense (4 or more yd. gain)	5	13
Turnovers including punts and on downs	5	8
Punts	4	3
Punt yardage	91	25
Average yards-per-punt change in field position	22.75	8.33

Here's how each series went:
Oakland series:

Plays	Distance covered	Result
3-6	32	TD, PAT no good
14-19	60	TD, PAT no good
25-33	2	punt
37-40	4	punt
43-46	14	interception
48-51	2	punt
56-58	-12	quick kick
66-68	25	TD, PAT good
74-78	44	TD, PAT no good

Bears series:

2	0	fumble
7-14	22	penalty on fake punt, over on downs
20-24	2	punt
34-36	0	interception
41-42	2	half-time
47	-1	fumble
52-55	2	punter sacked
59-65	1	punt
69-73	9	over on downs
79-82	2	interception

Oakland's success by play choice:

Pass to the left	1 for 11	11.00 yards per pass
Off tackle left	7 for 76 yards	10.86 yards per carry
Sweep left	3 for 27	9.00 yards per carry
Dive right	9 for 42	4.67 yards per carry
Off tackle right	1 for 1	1.00 yard per carry
Pass to the right	2 for 1	0.50 yards per pass
Sweep right*	6 for -14	-2.33 yards per carry

* not counting play #77 where players deliberately blitzed by permission instead of executing normal job description.

Cause of our failures:

Play	Cause
3	job description not carried out
5	poor tackling technique
14	poor tackling technique
16	poor tackling technique
17	job description not carried out
18	job description not carried out
25	poor tackling technique
27	poor tackling technique
44	job description not carried out
66	poor tackling technique
67	poor tackling technique
76	job description not carried out
77	job description not carried out (allowed to blitz because game was hopelessly lost)

Summary cause of failures:

Poor tackling technique	7 of 13	54%
Job description not carried out	6 of 13	46%

Comments on the game

Clearly, we primarily lost the game because of our often poor tackling technique. We devoted a great deal of time to tackling technique throughout the preseason and season. But apparently not enough. Oakland, in contrast, almost always tackled correctly. They hit low and wrapped tight for the most part. Their first tackler was usually all they needed. When they didn't tackle properly, typically against our fullback dive, our ball carrier dragged the Oakland players just like they dragged us. In terms of tackling technique, Oakland outcoached us.

Job descriptions not carried out

On play 3, the right linebacker was supposed to slide off the tight end and make the tackle. In fact, the ball carrier was by him before he slid off.

Plays 17 and 18 involved a substitute player. The starter was hurt. The substitute had played **left** defensive end extremely well in several games. This was the first time he had ever played **right** defensive end. The switch in sides may have disoriented him. He was also the safety who made the touchdown-saving tackle on the first defensive play and was hurt. It's possible his injury affected his play later after he went back in. I noticed his not crossing the line of scrimmage on plays 17 & 18 during the game and asked him why. He offered no explanation. The starter returned later in the game.

On play #44, the starter was back in at right end. He was supposed to penetrate to the depth of the ball. But that's easier said than done on Oakland's fast-developing off-tackle play. On that same play, the right linebacker was supposed to hold the tight end at arm's length and slide off to make the tackle. He did not do that. He may have been held. But we regard holding as no excuse. The player must break the hold or avoid it to begin with. We did not spend much time teaching players how to break or avoid holds. Our players were to operate on the assumption that the opponents would hold and get away with it and that we had to win in that "unfair" context.

On play #76, the right end (starter) lunged around the blocker for the ball carrier. We told our ends time and again that they must not do that. Rather they must stay at the depth of the ball and force the ball carrier to do the lunging. The most they were allowed to do was shove the blocker back into the ball carrier. They were supposed to hold the blocker/ball carrier pair at bay until the "cavalry" arrived to make the tackle. But this required more patience than our ends often possessed. We should have done a drill to emphasize this—a drill in which the end is forbidden to make the tackle. Rather he must just corral the ball carrier until his linebacker buddy makes the tackle.

Our right linebacker had the same problem as in play #44. Our right halfback played this as if it were a pass. He should have been in man-to-man coverage on the widest non-tight-end receiver to his side. He did not read run quickly enough. Reading the run takes judgment. Judgment comes from experience and this was a rookie who had not even been first string at the beginning of the season.

In the 1992 season, I wrote each position's job description (where to line up and what to do after the snap) on 4 inch by 5 inch Tyvek sheets. I punched holes at each end and put rubber bands through the holes. The rubber bands would hold the sheet on the boy's forearm.

When a kid has to move to a position he has not been playing all game long, I slipped a Tyvek job description on his forearm and told him to read it between plays. That seemed to eliminate the problem of a kid being shifted to a different position because of an injury or repeated failures by another player and not knowing what he's supposed to do in that position.

Strength of each side

Clearly our **right** side was weaker than our **left** in this game. Their two best plays were the off tackle left and the sweep left. When they tried similar plays to the **right** (our left), they got nowhere. Their dive right was more of an up-the-middle play than it was to the right side.

| Plays to the left: | 11 for 114 | 10.36 yards per play |
| Plays to the right | 9 for -12 | -1.33 yards per play |

Our left defensive end was perhaps the tallest boy in the league. We had several big players—not as many as Richmond—but we had some big ones. They were often asked by opposing players before games if they were **pee wees** which is the next highest age/weight level up. Our left end was once asked by an opposing junior pee wee if he were a **junior midget**. Junior midgets are **two** levels up. They weigh almost twice as much as junior pee wees. Before the Vacaville championship game, our left defensive end heard a player on the opposing team say, "Look at the size of that guy!" as he came out of the locker room. The Vacaville head coach sought our left end out after that game and said, "I guess we'll be seeing you in the NFL someday."

Our tall end, of course, met our weight limit of 85 pounds at the beginning of the season. So obviously he was slender. But a slender boy in shoulder pads doesn't **look** very slender. When he was coin-toss captain, he towered over the opposing captains. He was a second-year veteran. And he was as strong as he was tall.

Beach balls

You can see that in plays # 15 and 49. In both cases, Oakland tried to sweep his end including sending full-steam blockers at him. He reacted to the blockers as if they were beach balls. I burst out laughing when I saw these two plays on the videotape.

Our left linebacker was a second-year veteran, field captain of the defense, and probably the best athlete on the team.

Our left halfback was my son, a **three**-year veteran of the defensive line and linebacker positions.

Rookies on the right

In contrast, our right linebacker and right halfback were both rookies—**promising** rookies, but still rookies.

If I had it to do over again, I would have switched my son with the right linebacker. That would give us a veteran linebacker and a veteran end on each side. As it was, I had three veterans on the left and only one, the end, on the right.

And when the starting right end was hurt, I had **all** rookies on the right. That was the situation in play 17 and thereafter until the starter was ready to play again in the second quarter. When the starting right end was hurt, I should have moved the safety to **left** end, which he had played well earlier in the season, and moved the left end over to right end.

I'm not saying balancing the veterans would have won the game. No doubt we'd have weakened the left if we had been balanced. On the other hand, we were, if anything, **too** strong on the left. Oakland did worse running to our left side than **our** offense did overall against **Oakland's** defense.

It may be that Oakland's coaches detected a weakness in our right side when they scouted the Vacaville game the week before. Although they should have also seen that our left side was very strong and refrained from launching six disastrous sweeps, two ineffectual passes, and one failed off tackle in that direction.

Now that I think about it, distributing the veterans or best players equally on each side was something we made a point of doing in the 1990 season.

Players not lined up properly

You should note that not one defensive failure was caused by players not lining up in the right place before the snap. That was not the case in our jamboree. The reason we never had any players lined up wrong is that we only had **one** defensive alignment. And we practiced it a lot.

I never paid much attention, but I'll bet our opponents—including Oakland—had plays in which they were not lined up the way they wanted to be. The reason I'm so sure of that is that they had more than one defense. And as soon as you have more than one defense, you create the opportunity for confusion as to **which** defense the team is supposed to be in.

Attempts to confuse and surprise the **other** team are equally likely to confuse or surprise your **own** players. Plus I always figured the offense was probably somewhat confused on every play any way. And I felt that the offense was often blind to how we were lined up. There was no need for us to risk confusing ourselves with changes that may not be understood or even noticed by the offense.

Lack of gang tackling

We pushed gang tackling in practice. The line I often repeated to the kids was, "If you're not in on the tackle, you'd better have a note from your mother."

We also pushed going full speed until the whistle. We showed the kids game videos of players who **quit** going full speed before the whistle and pointed out how it hurt us on the play in question. We did a lot to encourage gang tackling, but clearly we did not do enough.

In the Oakland game, there were at least two plays, 5 and 66, where a ball carrier was hit by one or two of our tacklers—and everybody else pulled up as if the play was over. It wasn't. Oakland's ball carrier broke the initial tackle and ran free.

In 1992, we pushed gang tackling even harder—especially in preparation for the Western League Championship game against the Fairfield Falcons and their great running back, Gregory Reed. We tried some drills like having a large dummy set in a spot where the ball carrier was likely to go. We had the boys line up in their normal defensive alignment. On the snap, they did a normal charge as if they did not know where the ball was going yet. Then I yelled, "Gang!" and they all went to the dummy and swarmed it. We used a dummy instead of a scout-team player because being gang tackled is dangerous.

The other thing I did the week before Fairfield was talk constantly about gang tackling. I told them they were probably the best tacklers in the league as a team (which was true in 1992). But I said they were not good enough to stop Gregory Reed single-handedly. They had to gang tackle him. In scrimmage that week, once the first hit was made on the ball carrier, I'd yell, "Gang! Gang! Gang!" We tried to blow the whistle fast enough to prevent unnecessary risk of injury, but not so fast that the defense was unable to get into the habit of gang tackling.

During the game, I screamed, "Gang! Gang! Gang!" through my plastic megaphone every time we started to tackle the Falcon ball carrier. The emphasis on gang tackling in practice and during the game worked, too. In our game with the Falcons, we had the best gang tackling of any of the three teams I've coached—textbook gang tackling at times. Unfortunately, we did not get him every time. He broke loose four times and scored three touchdowns in their 19-7 victory.

Wide pursuit

I was pleased with our wide pursuit. We made a big deal of that and practiced it repeatedly. We told our players Oakland was very fast and that the only chance we had to stop them wide—once they broke out of the box between the ends—was to pursue at correct angles and at top speed.

In play 16, our pursuit angles and hustle got our players in front of an Oakland player which caused him to hesitate at which time he was tackled from behind.

In 1992, we pushed wide pursuit angles even harder in practice and had even more success. I discussed some of the lesson learned in the chapter on wide-pursuit angles.

Punt receiving

We never returned a punt all season in 1991. In the Oakland game, we probably had no chance to return one because Oakland's punter never kicked very far and Oakland's contain men were downfield fast. But we could have and should have **fair caught** the ball. That we didn't was my fault for not giving our punt returner any practice at it. Nor did I tell him to fair catch in pre-game preparation or during games.

Here's what happened on each Oakland punt:

Play 33	Landed at B47 and rolled to B30	fair catch would have saved 17 yards
Play 40	Landed at B24 and rolled to B14	fair catch would have saved 10 yards
Play 51	Landed at B19, Bears bounce to B19	fair catch would have saved 0 yards
Play 58	Quick kick	No one back to catch

So we gave up 27 yards by not fair catching. Of course, the reason the receiver did not fair catch was that he was afraid of muffing the ball and having Oakland recover. We beat Napa in the first playoff game on a touchdown set up by just that occurrence. But it seems that we ought to be able to reduce the number of muffs to a point that would make the percentages favor the catch. Plus there's always the possibility that the punting team would commit a penalty against the receiver by not reacting properly to the fair-catch signal. So good things can happen on a fair catch attempt as well as bad.

Oakland's defense

I was impressed by how well most Oakland players tackled. I wish I knew their secret for motivating their players to use correct tackling technique.

Their pass coverage wasn't so hot. The two interceptions they got were thrown right at the guys who caught them. But they left two receivers wide open for big gains in plays 10 and 14. Oakland appeared not to have assigned anyone to cover pass receivers coming out of the backfield.

Oakland's great strength was the tremendous **speed** and **tackling technique** of their linebackers. In their 7-3-1, they bunched the linebackers behind the middle of their line. That made it almost impossible for our fullback dive to gain four or more yards.

In our first game against Oakland, the fullback dive had consistently gained yards. As it did in our game against Vacaville the previous week. Apparently, Oakland decided they had to stack the middle to stop that play. And they did both. My fullback son only got as much as four yards once. He would typically run through the hole in the Oakland defensive line opened by our offensive line. Or the defensive lineman would grab him **high** allowing him to keep his legs driving. But the linebacker would come flying up to hit him low and hard and wrap him up tight. End of run.

Oakland apparently felt they could cover our sweep on sheer speed differential. Their parents were yelling about how slow our team was. You can hear them on the video which was taped from the Oakland side of the field. Our running backs would lumber toward end and the Oakland linebackers would come flying out to tackle us for a loss.

We probably should have thrown more passes like plays 10 and 14. I don't know how often we split out wide receivers. If Oakland responded to a wide receiver by putting a linebacker on them, we probably could have sprung our dives up the middle for more yards. And if they did **not** put anybody on the wide receivers, we could have thrown quick passes to them.

The Vacaville coach had beaten Oakland the previous year—and gone on to win the CYF championship. He told our offensive coordinator that his secret against Oakland was to run every play between the ends. Those plays sure didn't work for us.

Our offensive plays that **worked** generally featured at least one downfield block. Downfield blocks are tough on one-man dive plays. But there is plenty of opportunity for them on off-tackle and sweep plays. Oakland's offense was probably the best in the league at downfield blocking. I would say the key to beating Oakland's 1991 defense was to take their linebackers out of the game. That means:

- good fakes
- spreading out the offense
- assigning blockers to hit the key linebackers on each play.

What I did wrong

The main things I did wrong in 1991 as evidenced by our performance in the Oakland game were:

- Not motivating our players to use proper tackling technique throughout the season
- Not analyzing each game in the detail I have in this chapter
- Not teaching the players how to break holds
- Not seeing the pattern of weakness on one side during the game
- Not giving our punt returner fair-catch practice repetitions and instructions
- Not making sure everyone including substitutes understood their job description
- Not putting more emphasis on gang tackling.

In 1992, I generally **did** correct all those mistakes and we had a 9-2 record as opposed to our 1991 record of 7-3. Our kids were less talented as a group in 1992 than in 1991. But I was a smarter coach. Our offense and kickoff teams were also much improved in 1992.

In 1992, after he scouted our first playoff victory (26-0, six points by defense knocking ball loose and picking it up and running into the end zone) against the Delta Rebels, the Vacaville coach told our head coach, "Well, you guys are as good as they say." I was very pleased to hear that because I remembered previous years when the San Ramon Bears were 0-8 and 1-7 and one of the league's doormats. We beat Vacaville 26-0 (six points by defense on interception runback) the next week to win the 1992 Valley Conference Championship. In 1991, we also beat Vacaville in that game—but only by 6-0.

One of our 1992 losses (19-2 to Berkeley) came early in the season and was largely caused by four special teams failures. We later beat Richmond, who had beaten Berkeley. And we beat Vallejo, who had beaten Oakland 22-7 and I believe Vallejo either beat Berkeley or Oakland did. I suspect that we would have beaten Berkeley had there been a rematch in 1992.

When I analyzed our **other** 1992 loss—to Fairfield in the Western League Championship game—I concluded that there was not much I had done wrong. Fairfield's Reed was so good that if the key defensive players took one false step, or even a false **half**-step, he was gone. If I had the game to play over, I'd run a zillion sweeps in practice with the ball carrier getting a head start to simulate Reed's phenomenal acceleration. I suspect we could have fine tuned our ability to stop the sweep somewhat. If so, we might have held him to **one** or **two** touchdowns instead of **three**. But I doubt we could shut him out no matter how much we practiced. Beating a guy like that would require a whole team effort including a ball-control or high-scoring offense, excellent special teams performance, **and** a strong defense.

28

Our best playoff game

Our best game of the 1991 season was against Benicia. We scored 16 points on defense in that one. But the tape of that game is hard to analyze because the camera was stopped at the end of each play. So I have analyzed our best **playoff** game instead. At that stage of the season, we were getting better videotapes. Plus, Vacaville was a worthy playoff opponent. They had beaten Benicia 31-0 the week before to earn the right to play us for the Valley Conference Championship. Vacaville was the defending California Youth Football champion in 1991.

Play	Poss.	Down	To go	Ball on	Result	Comment
1	V	KO		B40	0	Kickoff to Vacaville, squib down middle, receiver deliberately fell down with it as soon as he touched it.
2	V	1	10	V45	1	Dive left. Stopped by left side of defense.
3	V	2	9	V46	-2	Fumbled hand off. Recovered by Vacaville.
4	V	3	11	V44	-4	Sweep left. Hit by two who did not finish tackle. Tripped by a third player.
5	V	4	15	V40	12	Punt to V47, bounced to B48. Returner realized late that it was a punt play.
6	Bears	1	10	B48	0	20-yard pass down middle. Almost complete. Receiver behind all defenders.
7	Bears	2	10	B48	-5	Sweep left. Two blocks but five unblocked defenders swarmed
8	Bears	3	15	B43	1	Sweep right.
9	Bears	4	14	B44	23	Punt to 33. Downed by Vacaville where it landed.
						Our left wide out ran down looking up at punt. He had to leave temporarily when a receiving team member blasted him with a block he did not see coming.
10	V	1	10	V33	1	I formation. Dive right stopped by our left side.
11	V	2	9	V34	-2	Sweep right. Ball carrier cleared our LE but saw LHB coming and reversed direction. LE grabbed shirt at V29. Ball carrier fought back to V32.
12	V	3	11	V32	3	Sweep left. RE and RLB dove and missed. RHB tackled.
13	V	4	8	V35	28	Punt to B41 bounced to B37.
14	Bears	1	10	B37	6	Dive right.
15	Bears	2	4	B43	2	Dive right.
16	Bears	3	2	B45	-5	Long count. Our guys jumped. Illegal procedure.
					6	Pass to fullback out of backfield. Cut in short of first down.
17	Bears	4	1	B46	3	Dive right. First down.
18	Bears	1	10	B49	1	Halfback flare pass right. Great block by lead back but blocked player still made the tackle because he was not put away.
End of first quarter						
19	Bears	2	9	50	1	Off tackle right. Tackle by LB. Blocker missed.
20	Bears	3	8	V49	-5	Drop back to pass. Ends came straight in unblocked.
21	Bears	4	15	B46	8	Fake punt pass to right wing. Illegal participation against Bears. 12 men on field. Declined??!!
22	V	1	10	V46	0	Dive right. Fumble on exchange to our LE.
23	Bears	1	10	V46	3	Dive right.
24	Bears	2	7	V43	6	Sweep right. Cut in behind blockers.
25	Bears	3	1	V37	-4	Dive right. Fumble on snap. Recovered by our team.
26	Bears	4	5	V42	2	Sweep left. Strung out. Over on downs.
27	V	1	10	V40	5	Dive left. 6 tacklers hit ball carrier. All high.
28	V	2	5	V45	2	Dive right. Stopped by left side of line.
29	V	3	3	V47	6	Dive left. Two tacklers hit high. Another had by one leg.
30	V	1	10	B47	2	Dive left. Hit at LOS then gang tackled.
31	V	2	8	B45	-2	Reverse to left. Played perfectly by our RE who contained while RT tackled.
32	V	3	10	B47	0	Dive left. No hole. Bounced to right. Tackled by LE and LT.
33	V	4	10	B47	15	LLB dropped back to receive punt. No punt. Safety moved to LLB. He was confused as to what to do. Sweep right. LE face masked. LLB and LHB missed. RE was blocked in. RHB came from other side of the field to make the tackle. No gain.

Play	Poss.	Down	To go	Ball on	Result	Comment
34	V	1	10	B32	-5	Dive left. Waist tackle for no gain. Illegal procedure.
35	V	1	15	B37	2	Off tackle left. RG missed. RE head behind arm tackle failed. Swarmed under by RLB, RT, RHB.
36	V	2	13	B35	4	Reverse to right. RE forced ball carrier to 9 yards behind LOS. But dove and missed. LHB overran. LLB missed. But missed tackles forced ball carrier to slow and allow pursuit to catch up.
37	V	3	9	B31	-5	Quick look-in pass to left split end. Played perfectly by RHB. Batted down. Illegal procedure.
38	V	4	14	B36	-3	Intended to be look-in to right tight end. He was well covered by three defenders including out-of-place LE. Pulled ball down and got sacked by RE and RT.
End of first half						
39	Bears	KO		V40	24	Kicked down the middle to our best returner. He fielded the ball on one hop at B31 and ran it up the middle to the V45.
40	Bears	1	10	V45	5	Dead ball offsides
					4	Dive right
41	Bears	2	1	V36	4	Dive right
42	Bears	1	10	V32	5	Dive right
43	Bears	2	5	V27	27TD	Off tackle right cut back against grain.
44	Bears	PAT	3	V3	0	Incomplete pass to right wing over the middle.
45	V	KO		B40	0	Squib kick to front line guy who caught and immediately dropped to knees—apparently as coached.
46	V	1	10	V47	0	Dive left. RT tackled.
47	V	2	10	V47	4	Dive left. RT was cut blocked. Hole in line. Excellent tackle by RHB and LLB.
48	V	3	6	B49	-5	Vacaville split right end out. As trained, our LE moved outside of offensive end. QB saw this and called time. After time out, right offensive end split way out as a flanker. Our LHB went out with him. Right flanker went in motion before snap toward our LE. Our LHB went in motion with him. When flanker was just outside LE, ball was snapped and flanker blocked LE in. Sweep right for 12-yard gain. But called back because flanker went toward the LOS during his pre-snap motion.
49	V	3	11	V46	0	Faked handoff then turned to pass. Whipsawed by our RE hitting low and LE hitting high. Apparent fumble recovered by Bears at V36. But referees ruled incomplete pass.
50	V	4	11	V46	30	Punt. Very high snap. LT there in time to block but wide to the left. Ball hit at B38 precisely where returner was waiting. But he scooted away and ball bounced to the B25.
51	Bears	1	10	B25	3	Dive right.
52	Bears	2	7	B28	-2	Sweep right. LT penetrated.
53	Bears	3	9	B26	1	Dive right.
54	Bears	4	8	B27	25	Punt to V48. Vacaville bounce but downed by right wideout.
55	V	1	10	V48	0	Dive right but huge traffic jam there.
56	V	2	10	V48	5	Sweep left. Our RE gave ground. RHB hit ball carrier hard but high at LOS. Gained 5 more yards. I yelled at RE, "Don't give ground! Stand and fight!"
57	V	3	5	B47	-4	Same play. RE did not give ground. Took on blocker. Ball carrier forced to go around RE deep. Saw RHB coming and reversed direction. Tackled immediately by LE pursuing through backfield in case of reverse.

Play	Poss.	Down	To go	Ball on	Result	Comment
58	V	4	9	V49	3	Dive right. Gang tackled after getting through hole.
59	Bears	1	10	B48	3	Dive right.
60	Bears	2	7	V49	2	Dive right.
End of third quarter						
61	Bears	3	5	V47	13	Sweep left. Great lead block by fullback but then quit. Guy that was blocked made the tackle.
62	Bears	1	10	V34	2	Dive right. Wide slot left to spread defense. Still three LBs in middle. Tackle by line.
63	Bears	2	8	V32	3	Sweep left. Lead blocker there but ball carrier cut in.
64	Bears	3	5	V29	-5	Illegal procedure.
			10	V34	2	Flare pass to back out of backfield. He stopped after catching and was tackled on the spot.
65	Bears	4	8	V32	-10	Punt right to returner who was at the V18. He ran right and got back to the V42 before being driven out.
66	V	1	10	V42	0	Sweep left. RE gave ground then stopped, slid off block, and made tackle.
67	V	2	10	V42	2	Sweep right. LE in good position but tried to arm tackle and fell down. LT also tried to tackle and missed. Dealing with LE strung out play. LHB threw down with high tackle.
68	V	3	8	V44	2	Dive left. Tackle by RG
69	V	4	6	V46	-5	Reverse to left. Handoff fumbled. LE unloaded on ball carrier right after he picked up the ball. Over on downs.
70	Bears	1	10	V41	4	Sweep right. One missed tackle.
71	Bears	2	6	V37	5	Dive right.
72	Bears	3	1	V32	0	Wide slot left to spread defense. Fumble to Bears.
73	Bears	4	1	V32	0	Off tackle left. No blocks. Over on downs.
74	V	1	10	V32	5	Dive left. Stopped at LOS but second effort.
75	V	2	5	V37	4	Off tackle right.
76	V	3	1	V41	3	Dive right. First down.
77	V	1	10	V44	-5	Apparent pitch option to right. QB was taking baby steps and was sacked by RG.
78	V	2	15	V39	0	Deliberate grounding look-in pass to stop clock. Almost instercepted by LE. It went threw his hands. 1:01 remaning.
79	V	3	15	V39	-7	Reverse to left. Ball carrier sacked by LLB.
80	V	4	22	V32	0	Quick look-in pass to right split end who had gone in motion. before the snap. Batted by LE. Almost intercepted.
81	Bears	1	10	V32	1	Dive right.
End of game						

Here is a statistical analysis of our win over Vacaville:

Category	Vacaville	Bears
Non-PAT scrimmage plays	38	33
Non-PAT scrimmage yards gained	20	97
Non-PAT scrimmage yards per play	.53	2.94
Penalties	15	25
Kickoff returns	2	1
Kickoff return yardage	0	24
Yards per kickoff return	0	24
Average field position after kickoff return	V 42.5	V 45
First downs	2	2
Non-PAT scrimmage successes on defense (less than 4 yd.gain)	22	30
Non-PAT scrimmage failures on defense (4 or more yd. gain)	11	8
Turnovers including punts and on downs	7	6
Punts	3	3
Punt (including return) yardage	70	38
Average yards-per-punt change in field position (punt team)	23.33	12.67

Here's how each series went:

Vacaville series:

Plays	Distance covered	Result
2-5	-5	punt
10-13	2	punt
22	0	fumble
27-38	24	end of half
46-50	-1	punt
55-58	1	over on downs
66-69	4	over on downs
74-79	0	over on downs

Bears series:

Plays	Distance covered	Result
6-9	4	punt
14-21	9	penalty on fake punt, over on downs
23-26	4	over on downs
40-43	45	touchdown
51-54	2	punt
59-65	20	punt
70-73	9	over on downs
81	1	end of game

Vacaville's success by play choice:

Reverse right	1 for 4 yards		4.00 yards per carry
Off tackle right	1 for 4		4.00 yard per carry
Sweep right*	4 for 10		2.50 yards per carry
Off tackle left	1 for 2 yards		2.00 yards per carry
Dive left	10 for 20		2.00 yards per carry

Dive right	5 for 8	1.60 yards per carry
Pass to the left	1 for 0	.00 yards per pass
Sweep left	5 for 0	.00 yards per carry
Pass to the right	3 for -3	-1.00 yards per pass
Reverse left	3 for -14	-4.67 yards per carry

* includes play #33 where our LE face masked for 15-yard penalty and play #48 where Vacaville flanker went in motion forward for 5-yard penalty.

Cause of our failures:

Play	Cause
27	poor tackling technique
29	poor tackling technique
33	poor tackling technique
36	poor tackling technique
47	job description not carried out
56	poor tackling technique
74	poor tackling technique
75	poor tackling technique

Summary cause of failures:

Poor tackling technique	7 of 8	88%
Job description not carried out	1 of 8	12%

The stats on this game make it look like two strong defenses played. Actually, the Vacaville **offense** was strong. They had beaten Benicia the week before 31-0. And all those points were scored by the Vacaville offense. When we played Benicia, our **offense** only scored 8 points and one of those was a PAT following a **defensive** touchdown.

Kickoffs

You can see the contrast between my approach to kickoffs and everyone else's in this game. We kicked off twice. Both times we squib kicked down the middle. Both times, the Vacaville player immediately downed the ball without attempting a return. That was precisely what I wanted them to do. True, they had decent field position near midfield. But they did not run either kickoff back for a touchdown. They didn't even run it back for a "first down" (10-yard return)—thereby forcing their offense to get one more first down enroute to a touchdown.

Vacaville's prime kick returner—the guy we most certainly did **not** kick to—**did** return one our **punts** (play #65) 24 yards in a play that was very scary until it ended. We could have lost the game if the punt return had broken loose for a touchdown instead of just 24 yards. If I had been in charge of the punt team, the punter would have been ordered to kick the ball where it could **not** be returned.

Now look at Vacaville's only kickoff to us in play 39 at the beginning of the second half. We did nothing special on the return. We just picked the ball up and ran it up the middle. But somebody on the Vacaville team blew their assignment and our returner went 24 yards. That was the first play of our only scoring drive—the **winning** scoring drive as it turned out.

Where did Vacaville kick? Right down the middle and hard. Who was there? Our best return man.

The kickoff is a very dangerous play—even when your team is as fast as Vacaville was and the receiving team is as slow as we were. If Vacaville had squib kicked as we did, there probably would have been no return at all—and no psychological lift for our team and corresponding downer for Vacaville.

Punt return team

Shame on me. Our punt return man apparently had it in his head that he should be extremely cautious about the decision to catch a punt. He never tried to catch one all year. As a result, mediocre punters often got excellent field position changes from favorable bounces. Vacaville's average field position change on their punts far exceeded ours 23.33 yards versus 12.67 yards. That's the kind of difference which loses games.

I should have **noticed** that we were not catching punts and taken action to either give the returner punt catching experience and training or found a different kid for the job. It basically did not penetrate my consciousness until the last playoff game against Oakland that we had never returned a punt.

I had admonished punt returners both in 1990 and 1991 that it was harmful to the team for punts to be allowed to bounce 10 to 20 yards the wrong way. But I never was successful in giving them proper perspective on the damage done by a **muff**—which can**not** be advanced by the punting team—versus the damage done by losing 10 to 20 yards of **field position**.

Returner out of position

On the first punt, play #5, our punt returner did not notice that there was a punt situation and that Vacaville was in a punt formation. I should have trained him to pay more attention to the down-and-distance situation and we coaches should have yelled, "Watch the punt!" before the punt team can to the line of scrimmage.

On play #33, we had the opposite situation. The punt return man dropped back to receive, switching places with the safety for the one play. But it was not a punt in spite of the 4th and 10 situation. In the video, the safety's confusion as to how to play linebacker was evident. The LHB was telling him to move over to be nose-to-nose with the tight end. The safety, who was formerly the left end, was trying to line up like a left end outside the tight end. He probably did not know that he was supposed to keep the tight end on the line of scrimmage and go with him if he escaped. I should have made sure that this player knew the linebacker job description and got practice time at that position even though he only had to play it occasionally.

Fair catch

The second punt, play #13, and third punt, play #50, should have been **fair caught**. We never practiced fair catching. We should have. In youth football, particularly at the Jr. Pee Wee level, fair catches should be the **rule**. That's because the vast majority of the punters can't punt very high or far. So the coverage is generally all around the returner when the ball comes down. In fact, I have never seen a single fair catch in four years in youth football games.

Play #50 could have led to us losing the game. The punt returner was standing precisely where the ball came down. But he scooted far away from it when he saw the punt team closing. The distance from the line of scrimmage to the impact point was only 16 yards. But the ball bounced to our 25-yard line. That was the **biggest play of the day** by either team in terms of field-position change. It was also Vacaville's **deepest penetration** into our territory of the day. If we had fumbled or thrown an interception during the subsequent series, it could easily have led to our losing the game.

Our offense only advanced the ball two yards on that series. Fortunately, our punter was probably the best in the league. He got off a 25-yard punt, which took a Vacaville bounce but was alertly downed by our right wideout. That put Vacaville back in its own end of the field. Except for two slight penetrations on plays #57 and 59, the ball stayed in the Vacaville end of the field for the rest of the game.

Punt blocks

As I mentioned earlier in the book, we blocked so many punts and sacked so many punters in the beginning of the season that we called our punt return team the "punt sack" team. We got no punt sacks on this day, however. We probably should have gotten one on the play that went to our 25. The snap was quite high. It had hang time. Our left tackle was in to block but went by it to the left. The rest of our line was slow in penetrating.

We should have practiced punt blocking more. Our early success made us overconfident and we failed to work on punt blocks. As I learned at a coaching clinic I took in February of 1992, you overload one side to block punts. We were not doing that. We just had everyone do their normal thing and hoped one would get through. That's too sloppy an approach.

Poor tackling technique

As with the Oakland game in the last chapter, poor tackling technique was the primary cause of our failures. Generally, the particular flaw was tackling **high**. Maybe we coaches should make a training tape of high tackles versus low ones to show how badly high ones work compared to low ones.

When the tacklers are high, it often takes five or six of them to bring the ball carrier down—and then only after he has advanced the ball another five yards while the six tacklers held onto him. That happened in play #27. In play #29, it took three guys tackling improperly to get him down and then only after he gained six yards.

Play #56 was a one-man tackle. But because it was high, the ball carrier got five more yards.

High tackles are the only kind that result in **face mask** penalties. Our left defensive end liked to tackle high. In both the Vacaville and Oakland games, he was penalized for grabbing the face mask. On that one play, he became Vacaville's leading ground gainer for the day—and he gave them one of their two first downs—on a play that otherwise was stopped for no gain.

On the other hand, low tackles only take one man and generally end the run on the spot. We had such a tackle—finally—on play # 33 after several missed tackles and a face mask.

The Flying Wallendas

The other common mistake was leaving their feet. Kids like to fly spectacularly through the air. It rarely works. But they keep doing it. Falling down should be noted when analyzing tape. The offending players should be spoken to about the problem. If they don't knock it off, try to replace them.

Job description not carried out

The only failure which was caused by not carrying out a job description was in play # 47. The right tackle was supposed to fill his gap. He's also supposed to be low. We told them a million times, "Low man usually wins." He got cut blocked—which is legal in the interior line—by the opposing offensive lineman. Low man won. The resulting hole allowed a 4-yard gain.

End giving ground

We had a problem with our right end giving ground on sweeps. We had told him that he was not to let the ball carrier get outside him. But he interpreted that to mean he should give ground so as to keep himself between the ball carrier and the sideline. That's incorrect. Giving ground opens a huge gap between the end and the tackle or linebacker. Frequently the sweep would work **inside** our right end because of his giving ground. That happened in play #56. That play ended right near our sideline. I yelled at the right end to not give ground—to stand and fight—create a pileup. We had said these things in practice previously.

Vacaville tried the same play again on the next snap. This time the right end gave ground momentarily, then took on the lead blocker. That created a small head-butting match which was in the ball carrier's way. The ball carrier went around it deep. That gave our pursuit a second to get wide. The ball carrier then saw our right half back outside and reversed field.

Reversing field on a sweep was not prudent against our team in 1991. We had been beaten in the same championship game the year before by two **reverses**. All during the 1991 season, we reminded our defensive ends to pursue **through** the backfield. And I recall no play in 1991 when the defensive end was not where he was supposed to be on a reverse. We didn't always **stop** the reverse. But none went for a touchdown like the two touchdown reverses in the 1990 playoff game against Vacaville. When the ball carrier reversed field on the play # 57 sweep, the left defensive end, who was probably the tallest player in the league, flattened him.

Our right end also gave ground on play # 66 but seemed to realize his mistake in mid play then stopped giving ground and slid off the block to make the tackle.

Blocking down on our end

Play # 48 is interesting. When I watched the video, I immediately saw what Vacaville was trying to do. That's because of the high angle of the video. During the **game**, however, I do not remember recognizing Vacaville's plan. During the game, I station myself on the **offense's** side of the line of scrimmage so I can see the play develop and yell, "Sweep!" or "Dive!" or whatever as soon as I recognize the play. From field level, my view of the **far** end was apparently obscured by the offensive backfield.

Vacaville tried to split their right end just a little bit outside our left defensive end. Our ends were taught to always position themselves at least one yard **outside** a tight end and at least two yards outside a wingback. So here we had a case of two opposing coaches each telling the end to get outside the opponent. The result was two guys dancing back and forth at the right end of the Vacaville line.

The Vacaville quarterback watched this dance and very wisely called time. I went out on the field but just had a general discussion. Had I seen what I saw on the video tape, I'd have said, "Watch the sweep to our left."

We actually had practiced the dance our end was doing. We taught our ends that they would occasionally encounter an offensive end who had been told to get outside of them so he could block down on them. Move back and forth, we told them, until the quarterback starts to call signals.

At some point, the offensive end must get set and not move for at least one second. At that point, you simply make your final move to the outside—or—if the end is really way out, move to the inside. Our defensive ends were supposed to be outside the offensive end or wingback unless the offensive player was **so** far out that the defensive end felt confident he could get to the depth of the ball untouched by any offensive player.

Motion man

The Vacaville coach apparently was told during the time-out huddle about the left defensive end's lack of cooperation with their desire to line up just outside him. And the Vacaville coach's solution was a pretty good one. He told the right end to line up as a flanker (not on the line of scrimmage) way outside the defensive left end—then go in motion before the snap so that he was where he wanted to be at the snap.

Actually, I had anticipated this stunt way back at the beginning of the preseason. The defensive job description sheet I handed out in August said this regarding the halfbacks,

[Line up] Two yards in front of the widest receiver other than the tight end. If your man goes in motion, go with him but stop when you get to the linebacker on

your side. If your man attempts to block our end, immediately blitz outside him and contain the sweep or reverse.

My son was the left halfback. When the flanker went out, he went out with him. When the flanker went in motion, my son went in motion with him. However, he did **not** blitz outside when the flanker blocked down on the left defensive end. The flanker's block on our left end was successful. The play swept their right end for 12 yards and a first down.

However, the Vacaville coach apparently made a mistake similar to the one I made on the play. I had not practiced this reaction to the motion man blocking down on an end since the preseason. Furthermore, I doubt my son was even at that position then. By the Vacaville game, he had forgotten about the need to assume contain responsibilities when the motion man blocked down on the end.

The Vacaville coach apparently also failed to give his flanker enough practice at this maneuver. The flanker went in motion **toward** the line of scrimmage which is a violation of the rules. It negated the 12-yard gain and first down and resulted in a five-yard loss for his team.

The golden five minutes

I noticed a phenomenon during the 1991 season: one team often blew away the other during the first five minutes of the game or second half. I think you can see that in this game.

We had been shocked in the Benicia game at how Benicia played in the second half. They apparently got fired up at half time and held our offense scoreless in the second half. They had done the same to Richmond in a game I scouted. Richmond was good enough to beat us 13-8 in 1991.

We resolved that we would not let that happen again. So we consciously spent the last few minutes of each half-time psyching our kids back up. Half-time is an emotional let-down. The adrenaline stops flowing. We started our usual yelling as the boys assembled for the run through the big paper sign held by the cheerleaders under the goal posts.

Coach: "What're the three parts of a tackle?!"

Players: "Hit! Wrap! Drive!"

Coach: "Louder! What're the three parts of a tackle?!"

Players: "HIT! WRAP! DRIVE!"

After they ran through the paper, we did it again as they assembled on the sideline. By the time the kickoff was ready, they were **fired up**.

Vacaville, in the meantime, was very **quietly** having a chalk talk. They seemed almost to be defiantly contrasting their calm, businesslike style with our loud rah-rah approach.

Then they very quietly kicked off and our fired up kids hit 'em in rapid succession with a 24-yard return, three dives of at least four yards each, and a 27-yard touchdown romp. Each of these runs went more or less right through the heart of their defense. A rapid-fire, 69-yard drive (including the kickoff return). I believe we used our no-huddle offense in this drive. We had previously no-huddled Berkeley right down the field to a touchdown in similar fashion in the first series of that game. Berkeley's coach even had to call a basketball-style time out to try to regroup—to no avail.

There was no other series like it all day by either team in the Vacaville game. After that, Vacaville got re-fired up by the game itself, if not by their coaches. But by then, it was **too late**. That one series was all we **did** that day offensively. But it was all we **needed**.

Gang tackling

We had more gang tackling in this game than in the next one with Oakland. I don't know why. I suspect that our kids got discouraged early in the Oakland game and let down a bit.

During the 1991 season, we never won a game in which the other team scored **any** points. Fortunately, we shut out all but two opponents. That was great and we're very proud of it. But it has a **down**side: your team doesn't get much chance to build come-from-behind character. And 8- to 11-year olds do not come with a lot of character in the face of adversity preprogrammed in at the "factory."

Our kids probably don't even remember the come-from-behind victories engineered by Joe Montana or Roger Staubach. They only knew taking the lead and keeping it. They got discouraged when they did not have the lead. We tried to engender a come-from-behind spirit, but I suspect it comes only from experience.

Our kids never came from behind to win a game—or even tie or take the lead temporarily. They **did** battle back on defense in the Richmond game to score eight defensive points after letting Richmond get ahead by 13. We probably should have created some artificial come-from behind drills or practice games to make up for the lack of come-from-behind game experience. We need some way to create a we've-been-here-before feeling about coming from behind.

Scout-team scrimmages accomplished that been-here-before feeling well as far as the opponent's offensive plays were concerned. Some similar artificial technique can probably accomplish the same for coming from behind.

Pass defense

Although our 8-2-1 and 10-1 are not supposed to be good against passes, we stopped Vacaville cold in that department. They tried four passes. Three were batted down with authority; the other barely left the quarterback's hand before he was slammed simultaneously by both of our ends. Indeed, the ball went **backwards** out of his hand and was recovered by us for a 10-yard loss. But the refs said it was an incomplete forward pass. The forward arm motion the referees saw was not evident in my video.

Each of the three passes that was batted down could have been intercepted. One was batted so easily the halfback was mad at himself for not trying to intercept it. Another went through our left end's hands between his legs. And the third was batted up in the air by the left end with both hands and almost picked off by our left halfback in tip drill fashion. We did not do a tip drill after the preseason. Another would-be pass was covered so well the quarterback looked, but pulled it down and was sacked.

May have led league in pass defense

I wouldn't claim that we were great pass defenders. Rather the quarterbacks and protection in Jr. Pee Wee football are so weak that there simply is not much of a passing threat. A few decent athletes watching the receivers and six guys with their ears pinned back pressuring the quarterback are about all you need.

In 1992, we evolved into a 10-1 defense that's supposed to be even worse against the pass than an 8-2-1. But our pass defense was probably the best in the league. We **intercepted** about half the passes attempted against us. Only about five were completed against us all season. Only one, in the first game, gained more than about six yards.

Delta tries to pass against our 10-1

The **first** time the Delta Rebels played us in 1992, they hardly passed at all—and we beat them 19-0.

The **second** time we played them was the first playoff game. They apparently decided that we were overplaying the run and that they could pass. They tried to pass six times in the playoff game.

One fell incomplete—and that was their **best** pass of the day. We intercepted four passes—one on a diving catch by our right cornerback who was also our quarterback—one by a defensive tackle. I alternately congratulated the tackle—who was a six-play player— for his interception—and chewed him out for standing up on the line of scrimmage when he's supposed to stay low and go sack the quarterback. "That was a great interception. Now tell me what the heck you were doing standing bolt upright on the line of scrimmage catching a pass when you were supposed to be in the backfield chasing the quarterback."

Defensive score on a Delta pass

The sixth Delta pass never left the quarterback's hand—at least not in the direction of the intended receiver. We had them on about their own two-yard line and they called time-out. I went out and said,

> *Hey. I don't want any measly safety here. A safety's only worth two points. Let's get six. Try to knock the ball loose then pick it up and run it into the end zone. If it's lying on the ground in the end zone, just fall on it. That's a touchdown. If you can't strip it loose, hold on to the ball carrier's shirt and let him take you out to the one-yard line. Then tackle him there and we'll try again.*

As a result of a successful sweep and penalty against us, Delta got out to about its own 20-yard line. Then their quarterback dropped back to pass rolling slightly to his right. Our right defensive end blasted him from the blindside, knocking the ball loose. Our left defensive end picked it up and ran it into the end zone for a touchdown.

Tackling yourself

When we scouted the Falcons game against Suisun, the Falcons blocked a punt around midfield. The ball went bouncing back behind the punter toward the Falcons' goal line. A Falcon flew after it and fell on the ball instead of picking it up.

The Falcons could have used that touchdown. The game ended 19-19 in regulation and the Falcons only won in the second and final overtime. Had the game ended in a tie, Suisun would have advanced in the playoffs rather than the Falcons because they beat the Falcons in the regular season.

The Bears players who were around me in the stands when the Falcon fell on the punt winced collectively and immediately started saying out loud, "Don't fall on it. Pick it up and run." They then laughed at how much they had been affected by our training. They winced because in our practices, falling on a blocked punt is invariably met with a loud, prolonged critique from me.

> *What in the heck was that? You had nothing but green grass between you and paydirt. There was no opposing player even going the right **direction** to tackle you. You could have had the first touchdown of your **career** right there. That was a **golden opportunity** and you blew it. They had **no** chance to tackle you. But you tackled **yourself**. Don't fall on that ball. Pick the darned thing up and run with it. It would have been **our** ball even if the **other** team fell on it. It was **fourth down**, remember? Falling on a blocked punt accomplishes next to **nothing**.*

That was all said in a pointed, exasperated tone with just enough edge in my voice to make it memorable. I would then toss the ball on the ground several times and make the player who fell on it pick it up and run with it. We also ran pick-up-fumbles-and-run-with-them drills in practice.

We blocked a punt in the 1992 Napa game and ran it in for the first score of the game. At the time, I commented to the other coaches on the sideline, "99% of the other teams in this league would have fallen on that." Napa never tried to punt again in that game. We won 27-7.

My San Ramon Bears teams have a Pavlovian response to balls on the ground: pick them up and run if at all possible. In two years we have scored four defensive touchdowns that way and advanced the ball before being tackled short of the end zone on other occasions. We have never lost a fumble recovery in a game because we tried to pick it up when we should have fallen on it. And there was only one time in two years in a practice scrimmage where I judged that trying to pick it up cost the defense a recovery. And then there was no field-position change.

In general, losing a fumble recovery because you tried to advance it only costs you possession—no yards. But the possible benefits of picking it up—touchdowns and favorable changes in field position—make the risk of loss very worthwhile indeed. Most coaches don't seem to realize that. They think losing a fumble recovery is a fate worse than death. I think losing a touchdown is the more important danger.

Beat them worse

We beat the **passing** version of the 1992 Delta Rebels by seven more points than we beat the **running** version—26-0.

We were scouted in our other 1992 playoff games. And all our playoff opponents apparently came to the same "We can pass against that 10-1 defense" conclusion. Vacaville threw a pass which we intercepted and ran back 60 yards for a touchdown. They threw another to their huge tight end. Our tiny middle linebacker batted it down with all the authority of a Ronnie Lott.

The mighty Fairfield Falcons, who beat us 19-7 in 1992 and went on to win the CYF championship, tried to pass several times against us. All fell incomplete—apparently because their quarterback was distracted by having to run for his life to get away from our eight-man rush.

Vacaville's 1991 passes were all **look-ins**. Our pass defense was probably strongest against look-ins. Look-ins were the type of pass I feared most because they are quick. Passes which take longer to develop don't have much chance in youth football because the offensive lines cannot pass protect.

Our linebackers were assigned to hold the tight ends on the line in our 8-2-1 defense. To the extent that they succeed, there will be no look-in. There will probably be no look-in even if they merely **delay** the departure of the tight end on his look-in pattern because the guards and tackles will be in the quarterback's face within a second or two if he stays right behind the center. Plus, our halfbacks were standing right behind the linebackers unless a non-tight end receiver was split out wide.

In the 10-1, we had the linebackers and cornerbacks line up on each shoulder of the tight end. When the ball moved, they were to charge forward driving their shoulder pads into the ribs on each side of the tight end. They were not to hold him on the line or cover him. Rather they were to simply run over him on their way to the ball carrier. If the play was a quick pass to the tight end, the quarterback was supposed to be sacked before the tight end recovered from the double-team steamroller.

So each tight end was sort of **double-teamed** as well as bumped while his quarterback was having to deal with a four-man rush through the center-guard and guard-tackle gaps. Vacaville threw their look-ins so fast that our very tall left defensive end had not yet left his starting point. He batted one with both hands and almost intercepted the other. With him there, the poor receiver was **triple**-teamed. One guy actually caught a look-in against us in the 1991 Manteca game. But he was so well covered that he only managed to gain about two feet on the completion.

One option play

On play # 77, the Vacaville team apparently tried to run a double option against us. A double option is one in which the quarterback either keeps or gives the ball to one other player. In the more common triple option, he either keeps or gives the ball to one of **two** other players.

Play # 77 was apparently a **pitch** option and the quarterback was running slow to allow the pitch man to get into a proper option relationship—typically four yards **outside** the quarterback and four yards **deeper** than the quarterback. It's not supposed to work that way. The quarterback is supposed to be watching the defensive end and the pitch man is supposed to get to the proper pitch relationship without the quarterback worrying about or looking at the pitch man. Both are supposed to run fast.

As Vacaville ran it, it was simply a very slow-developing play. The quarterback was clearly uncomfortable with it. And the pitch man was not where he was supposed to be. The quarterback was caught from behind by our backside (opposite of the play direction) guard.

I thought play # 77 was supposed to be an option. So did the public address announcer who said, "Loss of five on the option attempt" or some such.

Using the option as rarely as once a game shows a lack of understanding of option football. Stan Scarborough and William E. Warren wrote the excellent book, *Option Football Concepts and Techniques for Winning*. In it, they say,

> *...learning to run the option properly is a time-consuming proposition.*
> *...many coaches fail to realize that when they run the option play only as a complement to their power series, they fail to reap its full benefits...because their backs haven't practiced the play enough to get their timing and movements synchronized.*

Competent option teams run the option 70% of the time or more. Running it once a game is almost certainly doomed to failure. We have never seen an option team in youth football so we did not cover the option in our defensive coaching. Napa ran a wishbone **formation** when we first played them in 1991—and they apparently tried unsuccessfully to use the option at their jamboree—but they never used the option *per se* in our game. The wishbone is not a bad power formation, but it does not seem to have any advantages over more normal power formations like the I, wing T, or straight T.

If I had to defend against a true option team, I'd assign a linebacker to the dive man, the tackle to the quarterback, and the end to the pitch man and have them "slow play" it. That is, just shuffle along the line of scrimmage with your guy until he tries to cross it. Then tackle him.

General observations

Vacaville's best play in this game was sweeping right and hoping that our left end would draw a face mask penalty. That was the main play in their 24-yard drive, the only drive that went more than 4 yards.

Our kids were somewhat sloppy in their tackling. Vacaville was not strong enough on offense to get a score out of that sloppiness. The following week, Oakland was. Essentially, we played in two leagues in 1991: Oakland and the rest of the league. We were probably strong enough to win the rest-of-the-league championship. But we needed to improve significantly to beat Oakland.

No pattern of weakness is evident in Vacaville's success by play choice. Basically, it didn't matter what play they ran, we stopped it. Against a much stronger Oakland team the following week, clear weaknesses emerged. We used the same defensive line-up for both the Vacaville and Oakland games.

For more info...
Books

George Allen's Guide to Special Teams by George Allen and Joseph G Paccelli, Leisure Press

American Football Coaches Guide Book to Championship Football Drills by Jerry Tolley, self-published

Audibles, My Life in Football by Joe Montana, Avon Books

Bo by Bo Schembechler, Warner Books

Bootlegger's Boy by Barry Switzer, Berkley Books

The Boys Club Guide to Youth Football by Edward M. Torba, Leisure Press

Building a Champion by Bill Walsh, St. Martin's Press

Building a Championship Football Team by Bear Bryant, Prentice-Hall, Inc.

Championship Football by D.X. Bible, Prentice-Hall, Inc.

Coaching the Defensive Secondary by M. Schuster, Quality Coaching

Coaching Football by Flores & O'Connor, Masters Press

Coaching Football's Split 4-4 Multiple Defense by Pete Dyer, Parker Pub.

Coaching Football Successfully by Bob Reade, Human Kinetics

Coach of the Year Clinics manuals, annual transcripts of clinics taught by many coaches, Telecoach, Inc.

Coaching Team Defense by Fritz Shurmur, Harding Press

Complete Book of Linebacker Play by J. Giampalmi, Quality Coaching

Complete Handbook of Winning Football Drills by Don Fuoss, Allyn and Bacon

Defensing the Delaware Wing-T by Bob Kenig, Quality Coaching

Defensive Secondary: Coaching the Defensive Backfield by Greg McMakin, Quality Coaching

Directory of Football Defenses by Drew Tallman, Parker Publishing

Ditka by Armen Keteyian. Pocket Books.

The Eagle Five-Linebacker Defense by Fritz Shurmur, Quality Coaching

The Fighting Spirit, A Championship Season at Notre Dame by Lou Holtz, Simon & Schuster

The 5-2 Defense by J. Campbell, Quality Coaching

Football Coaching Strategies by AFCA coaches, Human Kinetics

Football Coach's Survival Guide by Michael D. Koehler. Parker Publishing

Football Drill Book by Doug Mallory, Masters Press

Football for Young Players and Parents by Joe Namath, Simon & Schuster

Football's Fabulous Forty Defense by Jack Olcott, Parker Publishing

Football's Modular Defense, A simplified Multiple System by John Durham, Parker Publishing Company, Inc.

Football Rules in Pictures by Don Schiffer and Lud Duroska, Perigee Books, Putnam Publishing Group

Football's 44 Stack Defense by Tom Simonton, MacGregor Sports Ed.

Football's Super Split The Underdog Defense by Bill Siler, Leisure Press

Football: The Violent Chess Match by Flores & O'Connor, Masters Press

Football Winning Defense by Bud Wilkinson, Sports Illustrated Winner's Circle Books

Football Winning Offense by Bud Wilkinson, Sports Illustrated Winner's Circle Books

Fourth and One by Joe Gibbs, Thomas Nelson Publishers

Friday Night Lights by H.G. Bissinger, Harper

Functional Football by John DaGrosa, A.S. Barnes & Company

The Fundamentals of Coaching Football, 2nd edition by George C. Kraft, Brown & Benchmark

Game Plan to Winning Football by Gordon Wood, Summit Group

Woody Hayes A Reflection by Paul Hornung, Sagamore Publishing

The Hidden Game of Football by Bob Carroll, Pete Palmer, and John Thorn, Warner Books

Hot Line to Victory by Woody Hayes, unknown publisher

How to Kick the Football by Edward J. Doc Storey, Leisure Press

Instant Replay by Jerry Kramer. New American Library.

Just Win, Baby by Glenn Dickey, Harcourt Brace Jovanovich

Tom Landry: An Autobiography by Tom Landry, Harper Paperbacks

Vince Lombardi on Football by Vince Lombardi, New York Graphic Society

Looking Deep by Terry Bradshaw, Berkley

Missouri Power Football by Devine & Onofrio, Lucas Brothers Publishers

Modern Football by Fritz Crisler, McGraw Hill

Modern Short Punt by Lou Howard, Prentice-Hall, Inc.

Multiple Monster Football by Warren Washburn, Parker Publishing

No Medals For Trying, A Week in the Life of a Pro Football Team by Jerry Izenberg, Random House

One Knee Equals Two Feet by John Madden, Berkley Books

Option Football Concepts and Techniques for Winning by Stan Scarborough and William E. Warren, Allyn and Bacon or Wm. C. Brown Publishers

A Parent's Guide to Coaching Football by John P. McCarthy, Jr., Betterway Publications, Inc.

Ara Parseghian and Notre Dame Football by Ara Parseghian, Men in Motion

Paterno by Joe Paterno, Random House

Pressure Defense Made Easier by Scott Pelleur, Quality Coaching

Principles of Coaching Football by Mike Bobo, William C. Brown Publishers

Pro 3-4 by M.McDaniels, Quality Coaching

The Right Kind of Heroes by Kevin Horrigan. Algonquin Books of Chapel Hill. (Inspiring story of the 1990 and 1991 seasons of the East Saint Louis High School Flyers football team which has a remarkable long-term record under Coach Bob Shannon.)

Rookie Coaches Football Guide by The American Coaches Effectiveness Program. Human Kinetics Publishers.

Run to Daylight by Vince Lombardi. Simon & Schuster. Classic. Excellent.

Saint Bobby and the Barbarians by Ben Brown. Doubleday. (Covers the 1991 season of Coach Bobby Bowden's Florida State Seminoles)

The San Francisco, 49ers, Team of the Decade by Michael Tuckman & Jeff Schultz, Prima Publishing & Communications

Secrets of the Split-T by Don Faurot, Prentice-Hall, Inc.

Simplified Single Wing Football by Ken Keuffel, Prentice-Hall, Inc.

The Slanting Monster Defense by Dale Foster, Parker Publishing

Total Impact by Ronnie Lott, Doubleday

Vince by Michael O'Brien. William Morrow & Company. (Life of Coach Vince Lombardi)

Youth League Football Coaching and Playing by Jack Bicknell, Athletic Inst.

Youth League Passing and Receiving by Ken Anderson and Bruce Coslet, The Athletic Institute

Winning Football Drills by Donald E. Fuoss, William C. Brown Publishers

Catalogs

Adelson Sports (Sells used, out-of-print football books), 13610 N. Scottsdale Road, Suite #10, Scottsdale, AZ 85254

Championship Books & Video Productions P.O. Box 1166, ISU Station, Ames, IA 50014, 800-873-2730 fax 515-232-3739

Coaches Choice, 302 West Hill Street, Champaign, IL 61824, 800-327-5557 fax 217-359-5975

Gridiron Communications, 707 Wellman Avenue, North Chelmsford, MA 01863 800-315-5580

Hoffman Research Services (Sells used, out-of-print football books), P.O. Box 342, Rillton, PA 15678, 412-446-3374

Majestic Licensing (associated with Pop Warner), 636 Pen Argyl Street, Pen Argyl, PA 18072, 215-863-6311

National Alliance for Youth Sports , 2050 Vista Parkway, West Palm Beach, FL 33411, 800-729-2057

National Federation of State High School Associations, 11724 NW Plaza Circle, P.O. Box 20626, Kansas City, MO 64195, 816-464-5400 fax 816-464-5104

Quality Coaching, P.O. Box 11051, Burbank, Ca 91510, 800-541-5489

Equipment

Adams USA, Inc., P.O. Box 489, Cookeville, TN 38501, 800-251-6857

Straight-on kicking shoes American Football Specialists, 1764 Plano Road, Suite 5, P.O. Box 50484 Bowling Green, KY 42104, 502-843-8393

training equip. (blocking dummies, etc.)
   Marty Gilman, Inc., P.O. Box 97, Gilman, CT 06336, 800-243-0398
Rogers Athletic Company, 495 Holley Drive, P.O. Box 208, Clare, MI 48617 800-248-0270
protective gear
   Riddell, 3670 N. Milwaukee Avenue Chicago, IL 60641, 800-445-7344
decals, emblems, award stickers, etc.
   SportDecals, 365 E. Terra Cotta, P.O. Box 358, Crystal Lake, IL 60014 800-435-6110
video editing
   Sports-Tech International, Inc., 2419 East Commercial Boulevard, Fort Lauderdale, FL 33308, 305-772-9155
World Sporting Goods, Inc., 1306 Stephens Road, Mobile, AL 36603 800-633-1270

Organizations

Membership in some of these organizations includes coaches liability insurance.
American Coaching Effectiveness Program, P.O. Box 5076, Champaign, IL 61825 800-747-4457
American Football Coaches Association, 5900 Old MacGregor Road, Waco, TX 76712, 817-776-5900 fax 817-776-3744
National Youth Sports Coaches Association, 2050 Vista Parkway, West Palm Beach, FL 33411, 800-729-2057
National Federation of State High School Assocs, 11724 NW Plaza Cir., P.O. Box 20626, Kansas City, MO 64195, 816-464-5400 fax 816-464-5104
Pop Warner Football, Pop Warner Little Scholars, Inc., 586 Middletown Blvd, Suite C-100, Langhorne, PA 19047 215-735-1450 Fax 215-752-2879

Periodicals

American Football Quarterly
The Extra Point, AFCA
Gridiron Coach Gridiron Communications
National Federation News, National Fed.
The Point, Pop Warner Little Scholars, Inc.
Coach and Athletic Director, Scholastic Coach
Youth Sport Coach, National Alliance for Youth Sports

Rule book

National Federation of State High School Associations (Contains catalog of officials' equipment and uniforms), 11724 Plaza Circle, P.O. Box 20626 Kansas City, MO 64195

Schools and clinics

Ultra Power Football Coaches Clinics, Frank Glazier
Offense Defense Instructional Football School, Football Camps, Inc.

Videos

There are zillions of football videos available in the various catalogs listed above in the catalog section.
Offensive Line Play of the Masters by Anthony Munoz and Jim McNally, Championship Technique Video
Official Pop Warner Football Handbook video, Majestic Licensing*Teaching Kids Football* by Bo Schembechler, ESPN Home Video

Addresses and phone #s

Algonquin Books of Chapel Hill, P.O. Box 2225, Chapel Hill, NC 27515
Allyn and Bacon, 7 Wells Avenue, Newton, MA 02159
American Football Quarterly, P. O. Box 963, Emporia, KS 66801, 316-342-2664
The Athletic Institute, 200 Castlewood Drive, North Palm Beach, FL 33480
Avon Books, Hearst Corporation, 105 Madison Avenue, New York, NY 10016
A.S. Barnes & Co. Inc., 11175 Flintkote Ave., San Diego, CA 92121
Berkley Books, 200 Madison Avenue New York, NY 10016
Betterway Publications, Inc., P.O. Box 219, Crozet, VA 22932, 800-823-5661
William C. Brown Publishers, 2460 Kerper Boulevard, Dubuque, IA 52001
Brown & Benchmark, 25 Kessel Courte, Suite 201, Madison, WI 53711
Championship Technique Video, P.O. Box 1526, Brookline, MA 02146, 800-628-1981
Doubleday, 666 Fifth Avenue, New York, NY 10103
ESPN Home Video, ESPN, Inc., ESPN Plaza, Bristol, CT 06010, 800-800-662-3776

Football Camps, Inc., P.O. Box 317,
    Trumbull, CT 06611, 800-243-4296
Frank Glazier, P.O. Box 3421, Stuart, FL
    34995-342, 303-470-8885
Harcourt Brace Jovanovich, Orlando, FL
    32887
Harding Press, P. O. Box 141, Haworth,
    NJ 07641
Harper Paperbacks, 10 East 53rd Street
    New York, NY 10022
Human Kinetics Publishers (Catalog
    contains other publishers' books too)
    P.O. Box 5076, Champaign, IL 61825-
    5076, 800-747-4457
Klemmer/Halley & Associates, Inc., 707
    Wellman Avenue, N. Chelmsford, MA
    01863, 508-251-8278
Leisure Press, 597 Fifth Avenue, New
    York, NY 10017
Lucas Brothers Publishers, 909 Lowry
    Columbia, MO
MacGregor Sports Education, Waukesha,
    WI
Masters Press, 2647 Waterfront Parkway
    E. Drive, Suite 300, Indianapolis, IN
    46214
McGraw-Hill, 1221 Avenue of the
    Americas, New York, NY 10020
Men in Motion, P.O. Box 428, Notre
    Dame, IN 46556
William Morrow and Company, Inc., 105
    Madison Avenue, New York, NY
    10016
Thomas Nelson Publishers, P.O. Box
    141000, Nashville, TN 37214
New American Library, P.O. Box 999
    Bergenfield, NJ 07621
New York Graphic Society, 140
    Greenwich Avenue, Greenwich, CT
    06830
Parker Publishing Company, Inc.
    Englewood Cliffs, NJ 07632
Pocket Books, 1230 Avenue of the
    Americas, New York, NY 10020
Prentice-Hall, Inc., Englewood Cliffs, NJ
    07632
Prima Publications & Communications,
    P.O. Box 1260 JMB, Rocklin, CA
    95677, 916-624-5718
Putnam Publishing Group, 200 Madison
    Avenue, New York, NY 10016
Quality Coaching (Catalog offering books,
    videos, and software), P.O. Box

11051, Burbank, CA 91510, 800-541-
    5489
Random House, Inc., 201 East 50th Street,
    New York, NY 10022, 800-733-3000
Bob Rexrode (Highly technical videos),
    1408 N. Ricketts, Sherman, TX 75090
Sagamore Publishing, Co., Inc., P.O. Box
    673, Champaign, IL 61824-0673
Scholastic Coach, P.O. Box 5288,
    Pittsfield, MA 01203-9826
St. Martin's Press, 175 Fifth Avenue, New
    York, NY 10010
Simon & Schuster, 1230 Avenue of the
    Americas, New York, NY 10020
Sports Illustrated Winner's Circle Books,
    1271 Avenue of the Americas, New
    York, NY 10020
Summit Group, 1227 West Magnolia
    Fort Worth, TX 76104
Telecoach, Inc., Earl Browning, Manager
    P.O. Box 22185, Louisville, KY
    40222
Jerry R. Tolley, Box 463, Elon College,
    NC 27244
Warner Books, 666 Fifth Avenue, New
    York, NY 10103

Your Opinion of this Book is Important to Me

Please send me your comments on this book. I'm interested in both compliments and constructive ciriticism. Your compliments provide guidance on what you want. And, with your permission, I'd like to use your favorable comments to sell future editions of the book. Constructive criticism also helps make the book's next edition better.

Evaluation of *Coaching Youth Football Defense*

Circle one: Excellent   Good   Satisfactory   Unsatisfactory

Circle one: Too Advanced   About Right   Too Basic

What part did you like best? _____

_____

What part did you like least? _____

_____

How can I improve the book? _____

_____

My promotional material includes brief comments by people who have read the book and their name, (company name in some cases), city, state, and occupation. I would appreciate any remarks you could give me for that purpose:

_____

_____

_____

Name _____   Team _____

Address _____

City _____ State _____ Zip _____

Feel free to leave blanks if you prefer not to answer all of these questions. I would appreciate receiving your evaluation even if you only fill out one line.

How long have you been a football coach? _____

What level do you coach at? _____

What part of your football team do you coach? _____

If your comments will not fit on this sheet, feel free to write them on the back of additional sheets. Please send your evaluation to:

John T. Reed
342 Bryan Drive
Danville, CA 94526

Newsletter

	Unit Price	Total
_____ one-year subscriptions to John T. Reed's Real Estate Investor's Monthly (12 monthly issues)	$125.00	$_____
_____ back issues (Please see catalog for list. <u>Minimum order is 3.</u>) 1 to 11 back issues	$ 8.50 ea.	$_____
12 or more back issues	$ 8.00 ea.	$_____
All back issues starting Feb. '86	$ 4.00 ea.	$_____

Special reports (48 pages, or more)

	Unit Price	Total
_____ Single-Family Lease Options	$ 29.95	$_____
_____ Distressed Real Estate Times: Offensive and Defensive Strategy and Tactics	$ 29.95	$_____
_____ How to Do a Delayed Exchange	$ 29.95	$_____

Books

	Unit Price	Total
_____ Aggressive Tax Avoidance for Real Estate Investors— **NEW 15th Edition**	$ 23.95	$_____
_____ Coaching Youth Football **NEW**	$ 19.95	$_____
_____ Coaching Youth Football Defense, 2nd edition **NEW**	$ 19.95	$_____
_____ How to Buy Real Estate for at Least 20% Below Market Value	$ 19.95	$_____
_____ How to Increase the Value of Real Estate	$ 39.95	$_____
_____ How to Manage Residential Property for Maximum Cash Flow	$ 23.95	$_____
_____ How to Use Leverage to Maximize Your Real Estate Investment Return	$ 19.95	$_____
_____ Office Building Acquisition Handbook (loose leaf)	$ 39.95	$_____
_____ Real Estate Investor's Monthly on Real Estate Investment Strategy	$ 39.95	$_____
_____ Residential Property Acquisition Handbook	$ 39.95	$_____

Cassettes (Two 60-minute cassettes in a binder)

	Unit Price	Total
_____ High Leverage Real Estate Financing	$ 29.95	$_____
_____ How to Buy Real Estate for at Least 20% Below Market Value, Vol. I	$ 29.95	$_____
_____ How to Buy Real Estate for at Least 20% Below Market Value, Vol. II	$ 29.95	$_____
_____ How to Buy Residential Property	$ 29.95	$_____
_____ How to Find Deals That Make Sense in Today's Market	$ 29.95	$_____
_____ How to Manage Residential Property for Maximum Cash Flow and Resale Value	$ 29.95	$_____
_____ How to Do a Delayed Exchange	$ 29.95	$_____
_____ Offensive and Defensive Strategy for Distressed Real Estate Times	$ 29.95	$_____
_____ Single-Family Lease Options	$ 29.95	$_____

Software

_____ Landlording™ On Disk software by Leigh Robinson

IMPORTANT—CHECK ONE: ☐ Macintosh ☐ IBM 5 1/4 ☐ IBM 3 1/2" $ 39.95 $_____

	Subtotal	$_____
Discount 5% for two or more items totaling over $100	$_____	
California residents: add your area's **sales tax** (except on newsletter subscriptions)	$_____	
Shipping: $4.00 for first item (Except subscriptions)	$_ 4.00 _	
$2.00 for **EACH** additional item	$_____	
(There is **one** shipping charge for any number of newsletter back issues.)		
	Total	$_____

Satisfaction guaranteed
or your money back

Method of Payment: _____ Check enclosed payable to John T. Reed   _____ Visa   _____ MasterCard   _____ Discover

Card # _____   Exp. Date _____   Signature _____

Ship to: Name _____ Telephone_____

Street Address _____

City _____ State _____ Zip _____ Fax _____

Please mail your order to: John T. Reed, 342 Bryan Drive, Danville, CA 94526
These prices are effective 3/1/96 and are subject to change. Source Code: 03
You can also **fax** your order to 510-820-1259 or **E-mail** it to JohnTReed@aol.com

**For faster service, ☎
phone toll-free:**
800-635-5425